BORIS JOHNSON is the Member of Parliament for Henley-on-Thames. He is a journalist and author of *Lend Me Your Ears*; *Friends, Voters, Countrymen*; *The Dream of Rome* and a novel, *Seventy-Two Virgins*. He lives with his family in London and Oxfordshire.

Visit www.AuthorTracker.co.uk for exclusive information on your favourite HarperCollins authors.

Also by Boris Johnson

NON-FICTION
Lend Me Your Ears
Friends, Voters, Countrymen
The Dream of Rome

FICTION
Seventy-Two Virgins

BORIS JOHNSON

Have I Got Views For You

HARPER PERENNIAL

London, New York, Toronto and Sydney

Harper Perennial
An imprint of HarperCollins*Publishers*
77–85 Fulham Palace Road
Hammersmith
London W6 8JB

www.harperperennial.co.uk

This edition published by Harper Perennial 2006
7

Parts of this book were first published in a collection entitled
Lend Me Your Ears by Harper Perennial in 2004

Lyrics from 'I Predict a Riot' by Kaiser Chiefs reprinted by
kind permission of Supervision Management & B-Unique Records

Copyright © Boris Johnson 2003, 2006

Boris Johnson asserts the moral right to
be identified as the author of this work

A catalogue record for this book
is available from the British Library

ISBN-13 978-0-00-724220-7
ISBN-10 0-00-724220-4

Set in Sabon and Frutiger Bold Condensed by
Rowland Phototypesetting Ltd, Bury St Edmunds, Suffolk

Printed and bound in Great Britain by
Clays Ltd, St Ives plc

CONTENTS

INTRODUCTION
When History Speeded Up

Crumbs, I thought, as I stood on the edge of the crater. Crumbs was the word. Or perhaps that should be fragments, little fist-sized fragments of house. Whatever explosive the US Air Force use in their bunkerbusters, it is powerful stuff. I was standing in the posh al-Mansour district of Baghdad, looking at the place where the Americans thought, in the last days of the war, that they had located Saddam Hussein.

It is hard to imagine the detonation that creates such a hole *from above*, not just destroying four houses, but somehow sucking up the earth beneath them, or blowing it down and out. They may not have hit Saddam, who was allegedly noshing in a nearby chicken and chip joint. But that hole nicely expresses what America did to his reign, and it sums up the range and irresistibility of America. When I first became a journalist fifteen years ago, America had not yet reached this pitch of technological virtuosity, of being able to drop a bomb on any house in any third world capital, at a time of her choosing. And she certainly did not have the licence to do so.

It was mesmerising, in April 2003, to stand in Baghdad and look at the contrast between the Americans and the

1

people they had liberated. The Iraqis were skinny and dark, badly dressed and fed. The Americans rode in their Humvees (a vehicle that is eloquently bigger than our Land Rover: more slouching, bigger tyred, cooler). The marines had the shades with the slick little nick in the corner. They were taller and squarer than the indigenous people, with heavier chins and better dentition. They looked like a master race from outer space, or something from the pages of Judge Dredd. It would be fair to say that Baghdad was not yet perfectly under their control. Everywhere there was shooting and looting, and a pall of smoke from the myriad bonfires, where Iraqis where barbecuing the street cables to get at the copper.

The conquest of Baghdad was made politically possible by the military reality. America spends more on defence than the next twenty-eight countries combined. We are left with a unipolar world, in which the Pentagon can not only call upon bases in Britain, and Turkey, and Cuba, but in the former Soviet republic of Uzbekistan, a place which, fifteen years ago, had missiles trained on the west. No, when I started out as a journalist, I didn't see any of this coming; any more than the residents of al-Mansour saw the bunkerbuster.

Perhaps there were some wise owls, like Francis Fukuyama, who had some intimation of how things would go, back in 1987, the year when I left university and looked for a job. Perhaps there were thinkers who could predict that Communism was about to collapse, that European integration would surge and then falter, that the anti-globalisation movement would arise, and then disappear up the spout of its own fundamental contradictions. Maybe someone foresaw the emergence of Tony Blair, the hobbling of the Tory party, and Islamic terror.

Perhaps you, clever reader, were among those who had already sussed out that the country would want to move on from the harsh vocabulary of Thatcherism, and that Britain would one day be suffused by the Age of Diana. Perhaps you even predicted that the apparently happily married young Sloane would one day be transformed into a martyr and icon of sentimental values. If you did have any such inklings, you were well ahead of me. Because in 1987, aged twenty-three, newly married and full up to the gills with the finest education England can provide, I didn't have the faintest idea what was going on. I am writing this on a delayed service to Paddington, late at night, staring at the darkened windows. I could no more have predicted the future than I could tell you what is out there in the night or when South West trains will get this blasted thing moving again.

My journalistic career began in the basement of a Mayfair hotel, where some plucky management consultants were trying to teach me their arts. Try as I might, I could not look at an overhead projection of a growth-profit matrix, and stay conscious. After I had sunk for the fourth time into a coma, and then jerked all too obviously awake, one of my fellow-trainees, a young thruster in a grey suit, could take no more. He was my age, and had also just signed on at the absurd (then) rate of £18,000 p.a. He nudged me and spoke in tones of disgust. 'Listen,' he said, 'if you continue to take this attitude I don't think you are going to get very far.'

I thought, and think, that he was a pompous squit, and I hope that he was an early victim of the management consultancy shake-out that followed. But as my ears burned, I knew he was right. I tiptoed to the telephone, rang a man called Peter Stothard, and found myself hired by the *Times*. To begin with, journalism was almost as confusing and depressing as management consultancy. Most journalists seemed just to sit in front of their Atex computer screens sending each other romantic messages, and then getting in a terrible state when they found they'd sent them to the wrong person.

Work consisted of placing a call, being told X was in a meeting, waiting half an hour, and then trying again. Looking back through the articles I wrote, I can find nothing of any merit whatever. I could not help wondering how long the *Times* could afford to employ such a heroically unproductive hack. In an attempt to step up my output, I started trawling the agency wires. All Atex users were able to call up Reuters or AP, and I soon noticed that there seemed to be big things afoot in Russia and Eastern Europe. And because the *Times* did not have staff correspondents all over Eastern Europe, I started to take a proprietorial interest in these stories.

It seemed to be one of the rules that you could rewrite agency copy, and claim it as your own, if you made at least one phone call to show that you had 'added value' to the story. With the help of beleaguered Foreign Editor George Brock, I soon built up a network of dons, at places like the London School for Slavonic and East European Studies, who would happily give a 'quote' about the matter in hand.

Had I the wit to see it, back in later '87 and '88, I might have detected a pattern in all this rubbish I was producing. I might have realised that not only was state socialism an inadequate means of satisfying material wants, but that it was about to implode. Everybody says that history started to accelerate in the late '80s. I am ashamed to say that I watched it without really grasping what was happening. I was too busy trying to get my byline on the story to wonder what the story might signify. It was only a year later, after I had left the *Times* in inglorious circumstances, that the process became obvious, even to me. The miserable members of the Warsaw Pact had not only been technologically out-generalled by Ronald Reagan. They were finally waking up to the reality that socialism, and the state enforcement of equality, is not only corrupting but inequitable: the *nomenklatura* will always get the shoes that are withheld from the masses. Yearly, almost monthly, they could see how they were falling behind the west, where the consumerist, technological miracle was taking place.

That's why the Ossies started driving their Trabants to the west. That's why the Berlin Wall fell, in November '89, six months after I had arrived in Brussels. And even then, in spite of all the indications they might have picked up in the foreign pages of the *Times*, the event was greeted in other European capitals with amazement and consternation. Thatcher seemed to try to stop German unification, and held a reactionary seminar at Chequers. The conclusion was that the Hun was either at your feet or at your throat. Mitterrand flew to Kiev for a mysterious meeting with Gorbachev, at which they tried, abortively, to think of a way of impeding the inevitable. One of the few European statesmen to grasp immediately the magnitude and irreversibility of the change was a Christian Lacroix-wearing, pipe-puffing former French socialist prime minister called Jacques Delors.

The other day I asked a twenty-five year old *Spectator* colleague whether she knew who he was. 'I know the name' she said cautiously. There, my friends, you have the glow-worm transience of journalism. Who knows how much of my life I have consecrated to writing up the doings of Jacques Delors? Months, years. Young people these days (pause to go purple) can't remember who he is!

The longer I stayed in Brussels – and I served five happy years – the more obvious it was that Europe would never work.

All journalists probably delude themselves that they may have influenced the history they are paid to observe; that their butterfly-flap triggered the storm. My boast, and I make it in the confidence that no one gives a monkey's, is that I probably did contribute to the Danish rejection of Maastricht. It was May 2nd 1992, and I was at one of those agreeable jaunts which punctuate the life of the Brussels correspondent: an informal meeting of foreign ministers at a scenic place called Guimaraes in Portugal. I remember going to a payphone at teatime that Saturday, standing in the dusty square and watching the dogs lying in the sun, and ringing Frank Taylor, the foreign editor of the *Sunday Telegraph*, to find out what had happened to my story. I thought it was quite good stuff, all about plans being incubated by Delors to create a European President, and centralise yet more power in Brussels, once the Maastricht treaty had been ratified. Frank thought it positively tremendous.

'We've made it the splash,' he said with his beardy chuckle, 'and I've called it "Delors Plans to Rule Europe".' Cor, I thought. That was a bold way of expressing it, and I wasn't sure that my chums in the EC commission would be thrilled. But the splash was the splash – the main article on the front page – and I happily consented. That story went down big. It may not have caused the dropping of marmalade over the breakfast tables of England, but it was huge in Denmark. With less than a month until their referendum, and with mounting paranoia about the erosion of Danish independence, the story was seized on by the No campaign. They photocopied it a thousandfold. They marched the streets of Copenhagen with my story fixed to their banners. And on June 2nd, a spectacularly sunny day, they joyously rejected the Treaty and derailed the project.

I would like to pretend, in a babyish way, that my despatch from Guimaraes was the root of it all. Someone from the *Sydney Morning Herald* did once argue that if I had not filed my piece about the 'Delors Plan to Rule Europe' the Danes would not have thrown out Maastricht;

the ERM crisis would not have happened; and John Major's government would not have been thrown into chaos, and so on. It's all nonsense, of course. The Tories had plenty of other problems; and the difficulties of the ERM were not solely a function of the Danish No.

The reason I became a sceptic about integration was that it continually involved a Procrustean squeezing or chopping of national interests. The one-size-fits-all ERM didn't suit us, which is why I have the gravest doubts about the single currency. And the same point can be made, in spades, about the plans for political union. Europe has been catastrophically disunited over Iraq. But people forget that she was catastrophically disunited over the first Gulf War, too. Not only did the Belgians refuse to send any troops. They even refused to sell us ammunition, a product Belgium has traditionally made in quantity. Chirac has been criticised for breaking with the Anglo-American coalition. But Mitterrand was almost as creepy in the first Gulf War, and this time round I have little doubt that he would have done the same. The wonder is that anyone still expects unity from Europe, on any really difficult issue of foreign policy.

Just as the Maastricht negotiations reached their mid-point, in June 1991, there was worrying news from the Balkans. Here we all were trying to forge a federal state, *e pluribus unum*, and the Serbs and the Croats were on the point of destroying federal Yugoslavia.

For three years the problem was left to Europe, and it was a disaster. There was a stage, right at the beginning, when they did consider sending an expeditionary force to oppose the Milosevic purges. Hurd argued vehemently against any such intervention; and from then on the strategy was pretty much to let the warlords get on with it, while doing what we could to alleviate the humanitarian disaster. Only after the siege of Sarajevo, and the appalling humiliation of the UN operation at Srebrenica, did the US decide that enough was enough. The Hour of Europe was over, and the Clinton administration implemented the policy of 'Lift and Strike', lifting the arms embargo against the Bosnian Muslims, and bombing the Serbs.

The lesson of Bosnia seemed pretty clear. Europe supplied dithering and appeasement. The Pentagon supplied violence, and a solution. Not that I saw any of the action myself, being mainly condemned to report the conferences and summits and nonsensical communiqués. Feeling a bit of a wuss, I rang the Foreign Desk during the first Gulf War, and begged to be sent out, along with Pat Bishop and Robert Fox, and all the other macho characters with their special Kate Adie warzone waistcoats. 'Hur hur', said the Foreign Desk. 'Nah, Boris, we reckon you're too valuable where you are.' Then I rang up during the Yugoslav crisis, being particularly jealous of Alec Russell, Tim Butcher and other reporters who had done some really gripping stuff. What do you think? I asked. Did our heroes perhaps need some assistance, from someone well-versed in pointless multinational negotiations? There was some cackling. 'Nah, Boris', the Foreign News Editor eventually returned, 'if you go to Yugoslavia you'll just take them all out to lunch.' This seemed to be some sort of reference to my expenses claims. 'You just stick in Brussels,' they chortled, 'and make sure you don't get hit by any profiteroles!'

This rankled, as you can imagine; and so when the next war came, I was determined not to be caught out. As Nato began to bomb Belgrade, with a view to driving the Serbs out of Kosovo, I went to see what it was like. This was now 1999, and a new concept was emerging in international relations: liberal imperialism. Gone was the old Hurdian instinct for appeasement and compromise. This was Blair and Clinton, the two uber-yuppies determined to create a better world, and to use smart bombs to do so.

In the morning, if the smart bombs had been dumber than intended, we would be taken to see the collateral damage. It was particularly sad, walking up a suburban street, where dead and injured were being taken out of their houses. I felt a surge of anger that my taxpayer's money was being used to fund this destruction, and I am afraid that pathetically, in a mumbled way, I apologised. It is difficult to be in an ancient European capital, under bombing, and not to oppose the bombardment.

I wrote what I hoped were some caustic pieces – not in defence of Milosevic, of course not, but against this manner of removing him. I think, in retrospect, that I failed to see the wood for the trees; and that has made me approach the second Gulf War with a more open mind.

There are many good conservatives and decent socialists who deeply dislike the New World Order/liberal imperialism business. They believe, like Enoch Powell, that Britain should avoid all foreign entanglements save where her interests are directly threatened. I am not so sure. They say we cannot do everything, cannot go around the world fighting every fire. That is true, but it is no reason to do nothing. I supported, and support, the second Gulf War on a strictly utilitarian calculation. The world is better for removing Saddam from power than keeping him there and allowing the Iraqis to suffer another twelve years of tyranny and economic sanctions. You can say what you like about Blair – and I have said and will continue to say some disobliging things – but he has participated in the toppling of two tyrants, Milosevic and Saddam, whom Major had left in power. And unlike the supposedly Eurosceptic Tories, Blair took not the blindest notice of European opinion, or the need to adhere to a common European position. The Kosovo enterprise was wildly unpopular in some parts of the Community, notably Greece. As for the second Gulf War, the split is the most sensational I have seen: France, Germany, Belgium, directly opposing an action supported by the governments of Britain, Italy, Spain, Holland, Denmark, and a comet tail of 'new European' states.

Confronted with a cold, hard choice, Blair went with the country that had the power and the money to do what he thought was right. He went with America, and with the Pentagon. And he won. All of which, of course, makes it much harder for mainstream Atlanticist Tories. How, we ask ourselves, are we meant to oppose the blighter? We thought Blair cosied up to Clinton just because Bill was a Democrat, and a fellow exponent of the aromatherapy mysteries of the Third Way. One of the joys of the first Blair term was going out to Washington, at the height of the Monica Lewinsky business, and watching him rally round the great philanderer.

And yet such is Blair's protean political personality that five years later he seems to have forged an equally close relationship with the teetotal, hot-dang, Bible-reading G Dubya Bush. Of course his own party hate it like poison. But what are we Tories supposed to make of it?

I began my journalistic efforts as the Cold War was ending. Fifteen years later, with the Cold War long buried, the winners and losers are, as I say, unexpected.

You might have thought the Tories would be triumphant, since the transformation was a spectacular ideological vindication. It proved what we had argued all along: that socialism was a hopelessly inept system for satisfying human desires. For years the Tories had been calling for freedom, and democracy, and free markets in eastern Europe and suddenly it all happened! What did Labour do in the Cold War? They turned their fire on Ronald Reagan, and Margaret Thatcher. They went on CND marches, ignored the Gulags, and took fraternal junkets to Moscow. And yet fifteen years later it is Labour which has adapted far more effectively to the New Order. With the end of the Soviet menace, the Tories were left still looking beetle-browed, and paranoid, and alarmist; but alarmist about what? Europe? Yes, the public was broadly Euro-sceptic, but with the best will in the world, it wasn't possible to turn Delors, and EU integration, into a threat to national security.

Where was the external threat to replace communism, against which the Tories had put up such yeoman resistance? China? Asylum-seekers? It didn't work. The Tories had lost a high card, and Blair followed Clinton in developing a new formula, that was attractive to an increasingly affluent country. He took the yuppyish Thatcherite values, which characterised the 1980s, and sanded off the rougher edges. You could still be a free-market liberal, he said; you could still be basically acquisitive and materialist. But under New Labour you could have it all in a caring, quivering-lip sort of way.

Our culture has probably become gentler, more touchy-feely, more politically correct, more *American* if you like, and that may of course be partly because we are richer. Per capita GDP has increased, at today's rates, from £12,637 to £17,096. The world has also broadly improved, in the sense that there were one hundred and fifteen countries which were classed 'free or partly free' in 1987. There are now one hundred and forty-five, though it should be noted that the number of unfree countries remains roughly the same. The wheels of capitalism turn ever faster and more productively. The House of Commons Library tells me that of the 2.7 million *Daily Telegraph* readers who might have read my first articles, it is likely that about 700,000 have now died. One or two of them, who knows, may even have kicked the bucket over breakfast, apoplectically choking on their toast as they read the latest news from Brussels. Amazingly, their ranks have been replenished by just as many others, who recognise the range and genius of that publication.

It is to the reader that all journalists owe the biggest debt: that huge, silent interlocutor with whom we feel we can converse on terms of such intimacy, and who sits in patient judgment over our babble. To those few, those faithful few who have reached this stage in the argument, I wish to leave this final, repetitive thought. Fifteen years after the collapse of communism, the biggest and most salient political fact in the world is American dominance. Japan was meant to eclipse her economically; and Japan, along with the other Asian economies, has been in serious difficulties. Russia is in a bad way. China grows fast, but shows no interest yet in impinging on the rest of the world. It is obvious that this American dominance is producing, and will continue to produce, a reaction; or rather a spectrum of reaction. Even in the Arab world, attitudes to America range from support and approval to the demented attacks of bin Laden's networks. America's performance in Iraq was formidable, and made Europe look ridiculous. But in the hearts of many moderate people, the very lopsidedness of the world demands some sort of compensation. The Iraq war not only undermines the case for Euro-federalism; it is also, paradoxically, a recruiting-sergeant for Europeanism.

Already, in Brussels, the kindly and charming bureaucrats are no doubt pushing aside their moules frites and doodling new plans on their napkins. Indeed, as I write these words, they are preparing for a new constitution of Europe. And good Lord Tony Blair proposes that there should be a new 'President of Europe', who should be, no doubt, a charismatic, glistering-toothed and straight sort of guy, with four children and an interest in rock music.

Where have I read that story before? Yes, at the risk of

12

flogging a dead horse, it was 'Delors Plan to Rule Europe', my path-breaking despatch from Guimaraes.

This time I have no idea how it will all turn out, though I stick to my central point: that it is very difficult to make a single political unit out of fifteen – now twenty-five – countries; and it is no use expecting to rival America, if you will only spend a relatively tiny amount on defence. All I will predict is that whoever comes to power in Britain, this country will continue to try to have it both ways; pretending a unique allegiance to both Europe and America, not because we are especially duplicitous, but because it is the sensible thing to do. We will stick with America while contriving to remain on the European 'train'.

And talking of trains, the Totnes to Paddington is finally pulling in. Don't ask how I could have written so much on one journey. We were diverted to Newbury, if you must know, because of something to do with signals. What do you expect? It's a Labour government, isn't it?

It is now May 2006 and almost exactly three years since the words above were written. You could be forgiven for thinking that history has entered a doldrums. Blair is still in power. Bush is still in the White House. People are still wrangling about the rights and wrongs of the Iraq war, with more of its advocates giving way to despair. China is still on the verge of becoming a global economic super-power – and, for reasons I describe later on, seems likely to hang around on that verge for quite some time. The Tories have stuck to the script, and lost another election. Has anything really changed?

Of course it has. The Labour government, that shiny piece of new technology in which the British people invested with such excitement, is now almost ten years old. The Blair machine is showing fatal signs of rust. And now, with that almost biological sense of rhythm, the British establishment is slowly preparing to transfer its allegiance to a newer, shinier, cleaner, greener proposition – the Cameron Tory party: still basically Tory, but also nappy-changing, bicycle-loving and kind to the ozone layer.

Iran has emerged as the new source of global panic, with some people panicked about Iranian nuclear capability, and almost everyone panicked about the American response. Even in the tranquil life of your columnist, there has been a certain amount of action and event, some of which is reflected in these pages. Yes, the winds of history have gusted as hard as ever these last few years. They have brought down a fresh litter of columns and a few more have now been kept and interleaved. You may sometimes think that's not how it is. But never mind, buster: this is how I see it.

POLITICS
From Thatcher to Blair

What made New Labour so hard to fight was that no one really knew what they stood for ...

Mr Blair has learnt a valuable lesson

Any businessman rolling the Labour Party's new improved Clause Four about his mind will instantly recognise the kind of texts that have inspired Tony Blair. Harping as the new constitution does on words like 'quality', 'service', 'endeavour', 'achieve', 'community' and 'prosper', it belongs unmistakably to a modern literary genre: the US-style corporate Mission Statement. In deciding to revamp the charter of Labour Plc, Mr Blair is mimicking the world's most successful companies.

For instance, in 1952 one 'Colonel' Sanders of Kentucky dipped a chicken drumstick into salty batter-mixture and (allegedly) pronounced: 'It's finger-lickin' good!' Ungrammatical, likely to encourage bad table manners; and yet the founder's words have been inscribed on countless boxes of Kentucky Fried Chicken. Recently, however, the strategy men in Kentucky have decided that this sentence is no longer enough, alone, to uplift the workforce and to convince an apathetic public of the moral dimension to selling fried chicken.

After what one can only assume was a full process of consultation with franchisees, Kentucky Fried Chicken has a new Mission Statement. Like the words of Sidney and Beatrice Webb, the honest exclamation of Col Sanders has been updated and blurred. KFC's goal in life is, I can reveal, 'to provide families with affordable, delicious, chicken dominant meals'. Notice the adept insertion of the hot-button word 'family'. 'Families' also appears, for the first time, in the new Clause Four.

In the development of their Mission Statements, the Labour Party and top corporations have converged from opposite directions. The 1918 Webb formulation has been junked essentially because Labour has so crushingly lost the argument about the role of commerce in society. Commerce, on the other hand, has understood that the public likes capitalism to sound caring. By 1995, both the Labour Party and Big Business have adopted identical methods of selling themselves. Both have produced Mission Statements in which the strategy is, within a few honed words, to achieve the smooth yoking-together of antithetical ambitions; or, to put it another way, to have one's cake and eat it.

Compare the 'Corporate Mission 1992–2000' of McDonald's Hamburgers, which strikingly resembles Blair's effort in language and tone. Perhaps conscious of accusations that they employ student hamburger flippers on Third World wages, McDonald's says: 'The company will be led by the needs of our customers and committed to the welfare and development of our staff.' See what taut equipoise is achieved between (a) the 'needs' of customers, chiefly for cheap food, and (b) the duty of McDonald's to its wretched staff. One might compare Labour's new balancing act, in which 'the rights we enjoy reflect the duties we owe'.

16

Like Blair, commerce has understood how valuable the Mission Statement can be for fudging a failure to stick to principle. One thinks of Anita Roddick's breathtaking assertion that the Body Shop's mission is 'to passionately campaign for the environment and for the protection of human and civil rights, against animal testing within the cosmetics and toiletries industry'. Brilliant, eh? On the one hand the Body Shop is (a) in favour of animals. On the other hand, it must, like Labour, deal with the world as it is, so (b) like the rest of the cosmetics and toiletries industry the Body Shop has to use products tested on animals.

Just such a recognition of reality lies at the heart of Tony Blair's new Labour Party constitution. The Fabian goal of public ownership is still there. But a future Labour Britain in which 'those undertakings essential to the common good are either owned by the public or accountable to them' must face up, Blair admits, to the existence of 'a thriving private sector'.

Statements of this kind give an opportunity for a delicate adjustment of stance. Remember KFC's wonderful new aspiration to provide 'chicken dominant' meals. Yes, even as the menu at KFC is no longer in thrall to chicken, so Labour is no longer dominated by the Unions. Just as a KFC Family Feast now consists of additional fries, cole-slaw, BBQ beans and Sara Lee apple pie, so New Labour will also co-operate, says the revised constitution, with 'voluntary organisations, consumer groups and other representative bodies'.

Not least, the Mission Statement is an opportunity for rhapsodising. Take the sweep of ambition of Ben and Jerry's ice-cream, which is apparently intended to 'improve the quality of life of a broad community, local, national and international'. Just so is Labour committed to working with 'international bodies to secure peace, freedom, democracy' and so on. A mission statement can say what the firm does not want. Pret A Manger, the fashionable new sandwich chain, says, 'We ruthlessly avoid preservatives, additives and obscure chemicals.' Tony Blair's new-look Labour is still hostile, we gather, to the wealthy few.

The similarity between Labour's new Clause Four and the most right-on commercial Mission Statements is uncanny. I don't know whether John Prescott is the sort of ex-sailor to make use of the Body Shop. But I could swear he has cribbed Roddick's vow 'to *courageously* ensure that *our* business is ecologically sustainable, meeting the needs of the *present* without compromising the future'. Labour's new Clause Four calls for a 'healthy environment which we protect, enhance and hold in trust for future generations'. The new Labour Party speaks of 'solidarity, tolerance and respect'. The Body Shop offers 'honesty, fairness and respect'.

It would be dangerous, though, to mock. My purpose is not necessarily to debunk Labour's new constitution. After all, these companies whose guff-filled Mission Statements Mr Blair imitates are phenomenally successful. If Anita Roddick can persuade millions of people to buy her delightful coconut oil shampoo or taramasalata facial scrub, then why should identical techniques not persuade us all to vote Labour?

Where is the Tory Mission Statement? One thing is certain: more people will buy Big Macs in 1997 than will vote Tory. The time is approaching when the Tories may have to consider following Blair's lead, sacking Mr Hanley, and putting Colonel Sanders in charge of Central Office.

And no one knew what Tony Blair really believed in.

Who was fibbing – the old Blair or new?

There is a rather good parlour game where you pick up the Bible or Shakespeare or Baedeker, or, even better, the Koran, and quote a passage until you start improvising parodically, while the listener has to guess at exactly which point you departed from the text. Well, I thought I would give you some Tony Blair. All you have to do is yell or whistle as soon as you think I am starting to send up Blair's efforts to sound like a Tory. Ready? Here goes. This is Blair in the spring of 1995:

'Duty is the cornerstone of a decent society.'

'I believe Margaret Thatcher's emphasis on enterprise was right.'

'Parents must be warned that non-attendance by children can lead to court.'

'Top-rate tax does not equal wealthy any more.'

'I am in favour of capital punishment for those who kill policemen.'

All right, I admit it, I made the last one up. But you take the point, I hope.

This is the brand of 'socialism' that is about to administer the most unholy drubbing to the Tory party in the local government elections on 4 May, and, some would have us believe, precipitate the downfall of Mr Major. As *The Spectator* went to press, Blair's chances of losing the vote on changing Clause Four dwindled to vanishing point.

The Labour leader is by any standards formidable in his public relations. Like a master organist he flits between the stacked keyboards of the press, playing us all simultaneously without hitting a bum note. His handling of the 'teachers' who frightened Blunkett's dog was assured, turning a minus for Labour into a plus.

Such is the lust for change, the desperation to trust him, that the electorate would seemingly forgive anything. Should they?

In theory, it is a measure of a statesman's fitness for power whether he is *tenax propositi*, whether he adheres to principle. So let us play another game, the one that the BBC would play, were its presenters a tiny bit tougher on what we are invited to call 'New Labour'. The game is an old, crude politician's stand-by. I only resort to the trick because it is so unfashionable and because Labour is still handled with such deference. This game is called 'But You Said, Mr Blair – And I'll Read It To You'.

We've all heard of Blair the Moderniser. Blair the Moderniser has reassured Middle England that he isn't going to tamper with the Tory trades union law which largely restored confidence in Britain overseas. But there is another character: we might call him Ur-Blair. Here is Blair the Archaiser on the subject of the 1984 Trade Union Act, an essential, democratic reform which made strike ballots compulsory: 'It is a disgrace that we should be debating today the taking away of fundamental freedoms for which British trade unionists have fought . . . We shall oppose the Bill, which is a scandalous and undemocratic measure.' Young Tony was scarcely less Spartish, Hansard reveals, about the 1982 Act and the restrictions on secondary picketing.

Anyone can change his tune, especially in response to four election defeats. But it is more difficult, one would think, for a politician to change his or her instincts. The important question for us all, as voters expecting a Labour government, is, When were they telling the truth about what they really thought, then or now?

One of the pair, Ur-Blair or Blair, is lying. I am fairly sure the fibber is, or was, Ur-Blair the Archaiser. In other words, what you *now* see is what you get; he *really* is a social democrat-cum-Tory who happens, amazingly, to be leading the Labour Party. Many of the converts among us will want to see it like this. They will be inclined to be indulgent of Ur-Blair. They will know why he said things like, 'We'll negotiate a withdrawal from the EEC, which has drained our natural resources and destroyed jobs' in his 1983 election address. He said them, fingers crossed, because he was a bright young man who wanted to get on in the Labour Party, like those Tories who stoutly defended the ERM in 1991 and 1992 and then repented.

The more interesting question, perhaps, concerns the rest of them. Which set of propositions reflects the true instincts of the Shadow Cabinet, the senior figures whom Blair must heed, especially if, as seems likely, he has a small majority in Parliament? Were they faking it for all those years, and did they decide – about a year ago – to tell the truth? Or are they dissimulating now? It should not be too tiresome to repeat that the entire Shadow Cabinet was opposed to every one of the Government's privatisations, that 14 of them are known to have been members of CND, that six of them voted against Britain's membership of the EU.

I wonder if these colleagues of Mr Blair can really have lost the emotions that actuated them then, that made them want to go into politics: the deep distrust of capitalism; the hatred of the profit motive; the wariness of commercial competition; the class anger; the instinctive belief that business is best organised by the state; the urge to take and redistribute money.

Which is the real Jack Straw on the subject of education? There is the Jack Straw who has beamed at Tony and Cherie Blair's decision to send their son Euan to a grant-maintained school. Or there is the Jack Straw who at a local government conference in 1992 called Tory plans for opting out, which broadly took power over children from left-wing councils and gave it to parents and governors, a 'disreputable and failing system'. In a press release of 1988, the old Jack Straw, Ur-Straw, said City Technology Colleges and opted-out schools are 'designed systematically to sabotage the central value of the comprehensive school'. As recently as 1991, he wanted to axe the 'wasteful' City Technology Colleges, thereby, he said, saving about £50 million.

I have an idea which is the real Jack Straw. Think into the mind of someone who believes that 'the monarchy is a deeply decadent and detached system for which we are all paying'. He is obviously an overgrown student socialist.

Which is the real John Prescott? Is he the man who, with Blair, turned Clause Four into a kind of fast-food mission statement, or the man who told us all in February 1994 that 'I come from the bowels of the trade union movement. I am a typical creature of the movement.' The psychologically convincing Prescott, surely, is the one who said in May 1994, 'I don't believe in ditching Clause Four because I do believe there is a role for public ownership'; the one who told *Labour and Trade Union Review 1990* what he would do with the Tories' employment reforms: 'There's nothing you can keep of this legislation. It all has to go.'

We are told by New Labour and New Blair that a minimum wage would not cost jobs. But Ur-Prescott gave the game away on Sky TV on 18 March 1992: 'I think you have to accept that there will be some shake-out of jobs in certain areas.' Again, Tony Blair has been ingeniously vague about what New Labour would do to our tax bills. He's not saying anything on tax, except that the Tories have lied and robbed.

But wait, here is Prescott, only last year: 'There's certainly going to be a higher top rate than we have ... You can argue about what that might be, but if we want a fair tax system, you're certainly going to have that.'

And which is the real Labour policy on nationalisation? Tony Blair's office told me that suggestions that Labour might take control of some industries were 'rubbish'. But according to the master mariner and deputy leader in the *Morning Star* 30 August 1986, 'The public utilities should be returned to public ownership and there should be state intervention where capitalism fails...' Or take Frank Dobson, who said in the House on 2 July 1991, 'We have said all along that we will bring the National Grid Company back into public ownership. It will be a high priority, I assure Hon. Members.' Margaret Beckett, Robin Cook, Tony Blair, Ann Taylor: all have called for water to be returned to the state sector.

As for their policy on the single currency, well, the answer is Yes. As Blair put it in the House of Commons, 'The answer is unequivocally Yes'; or, as Prescott said on the *Today Programme* on 15 June 1991, 'Yes, we're against a single currency.'

Now it will be up to Jeremy Hanley, or whoever succeeds him as party chairman, to persuade the electorate that New Labour is really Old Labour, that they are still the same under the skin. It is, he must suggest, a little like the film *Invasion of the Body Snatchers*. They have seized a plausible guise, while underneath are invisibly gibbering creatures from political outer space.

In fairness to Labour, the party is changing under Blair. Some leftish MPs report that they receive the odd letter of protest from constituents lamenting the loss of radicalism. Old-fashioned constituency associations have been deeply offended by the Blairite decision that 50 per cent of all candidates must be women; and a revolt is brewing on that score. But those 80,000 new members who have joined since he became leader are, it is said, diluting the hard-left activists.

It should be recorded, too, that some of the old-style

Labour Left don't really believe that the U-turn will become an S-bend when New Labour comes to power. 'It's like Gorbachev's Communist Party in the Soviet Union,' says one sad and distinguished Labour MP. 'They just go along with whatever the leader says.' They've been lobotomised by defeat, he argues. The Shadow Cabinet are not only docile now, they would be docile in office.

'Maybe I'm too pessimistic, but I don't think John Prescott is going to kick over the traces once he gets into power. John is a good guy but he loves his Jaguar. Meacher has never really rebelled. Cook will go along with almost anything.'

Remember, though, that these are criticisms from the Labour Left. For believers in common sense, there is only one way to test whether New Labour's conversion is sincere, and that is to put the following questions to Blair and Co:

Will you reduce the burden on posterity by following the Government in encouraging private pensions? Will you discourage spongers by keeping the Jobseeker's Allowance? Will you maintain Mr Lilley's attempts to stop malingerers from claiming Disability Benefit? Will you keep compulsory competitive tendering for local authorities?

I believe the answer to all those questions, and others like them, is No. That is a fact that should be exposed. Mr Gordon Brown is apparently telling his friends that Labour has done enough allaying of middle-class fears. Soon, he says, Labour will have to spell out its positive policies.

Come on, New Labour. Now is the time to go on the offensive and tell us what you really think. It is the Tories' only hope.

Major's position became so grim that he finally turned on his critics, resigned as leader of the Conservative Party, and dared them to challenge him. John Redwood did, and lost.

So much for the pen and dagger men

Once the drumming of feet had died away last night in the committee corridor, and mobile telephones of the TV men had ceased to beep like crickets, a soft noise could just be heard, if you strained your ears, in the newspaper bureaux above the ministerial corridor. It was the gentle mastication of humble pie on the part of much of that which used to be called Fleet Street, and – for there is no point in denying it – your reporter had a mouthful himself.

It was Major One, Hacks Nil. 'Not for the first time the pundits and commentators have been absolutely routed!' said Gillian Shephard. And the Prime Minister himself was careful, in the final words of his triumphant statement on the steps of Number Ten, to plant his foot figuratively on the mounded bellies of his real adversaries; not in Westminster, he said, not in the constituencies – no, he knew where the real enemy was:

'This has been settled in Westminster, not by commentators outside Westminster with their own particular views!' he cried. Before the result was flashed through the steaming committee corridor, and before it was clear that Mr Major was at least reasonably safe, the view of Major loyalists about the behaviour of the press was barely printable.

In the lobby corridor shortly before the result, I was confronted by one normally genial minister whose face went red as he abused the stance taken by your correspondent, with a string of profanities that turned heads for 20 yards. In the run-up to this leadership election, ministers have believed that there is what Harold Wilson called 'a small group of politically motivated men', Right-wing journalists in cahoots with the parliamentary Eurosceptics, determined to bring down the Prime Minister.

For the last four years, they believe they have launched their cowardly darts against John Major, actuated either by a misplaced intellectual snobbery or resentment that he is not Mrs Thatcher.

These pinpricks, though, have been nothing to the extraordinary barrage of artillery trained on Mr Major yesterday by what was once the loyal Conservative press. *The Daily Telegraph*, *The Times*, the *Daily Mail*, and almost all the rest of Fleet Street bar the *Financial Times* and the *Daily Express*, were convinced that Mr Major was leading his party to defeat in the next general election, and that he should therefore go. Such 'disloyalty' has enraged ministers. They see journalists as grossly inflated and self-important figures, irresponsible bomb-throwers.

They would sever all relations, were it not for the reality that, as with other terrorists, politicians have no choice but to talk to them. Across much of the party in the country, there is a parallel outrage at the behaviour of the press.

'Why can't you give John Major credit for what he has done?' local Tories demand. 'Why is he never congratulated for his success in bringing about sustainable economic growth and delivering the makings of a lasting settlement in Northern Ireland?'

Why indeed? Why has he taken such a pasting? Before we discuss the objections of principle to John Major's premiership, we should not forget the iron law of Fleet Street: you build 'em up in order to knock 'em down.

When John Major was a younger MP and rising fast, he cultivated political editors. Members of the Downing Street lobby say he was charming, personable, a man who caught your Christian name first bounce and lobbed it back. He was always on everyone's reshuffle list as a man likely to make the Cabinet. And once he had attained great office, and was no longer able to cultivate journalists with the same familiarity, it was always likely that relations would decay.

As Prime Minister, his great attraction was initially his very ordinariness, his decency, expressed in his campaign for a 'classless society'. But it is the professional deformation of journalists on broadsheet newspapers to be in search of Grand Ideas for their columns, and John Major did not provide them. They were never likely to be satisfied with a Major 'vision of Britain' which seemed to revolve around the frequency with which lavatory facilities occurred on motorways. They began to say that Mr Major had no real ideological backbone; and it was his mistake to be too sensitive to these jibes.

Unlike Mrs Thatcher, who some would say was eventually toppled because she failed to listen to her critics in the press, Mr Major listened too much. He seemed to care too intimately what was written about him by men he imagined sitting in book-lined rooms, with fancy waistcoats and fancy degrees.

He was known to be wounded by impertinent pseudo-psychological profiles. The journalists smelled vulnerability, and they piled on their attacks more thickly, characterising him, without much evidence, as a man who might wear his shirt tucked into his underpants.

Mr Major's best defence – and it has proved highly effective – is to inspire feelings of sympathy. Unlike Mrs Thatcher, though, he did not inspire fear; and to that extent Mr Major must blame himself for the way some back-benchers and the press engaged in bidding each other up in their insolence.

All this though is in a sense secondary. The press can in

no way be blamed for the axial moment of Mr Major's prime ministership, when the pound crashed out of the Exchange Rate Mechanism. One can blame the Bundesbank for failing to do enough to help; one can blame the speculators.

One might conceivably follow Douglas Hurd, and blame *The Sunday Telegraph* for encouraging the Danes to vote No in 1992, and so triggering the Maastricht crisis. But one cannot blame Fleet Street for the decisions of Messrs Major and Lamont to stay in the ERM long after it had ceased to be economically defensible, squandering billions and sending thousands of businesses to the wall.

It was not the press which landed some of the most damaging blows to the Prime Minister's authority. It was Norman Lamont, his former Chancellor and campaign manager, who said in the House of Commons, that he gave the impression of 'being in office but not in power'. It was Tony Blair who said that 'I lead my party, while he follows his.' Above all, the row over Europe has not been a mere figment of the imagination of the press.

It has been obvious to a wide section of his backbenchers – not least the 89 who voted for John Redwood – that the Prime Minister's March 1 statement on the single currency was less than decisive. The press did not cause the Conservative Party to plunge to defeat in the local and European elections.

The press has the power to convey its own public dissatisfaction to the Prime Minister. But it does not have the power to break him. Last night's result proved that.

And still the middle-of-the-roaders were flocking to Blair.

Who *are* all these people?

The taxi throbs deep into the evening of darkest Dulwich, into SE22. It is a voyage of discovery. I have come in search of a new and mysterious group of people whose importance is known, but whose characteristics are, as yet, imperfectly understood by political science. 'No one knows who these people are,' one of Tony Blair's advisers confessed to me. 'We're rather curious, actually.'

As of this month (September, 1995), the Labour Party claims to have 351,000 members, almost doubling its strength in 15 months; a figure all the more remarkable when you reflect that across Europe political party membership has been in chronic decline. Gone is the mass adherence to Christian Democracy and Social Democracy, and their counterparts in Britain, which gave the Labour Party a million members and the Tories an amazing 2.8 million in 1952. These days we devote our energies to the RSPB, to campaigning for Aids sufferers, to chaining ourselves to lorries carrying veal calves.

Only one party is bucking the trend, and most of its 100,000 new signings in the last year are attributed to one man: his flashing eyes, his floating hair, his chipped front tooth. When Tony Blair addresses the Labour Party conference next week, much will be made of the 'head and shoulders' argument: that Blair may indeed be a social democrat, but that the party as a whole has failed to move, and remains wedded to punitive redistribution and public spending. In the run-up to the next election, that must be the chief burden of Tory propaganda.

So it will be all the more vital for Blair to prove that the party *is* changing, from the grassroots up. The taxi stops at a tiny terraced house in Grove Vale. We are there:

29

at the HQ of the Dulwich Labour Party, where they are recording 80 new members per month. Through the dusty front-room window, I can see the shadowy forms of men and women of various ages. On closer inspection, they are drinking wine and orange juice.

They are not so very different from you and me, in tidy sweaters and skirts. These are the specimens, the new members of the Labour Party, very kindly assembled for me by Tessa Jowell, MP for East Dulwich, who is not only highly energetic and intelligent but also 'close to Tony'. As Peter Snow likes to say when the general election results are coming in, this is only a first sample. The reader is warned that our methods are not, cannot be scientific. But after spending more than an hour drinking Bulgarian Merlot and eating taco crisps with about a dozen new members, it seems that Blair is right to say that the party is changing. Blair's old Labour deputy, John Prescott, were he here, would hang his head; and yet there seems no reason, *prima facie*, for Mr Major to be altogether discouraged.

On the wall is a nicotine-stained map of the constituency and a 1930s poster with the slogan 'Tomorrow – when Labour Rules', depicting the workers in various attitudes of triumph. In the past, perhaps, this was the place for cloth-capped harangues and pipe-fuelled disputations about free collective bargaining. No longer. Barbara Richardson, a JP in her mid-40s with short hair and a cerise suit, tells me she has to push on shortly, and so briefly explains why she joined new Labour. She had been a social worker in the area (as had Tessa Jowell) and a member of the Norwood Labour Party. But she had despaired.

There was 'Red' Ted Knight. There was the way the party would not let her send her children to an independent school. And there was Neil Kinnock. 'I couldn't stand Neil Kinnock,' she says, and admits she feels guilty for saying so. Her view is shared, with less intensity, by a couple of others here. 'I was driven into the arms of the SDP – and I met some very nice people in the SDP,' says Barbara. So why did she rejoin? Unprompted, she hits the coconut: 'It was mainly because of Tony Blair'; which is the reason given by a quarter of new members in an April survey by *Labour Party News*.

It is also the reason given by Tom Ward, a bearded 19-year-old Carthusian wearing a Jim Beam T-shirt, who is just going up to Pembroke College, Oxford. 'I wanted to be more of an activist, and Blair made it acceptable to someone with a public-school background,' he says. At this point Ward is interrupted by John McTernan, the man acting as my cicerone in the world of the Dulwich Labour Party.

McTernan is a sophisticated Scot who was head of the debating Union at Edinburgh University, and who is now a big wheel in the local party. He wants to make sure I have got the point. 'This,' he exclaims, with the excitement of a scientist showing a visitor the world's first cyclotron, 'is New Labour! Tony Blair is the issue,' he continues. 'He is the first political leader in Britain since Margaret Thatcher whose distinctive social values could change the way we live our lives.'

That is a bold assertion. It is true that there must be many people who would have been quite uninterested in British politics had it not been for Mrs Thatcher. Is Blair about to re-order political life in the same way? I try the proposition on one of the younger types, a grinning chap of 30 wearing a beige leather jacket. He is called John Balme and was educated 'at the same school as Mrs Thatcher's son' (Harrow) before reading classics at King's College, London. Mr McTernan put it to me, 'New Labour comes from an interesting mix of backgrounds.'

Balme, it seems, joined less out of admiration for Tony Blair than out of respect for the memory of John Smith, whom he describes as 'the greatest prime minister we never had'. Certainly, Balme is enthusiastic about Blair. But it would be an exaggeration to say he is enthused by Blair's ideology. 'I think he could nail something down,' he says, meaning, for instance, that Blair could spell out what he intends to do with the privatised industries. But other new members admit they are rather unclear as to what their leader really represents.

'I still haven't quite been able to place him,' says Ian Richardson, a 72-year-old former *Birmingham Post* journalist wearing a woolly tie and stout brown shoes. Richardson has drifted across the political map. He almost became a communist in the 1930s. He voted for the Tories twice in the 1950s and once, to his shame, for Mrs Thatcher. But he describes himself as 'temperamentally a Labour man'. Again, though, he does not appear to hunger for any specific agenda from Mr Blair.

He is actuated more by rage against the Tories. I should have mentioned rage earlier. It is almost universal here. 'I'd like to shoot them all,' says Richardson, meaning all Tory ministers. He is angry about what he sees as the running down of the NHS. 'I have a handicapped child and I am 72,' he says in his educated voice. 'If I became even more Alzheimerish I might be faced with the possibility of having to sell my house. Where's the money for the oil and gas?' he demands, and there is a terrific amen-ing.

When I feel obliged to point out, like some hapless Tory candidate, that the economy is recovering, unemployment falling, 3 per cent growth, lots of lovely cheap houses, I come under fire from Judith Fitton, a woman in a blue denim dress who used to be first flute in the English National Orchestra and who has two grown-up children. 'You're sort of all I'm all right, Jack, aren't you?' she says consideringly. 'You don't know what it's like to try and get housing.'

The white-haired and white-sweatered curator of the River and Rowing Museum at Henley on Thames is also 'angry'. Mr Chris Dodd is in a strop because the Millennium Commission has failed to stump up for his project.

'It's their incompetence and their inability to take their hands off things,' says William Millinchip, another ex-journalist.

'Homeless beggars are something you associate with the Third World,' says Jenny Wick, a sweet-faced 60-year-old who is just dashing off to her swimming class.

'What has got my goat,' says Dodd, 'is that I don't believe anything this Government says.'

'My 80-year-old aunt in Halifax hasn't got any water,' says Jenny.

What we have here is nothing more original than middle-class leftish whingeing against the Government. All these folk here tonight have probably come from the slightly swankier Ruskin ward of Dulwich, with its semi-detached Edwardian houses. According to Tessa Jowell, her association has just been joined by the former British ambassador to Bogota and the deputy women's editor of the *Sunday Express*. They are decent, caring people who have decided that they can help their fellow man, and perhaps themselves, by putting Labour in power.

That does not mean that they were ever natural Tories, or that Mr Major need utterly despair. Successful though the Labour membership drive is, the party is only now approaching the membership levels of 1983; and at least a third of all the recruits are what Mr Blair's office describes as 'SDP retreads'. What these people in Dulwich have in common, it seems to me, is that they are angry middle-grounders who have given up on the idea of a centre party and found that Labour membership is no longer socially embarrassing. Almost all of them have at one time voted either SDP or Liberal.

It is not good news for the Tories, certainly; but it is worse news, surely, for Mr Ashdown. 'That's the strength of Labour's new membership,' explains McTernan. 'We're coming back to our true home.' If Mr Blair wants to turn his party into an SDP Mark II, he will have these people's undying support.

At one stage even the Daily Telegraph editorial column seemed half to succumb.

The 'new' gospel

Anthony Charles Lynton Blair is an attractive politician, who yesterday delivered a calculating and confident speech expressed at times in the hot-gospelling language of the star of a religious rock musical. Many will have been pleased to hear a politician infuse his discourse with such moral vigour, even if they may be irritated to hear Mr Blair proclaim that socialists have a monopoly on morality. Like most of the Labour leader's speeches, this sermon was pitched squarely at the disgruntled middle classes, and most of it could have come from the lips of a One-Nation Tory.

Mr Blair pledged to swell the ranks of policemen on the beat, for instance; and he appealed to traditional conservatives by suggesting that the sexual revolution had produced insecurity and spiritual doubt. To the remaining Scargillites in the hall at Brighton, he gave a warning that 'New Labour' was the party of patriotism and national unity, not class warfare on behalf of the international proletariat. The speech owed less, though, to Disraeli and John F Kennedy, than it did to the last Labour leader to rival Mr Blair in cleverness and sleight of hand.

In the year of Lord Wilson's death, and with Mary Wilson sitting behind him, Mr Blair paid conscious homage to Harold Wilson's 1963 pledge to deliver a new Britain forged in the white heat of the technological revolution. He echoed Harold Wilson, too, in the fundamental fraudulence of his rhetoric. 'Feel New Britain come alive,' rhapsodised Mr Blair. 'Feel the vitality that can course through this country's veins and make it young again.' It was not quite clear, however, what elixir was on offer. Apart from the renationalisation of British Rail, there was one new concrete promise: that every child of five, six or seven shall be educated in a class of fewer than 30 pupils. This, said the Fettes-educated Mr Blair, would be paid for by cancelling the assisted places scheme, and the chance of thousands of children to attend independent schools.

Mr Blair's central economic proposition was that the nation would be rejuvenated by the use of the information superhighway, the fashionable system of electronic communication. Never mind the irony that British Telecom, which would supply the network's infrastructure, would never have been privatised under Labour. Important though the information superhighway may be, it hardly amounts to a credible cornerstone for an economic strategy; and yet that is where it stood in Mr Blair's 'vision'.

For the rest, the Blair prescription for recreating a 'young' Britain was at best dubious. Labour would revivify the constitution by creating new tiers of bureaucracy in the form of regional assemblies for Scotland and Wales.

Businesses already groaning beneath the weight of regulation, would face, as *The Daily Telegraph* revealed yesterday, the extra costs of Labour's 'agenda for rights at work', including the Social Chapter. On the central question of how Labour's aims would be funded without an explosion in public spending, Mr Blair was silent.

As a piece of inspirational guff, the speech rated an

alpha. As a coherent economic and political call to arms, it was less than satisfying.

Many believed that the real fault-line, and the best hope for the Tories, lay in the split at the top of Labour.

Tony has the smile but Gordon has the brains

It was confrontation time last night (January, 1998) in Downing Street, apparently. A livid Tony Blair flew in to have it out with the Chancellor of the Exchequer. 'Brown faces Premier's wrath' said the headlines. Blair wanted an explanation from Gordon, we were told, and it had better be good.

There he is, thousands of miles away in Japan, when he hears that the Chancellor has been stabbing him in the back: whingeing, in fact, in an 'authorised' biography, about his failure to become Labour leader and about his 'betrayal' by the Blairites.

Oh, to have been a fly on the wall last night as Blair read the riot act to Brown! This is dynamite stuff, a split between PM and Chancellor. We do not yet know in what terms Blair reproved his erstwhile friend, and yet I doubt if he was too stern. What can he possibly say?

Brown is unsackable and impregnable. Indeed, as one Labour source put it yesterday, 'Blair is the President and Brown is the Prime Minister'; or, to take a showbiz metaphor, does anyone remember a pop group called Wham? There was Andrew Ridgeley and George Michael. You *must* remember: wham/bam/I am/a man was one of their hits.

The essence was that they were a duo, blood brothers, just as Tony and Gordon were the golden young modernisers of the Labour Party. All went well with Wham until it became obvious that George, the brooding, heavy-jawed one, had all the talent – and Andrew, well, Andrew was more of a pretty face. So they split up amid much acrimony and tears; and if you doubt the analogy, look at the respective roles of Gordon and Tony and ask yourself, which is truly First Lord of the Treasury?

In today's Britain, half the national wealth is already taken by Gordon Brown and allocated to other departments for spending, which gives a sense of his natural dominance in Whitehall. Gordon has gone further. Such is his authority over Welfare to Work, his brainchild, that the Department of Social Security was not even informed of the decision to extend its scope beyond the 18- to 25-year-olds. When the Chief Whip, Nick Brown, totted up the numbers of potential rebels over single-parent premium, who saw his report first? Not Blair, nor anyone in the Prime Minister's office. No, it's got to be Gordon.

Gordon Brown and his small team took the momentous decision to give the Bank of England independence, and then sold it to Blair. Gordon reaches across Whitehall to the departments of Education and of Social Security to take control of welfare reform, the one policy on which Labour has asked us to judge its performance. It is a rule of thumb that in every important department of state, there is a minister loyal to Gordon Brown. There is Andrew Smith at Employment, Nigel Griffiths at the DTI, Doug Henderson at the Foreign Office. Gordon Brown lobbied hard to install Harriet Harman at Social Security.

To inspire such loyalty bespeaks a certain intellectual aura, and he is by far the brightest star outside No 10. At one time, that accolade might have gone to his old enemy from Scotland, Robin Cook, the man who believes he should have been Chancellor. Poor Mr Cook has had too many appalling experiences in airport lounges. Worse, he has allowed himself to be bullied by Alastair Campbell: anyone with gumption would have paid for his mistress to travel with him from his own pocket. And while Cook writhes between the hammer of his wife and the anvil of No 10, the single biggest foreign policy dossier – EMU – is, apparently, entirely out of the hands of the Foreign Office.

Gordon Brown is so self-confident that last year he and his officials made an attempt to bounce the Prime Minister into supporting early entry to EMU. Someone in the Treasury briefed the *Financial Times*. The market reaction was so extreme that Blair was forced to call a halt. Charlie Whelan, Gordon's trusted press man, was overheard dictating the future of the pound in the Red Lion pub over a mobile phone. Has Whelan been reprimanded? Of course not.

He spins away, independently of Downing Street, allowing the television cameras into the Treasury, and admitting that he sometimes misleads; and the reason Blair allows the Brownies to get away with it is, simply, guilt.

As Paul Routledge's new biography makes clear, Brown is still bitter about the leadership election of 1994. It had always been the understanding in the Brown-Blair duo that Brown was the one who would stand for the leadership. Peter Mandelson, in theory, would support him. Brown still feels the treachery of Mandelson, who wrote a cunning letter to the effect that he would support a Brown candidacy, but that it would gravely damage the Labour Party.

He still smarts from the smears, emanating from the Blair camp, that he was homosexual. The reality, perhaps, is that Brown was always likely to lose a race against Blair. He was too dour, too Old Labour, for the task Mandelson had in mind. But it was Gordon Brown who had the credentials. Blair just had the teeth. Brown's family were farm labourers, while Blair's father was a *Conservative*!

Brown had a first-class degree in history from Edinburgh before he was 20 and was made Student Rector. Blair achieved a second from Oxford and played in a band called Ugly Rumours. Brown has written books on obscure Scottish socialists and on the case for a Scottish assembly. Blair has hoovered up his friend's ideas; and if evidence were needed of this, ask yourself, what is the slogan for which Blair was best known before he became Prime Minister?

That's right, it was 'Tough on crime, tough on the causes of crime'. And who minted that phrase, and innocently offered it to his buddy? Gordon, outmanoeuvred by a man two years his junior. Brown is the animating intelligence of the modern Labour Party; Blair is the man who takes the policies, and puts a nice shine on them.

It is, in a way, a good fit. They complement each other. Brown is in the Treasury at 6am, dreaming up wheezes for stinging the middle classes. Blair goes on television to reassure those about to be stung. This week we hear that Labour proposes to tax the universal benefits that currently go to the middle classes. Child benefit, disability living allowance, maternity benefit could be reduced for the better-off, without any countervailing cut in tax. So Blair will tomorrow go on the stump in Birmingham to assuage public anxiety about his plans – or rather, Gordon's plans.

And yet the double-act has its strains. The two men have different priorities. Tony Blair wants to end this parliament claiming that he has kept his promises, kept faith with the ex-Tories who flocked to his banner. When one talks to Gordon Brown one feels he is actuated by a sense of social injustice; he wants redistribution of wealth.

Gordon wanted a top rate of tax of 50p. Blair said no. Gordon proposed to axe tax-exempt savings of more than £50,000. Now Downing Street is saying the policy was 'badly presented'. Gordon Brown is consciously positioning himself, in the words of one MP yesterday, as 'the soul of the Labour Party'. Blair may have nothing to fear from his friend in the short term, since their interests so largely coincide. In the longer term, though, he might remember Machiavelli's dictum that it is wise not to trust a man who knows you have done him wrong.

But if Blair was an actor, he was brilliant at it. He borrowed from everyone, even his supposed ideological foes.

He went on and on, but he's no Mrs Thatcher

Give that man a handbag! And while you're at it, tell him to wear a powder blue suit and a pineapple-coloured wig next time he wants to impersonate this century's greatest peace-time prime minister.

We have had Tony the public school prefect with his half-time pep talks. We have had the bursting-chested evangelical. Yesterday we had a shameless piece of drag artistry.

The road is long. There is no backing down. There Is No Backing Down. TINBD, said our leader and his eyes flashed with something like the Caligula gleam of our lamented Leaderene. As Mr Mandelson, a man who claims to have forsaken the arts of spin, suavely confided: 'Basically, it's Tony's equivalent of the Lady's Not For Turning Speech of 1981.'

That's right. You turn if you want to, you moaning minnies, said Tony, showing the world he had all the *cojones* of La Dama di Hierro. 'Backbone not back down,' he barked at the conference. Straighten up, you 'orrible lot!

In true Thatcherian style he flailed at vested interests, or at least a judicious selection, and it would be dishonest to pretend that the tough-guy passages did not warm the brutal cockles of my heart. Teachers would have to brace up and get used to performance-related pay, he scolded. And they clapped!

Industry! chided the Prime Minister. What a shower. Dithering bosses and idle workers; well, he attacked the bosses anyway, only murmuring something about 'lack of productivity'. Bashing the workers is still going it a bit for Tony, but one lives in hope. He was pro-car, just like Herself.

'Family life has changed for good reasons as well as bad,' he said. You mean a Labour leader actually thinks there could be *bad* reasons for family breakdown, morally bad? One could almost hear the sucking of teeth.

The welfare state was being ripped off by scroungers, said Tony Blair, and such is the lobotomised state of his party that they clapped that, too. He said he was proud of cutting corporation tax to an all-time low. This did not elicit applause. But it could, of course, have come straight from an oration by the former Tory leader. All he had to say was 'We are a grandmother' or 'No, No, No', and the act of homage, or plagiarism, would have been complete.

Blair has tried this stunt before. He saw before the election that there was a significant group of erstwhile Tory voters who warmed to Mrs Thatcher's style of leadership, and felt disappointed by the less bone-crunching style of her successor. 'Say what you like about her,' said this type of disgruntled Tory, 'at least she knew what she thought.'

That was why Blair began cunningly to put it around that he 'admired' Mrs Thatcher; he allegedly sought her advice; he sucked up to useful idiot Thatcherites in the Right-wing press, who could be relied upon to bash Mr Major. And since the election we have been repeatedly tipped the wink that the Thatcher era is programmatic of the Blair reich.

Like Thatcher, Blair wants to be seen as a leader at war with the fainthearts, the wets, the Left in his own party, calling for a U-turn as recession bites. That was why so much of yesterday's speech was about 'challenge', that fierce flared-nostril exhortation to rise on the stepping stones of our dead selves to higher things. He even challenged the media not to wreck his moralising by unkind prying into the private lives of Labour ministers: a bit rich from a man whose party profited so grossly from the exposure of the sex lives of Tory ministers during the 'Back to Basics' fiasco.

But there is another and more important way in which Blair yearns to be compared to Thatcher. Hers has gone down in history as a time of ideological triumph, in which the ideas of the Right vanquished those of Mr Blair's party. Mrs Thatcher pioneered a revolution which was imitated in one way or another, around the world; and *that* is the analogy which Blair hopes will be drawn.

That is why he was sycophantically introduced yesterday as the model of aspirant leaders from Germany to Japan. That is why he banged on so relentlessly about the 'Third Way'. Emptying his sentences of verbs, he tried impressionistically, with blobs of vacuous uplift, to explain what this meant. 'And in this new era, a new agenda. Economies that compete on knowledge, on the creative power of the many, not the few. Societies based on inclusion, not division. Countries that are internationalist not isolationist, this is the "Third Way" . . .' If you can make head or tail of that, my friend, you ought to be a Labour spin doctor.

Mrs Thatcher never tried to define Thatcherism, in advance of the fact, with a lot of de-verbed drivel. The term was coined for her, once her achievements were so palpable. Why does Blair bother with the 'Third Way'? Because Blair's deepest fear is that there isn't really any such thing as Blairism.

In Mrs Thatcher's first term she embarked on a programme of reforming the supply side of the British economy and containing government expenditure. In a way, the problems facing the incoming Labour government have been of comparable magnitude: how to reform the welfare state, and how to reach a settlement in Britain's relations with a federalising Europe.

On both these questions, Tony Blair's approach is more striking for its continuity with Tory governments, than any revolutionary 'Third Way'. He did put in Frank Field to think the unthinkable about welfare. Mad Frankie duly unthunk it, and was kicked out for his pains, along with Harriet Harman.

The Left of the Labour Party see that as a victory, and they are probably right. As for his European policy, it is identical to that of John Major and Douglas Hurd. Make up our minds on the euro in due course, keep a seat at the table, oppose interference in the nooks and crannies of our national life.

It is not that it is a bad policy; but sorry, Tony, it lacks that Thatcherian zing. Which brings us to the final attribute of the Thatcherian epoch which Blair undoubtedly hopes to emulate: longevity.

Looking at him yesterday, and looking at the state of the Opposition, one could indeed see him going on and on and on. But if this is the 'year of challenge', as he kept saying, next year could be the year of raiding our wallets, as Labour's extravagant spending commitments coincide with the burdens of a recession.

One day, in a way we cannot foresee, this demi-god will complete his imitation of Thatcher. He will be turfed out with tears and ignominy. It is the common fate, as Enoch Powell said, of all politicians.

There were some Labour disasters, and they were gloriously self-inflicted.

He lived by Spin, he died by Spin

Weep, O ye shirt-makers of Jermyn Street, ye Cool Britannia tailors and whatever exists of human finer feeling. In the Ministry of Sound, the tank-topped bumboys blub into their Pils.

In the delicatessens of Elgin Crescent, the sawdust is sodden with tears. For months, years, Carla Powell will go into mourning, her plumage as black as night. For Mandy is dead, dead ere his prime!

Yes, one can already hear the chokes and the sobs, even from those Left-wing quarters that were yesterday calling for his pomaded scalp. 'So noble', 'So honourable', 'Fell on his own sword', 'A good end – so unlike the other lot!'

In the soft-lit Soho drinking clubs frequented by Mandy and his pals, his deed will be likened to Captain Oates stepping out into the blizzard to spare his comrades. We are asked to imagine a kind of pre-Raphaelite scene, 'the self-sacrifice of Mandy'.

On one telephone, Blair, haggard, appalled, pleading: and on the other, Mandelson, unswerving, resolute, his convex brow transfigured by a strange shaft of light. Blair: 'Peter, reconsider, I beg you!' Mandelson: 'My mind is made up. I must go for the good of the party,' and so on.

That is how Mandy would like us to imagine the events of the past 24 hours. Alas, it does not square with the facts. This time on Tuesday, Peter Mandelson was saying, 'I have done absolutely nothing wrong' and 'I won't quit'. He was writing complicated self-justificatory letters to Elizabeth Filkin, the Parliamentary Standards Commissioner, all about the loan from Geoff and the absolutely-above-board, Midland-Bank terms on which it was agreed.

Downing Street was announcing that this was 'not a hanging offence', and some of us were so dunderheaded as to believe the spin doctors.

We thought Blair and he would stand shoulder to shoulder, and I should like to make clear that, when I wrote yesterday that Robinson would go and Mandelson would 'survive', this was, ahem, correct in the purely biological sense, the Gloria Gaynor sense.

It is now clear that Mandelson was hanging on by his cuticles and it was Tony who was suddenly remote, down the line, watching events in Chequers. And what was he watching? He was watching this space, or spaces like it. In the end, it was the sheer volume of coverage in yesterday's papers – the multiple avenues of inquiry whose end one could not quite see – that convinced Ali Campbell that Mandy must go.

He lived by spin. He died by spin. Do not for one minute believe that this is some ingenious 'tactical' resignation, *reculer pour mieux sauter*, that will simply win sympathy and speed his comeback. Peter Mandelson will ever bear the epithet 'disgraced', as in 'disgraced Cecil Parkinson'. That is what a resignation is. It is an admission of guilt.

Mandelson has not resigned because he has caused embarrassment to the Prime Minister through the wilful misrepresentations of the press. He has been chopped because (a) there are unanswered questions over his Britannia mortgage application; (b) he would seem to have broken the letter and spirit of the Code of Conduct; and (c) he was hopelessly compromised as the chief regulator responsible for this country's business and financial probity, since one of the main targets of his department's investigations had lent him £373,000, at such advantageous rates that Mandelson had, effectively, already received a present of £10,000.

It is almost incredible folly, and the Tories must be

staring with that look of amazed joy that you see in war films, when a bomb falls miraculously down the single chimney pot into the fortified nerve centre of the enemy. Mandelson has been integral to New Labour, both to what is good – and a lot of it is good, if one takes Old Labour as the yardstick – and what is bad.

In so far as the party has moved to the Right and abandoned some of its hostility to enterprise, he must take his share of the credit. True, he has been happily festooning business with more red tape, imposing Euro-regulations on hours of work and so on; and yet there is no mistaking his popularity with the CBI, or their sense that he has made a good start.

And in so far as New Labour is flashy and meretricious, Mandelson must also take the blame. If anyone is responsible for the triumph of style over substance, he is. He is a marketing genius: and he saw that you could take a red rose, and add flashing teeth, a quivering lip, gobbledegook about the 'Third Way' and pretend that it was something new and wonderful.

The danger for Tony Blair, now that Mandy has gone, is that the lipstick, the varnish, the gloss will start to come away . . . and behind the gloss? What do we see? Just a load of politicos on the make: men and women actuated by nothing nobler – and nothing worse – than the urge to govern, to take on the trappings of power, to be wooed by media moguls and have their ears nibbled by society's loveliest hostesses: not so very different, in fact, from the last years of the Tory party.

Mandelson was the man whose inventiveness with image and message did so much to make this party seem special; and now New Labour seems less special, and the vacuities of its leader less protected. He had one further, vital function. I don't mean the Millennium Dome, though you may be wondering, parenthetically, who will speak now for that monstrous puffball (the answer is the glamorous Chris Smith).

Who will have the pzazz to con everybody into going there, as I am sure Mandelson would have done? My name is Ozymandelson, king of spin; look on my works, ye mighty and despair. No, more important than his function as chief Domocrat, he was to be the man who finally reached a settlement between the British people and the European Union.

Mandelson made no secret of his desire to emulate his grandfather, Herbert Morrison, and become Foreign Secretary. The fact that Robin Cook has had such an abysmal year can be at least partly attributed to Mandelson's hot breath on the back of his neck. Mandelson is a key player in the European Movement, a man whose judgment Blair utterly trusted on the question of when and how to take Britain into the single currency. Will he trust Mandelson's judgment now? Why should any of us trust that judgment?

This is a disaster that arose, in the classic tradition, from an earlier evil done to another. We may never know quite how this story reached the ears of Paul Routledge, the journalist and partisan of Gordon Brown: but I wonder whether it can be wholly unconnected with the sense of wrong that Gordon still feels, after Peter backed Tony, and not him, for the leadership in 1991.

In the very genesis of New Labour there was bloodletting and backstabbing: and now the miasma has claimed its first and most spectacular victim. Mandelson, we may be sure, will have his revenge. The tragic cycle of New Labour has begun.

Still struggling to define the meaning of New Labour, those close to Gordon Brown were starting to talk about imitating America. But were they prepared to do what it took?

American revolution

A curious consequence of the end of the Cold War is a change in left-wing attitudes to America. Now that we no longer depend on the United States to protect us, or to uphold freedom against tyranny in Eastern Europe, left-wingers seem to have dropped their loathing of Uncle Sam. If reports are to be believed, both Gordon Brown and Tony Blair are in thrall to a book by Jonathan Freedland, a *Guardian* columnist, called *Bring Home the Revolution*. Many of Mr Freedland's sentiments were echoed in Mr Blair's egregious attack, last month, on the forces of conservatism.

The Freedland thesis, broadly, is that America is a very wonderful place, for two reasons. The American people are bursting with enterprise and a spirit of get-up-and-go; and they have a real sense that they, The People, are in charge of their own democracy, in that they tug their forelocks to no man, and regard the very President of the United States as their servant, not their master. How marvellous it would be, says Freedland, if we in Britain could import that spirit of classlessness and gumption. The answer, he suggests, is to remember that British thinkers inspired the American revolution, and the end of the rule of George III over the North American colonies. Let us bring the revolution home, he urges, and step number one is, of course, to get rid of the monarchy.

Abolish the Queen, he says, and suddenly a huge symbolic weight will be lifted from the shoulders of the British people. The great invisible apparatus of class will be magicked away, and a new nation will be born: unstuffy, undeferential, dynamic and exploding with new ideas for Internet startups. Though Mr Blair and Mr Brown have been careful not to echo the Freedland line on the monarchy itself, they are avid supporters of the underlying thesis: that we need a new idea of 'Britishness', in which the oppression of ancestral symbols is cast off, in favour of a 'new nation' of equal citizens, each thrusting vigorously in the best American way.

Now it would be possible to do battle with the Freedland argument, and reply that the Queen is held in harmless affection by the majority: that any replacement – as the Australians have just shown – would almost certainly be worse, in the sense that he or she would be the product of party politics; and that, in any case, the existence or otherwise of the institution of monarchy (or, indeed, the hereditary peerage) has no bearing for good or ill on the spirit of enterprise, or democracy, in this country. But that, in a way, would be too kind to Mr Freedland, Mr Brown, Mr Blair and their hilarious mistake.

You don't have to be the new de Tocqueville to see that America's stunning economic success has little or nothing to do with getting rid of the King in 1776, and everything to do with the American approach to business; with their cult of success, and their ability to bounce back from failure. Why has American business prospered so mightily, and why has America found it so easy to create jobs? Because, for one thing, total taxation in America is about 32 per cent of GDP, while it is slightly over 40 per cent in this country; and because employment regulations are nothing like as onerous as those in Britain. By all means let us bring home the revolution, if that means cutting taxes by 20 per cent, and creating the true, American conditions for enterprise. If Gordon Brown means what he says, he will presumably halt the astonishing rise in taxation under Labour, now the fastest increase in any European country. And, as for importing the American love of democracy, we say yippee, and it couldn't come a moment too soon.

By all means let there be elections for the municipal dog-catcher, as Mr Freedland suggests, and let the British recover their sense that We The People really run our country. It is a striking feature of American democracy that the Americans will not tolerate the subjugation of their sovereign will to international bodies. The United States habitually ignores the rulings of World Trade Organisation panels. Which country is against the establishment of a supranational Court of Human Rights in The Hague? Not China, not Indonesia, but the United States. One need not go as far as some American politicians, who think the UN represents an unacceptable intrusion. But perhaps there is something in the American love of national self-government; perhaps that is one reason why their democracy feels so healthy to Mr Freedland: the Americans still believe that the politicians they elect are running their country and having an impact on their lives.

So come on Freedland, come on Brown and Blair. Let's bring home the revolution; let us do honour to the Anglo-Saxon principles of democracy still alive in America, and end the cession of sovereignty to Europe. If Mr Freedland and his Labour supporters had the slightest intellectual honesty, they would recognise that the American revolution was based on one founding principle, which is wholly incompatible with the euro, and the growing economic government of Europe. It was called No Taxation Without Representation.

As I have chronicled elsewhere, the Tories were given another stuffing, and William Hague, who will one day be Chancellor of the Exchequer, at the very least, threw in the towel.

This is no fight for the Tory soul

Right, I can't take it any more. If one more well-meaning person begs me to consider that the Tory party is on the verge of extinction, I think I will jump in the Thames. You never heard such needless pessimism, much of it from the readers of this newspaper. Oh, there will be a plague of boils if so and so becomes leader, says one group of correspondents. Plague of boils? says the other group. We'll be lucky. Why, if the other chap becomes leader, there will be a plague of boils and a blood-red moon, a murrain on our cattle and our children will all get nits.

Nits! says the first group. That's nothing. If so and so becomes leader they will be mutant shampoo-resistant nits . . . and so on and so forth. Come on, folks. Let's get a grip here. It is true that, under the curious algorithm used to produce a new leader, the Tories have just left a brilliant candidate by the wayside.

You could at this point compose an enormous sermon about why he lost, the hidden agenda of the newspapers, the slightly fascistic tone of some of the articles about 'fatherhood'. You could prose on about his inner torment, complex personality, artistic temperament, proud Spanish origins and blah blah fishcakes. But since Michael Portillo lost by only one vote to the man everybody said was the front-runner, I think you will agree that any such article would be an inverted pyramid of piffle.

So we are left with two candidates, and already this is being portrayed as a Manichean struggle between light and dark, yin and yang, Tom and Jerry and all the rest of it.

On the one hand, according to one group of gloomster letter-writers, there is the man who wants to scrap the pound and turn Westminster into a branch of the Brussels Bundeskanzleramt. Oh yes, they go on, he wants to drive the Euro-sceptics into priestholes, and force all our children to learn the choral part of Beethoven's ninth, and tattoo the hideous 12-star Euroemblem on to the very bellies of our once-proud football hooligans.

Ha! say my other group of correspondents. But if we go off with the other chap, he'll lead us into some Right-wing cul-de-sac redolent of the 1950s, full of authoritarian morality and secret sock drawers with leopardskin accessories. The air will resound to the thwack of the sjambok against the riding boot, and the men will look like Terry-Thomas, and the public will think the Tories are more irrelevant than ever. Those are the symmetrical doomsday scenarios, and they are both, of course, utter nonsense.

Everybody now agrees with Michael Portillo's analysis: that the party failed in some sense to 'connect', seemed to cherry-pick a few relatively minor issues, and didn't seem to have anything to say about public services. If you read the manifestos of Clarke and Duncan Smith, they are saying almost exactly the same thing about the way back.

So let's stop this pretence that either of the two remaining candidates would cause the end of civilisation as we know it. Call me a blithering optimist, but it is time we looked at this question from the other end: not at the damage either man could do, but at the great virtues of both of them.

Here is Iain Duncan Smith, a young man, affable, amiable, able, who was identified by this column in 1994 as the future of Conservatism. He has oodles of children (though I hasten to say that this is not remotely important). He has lived and worked in what politicians and journalists touchingly call 'the real world', and in his straightness he would provide a splendid contrast to Tony Blair.

Then there is Ken Clarke, who also has bags of hinterland, jazz, cricket, Angevin kings and whatnot. He also has children (not that … etc) and a brilliant wife who does tapestry. He is massively experienced in government, and with his boisterous, biffing, bonhomous temperament and his great spinnaker of a belly he would provide a splendid contrast to the actorishness of Tony Blair.

It is true that they do not agree about Europe. Duncan Smith would be able to lead the Tory party during a referendum campaign, in full-throated defiance of the single currency. Clarke would not, though he would allow full-throated defiance from the rest of his party.

The question is whether this would make any difference (a) to the fate of the pound and (b) to the fate of the Tory party. My hunch is that the referendum result would be completely unaffected. The experience of other countries' euro-referendums is that the best way to achieve a 'No' is to ensure that the political establishment is in favour of a 'Yes', in which case the public has the exquisite pleasure of telling them all to go to hell.

If Blair were so foolish as to call a referendum, he would almost certainly get the bum's rush whether Clarke were the leader or not, and a pretty delirious experience that would be. As for whether or not it would be a disadvantage to the Tories to have this split at the top during a referendum campaign, I wonder. We had a more or less united position during the last election (though it was too weak for many of us), and we didn't exactly storm to victory. Among the acute observations that Michael Portillo made during his campaign was that Europe would not have the same salience during the next election.

Let us see which of the two comes up with the most interesting stuff, over the next few weeks, on public services, but also on the issues that are starting to interest affluent Britain: the environment, globalisation, even the Third World. Whatever happens, let no one say that this is a struggle for the Tory party's soul. There is no such thing. The Tory party is a vast organism animated by a few vague common principles such as tradition and love of country, and above all by the pursuit and retention of power.

In spite of their colossal majority, Labour ministers showed their splendid gift of self-destruction.

Now can Blair make Mandy Chancellor?

Drat. Double drat. I had just come up with a brilliant campaign for the Tories. It was the Keep Stephen Byers campaign. By the sixth month of his epic resistance, as tenacious and demented, in its way, as the German survival under the Soviet shelling at Stalingrad, it had become clear that there was no longer any advantage in removing him from office. The Tories should have recognised that he had achieved landmark status in our national culture, and slapped a preservation order on him. His place on the Labour front bench should have been blue-plaqued, in tribute to his personal evolutionary breakthrough: the prehensile buttock.

The Byers seat in the Cabinet should have been designated a Site of Special Scientific Interest – a unique habitat for a new and remarkable form of human limpet. English Heritage, English Nature, the Council for the Protection of Hopeless Politicians, every quango in the book could have been mobilised to protect Mr Byers from the bulldozer; because after months of ludicrous falsehoods and incompetence, he had become a Grade I listed monument to Labour mendacity. Byers incarnated all the vacuity, the spin-driven vanilla-flavoured candyfloss nothingness of this Government. It was surely the duty of all good conservatives to conserve him, and keep him before the public as a constant reminder of what Blair and co are really all about. It was of course about 24 hours after this inspiration had hit me that Mr Byers was accorded the bizarre privilege of resigning from Downing Street, which shows, perhaps, that Labour minds were working on lines similar to my own.

By giving him the Downing Street send-off, Tony is sending a signal that Stephen is still a much-loved disciple, but one who has been cruelly martyred. Like the eponymous saint, Stephen has been pelted to death – only this time it's by the missiles of Fleet Street, says Labour. He has been hounded out, silenced by the cacophonous yapping of the press; or at least that is the Downing Street spin, and it seems to be working. I was pretty shocked on Tuesday afternoon to witness the response of some of the female staff at *The Spectator*, when Byers was saying bye-bye. There were oohs and aahs, and there may even have been a brushing away of a tear by Kimberly Fortier, our generally tough-minded American publisher.

What's the matter? I yelled at them. How could they fall for the fellow, just because he looks all suave and neat and sorrowful? He hasn't been the victim of a concerted media campaign, I reminded them. He's been the victim of his own intergalactic bungling and ineptitude, which he has repeatedly covered up with lies. If there is one man to be singled out for causing the current chaos in the railways, that man is Stephen Byers. No one knows when Railtrack will come out of administration, where it is being cryogenically preserved by lawyers and accountants. It may be November. It may be longer.

No one knows when someone will get a grip on the

company, restore morale, and sort out the delays caused by infrastructure faults, which rose by 45 per cent in the two months after Byers's Mugabe-style expropriation of October 2001.

What we do know for sure is this: that with the bill from Ernst and Young and everyone else running at £1 million per day, and with the cost of compensation to shareholders already standing at £500 million and climbing, Byers has pulled off a stunning feat. The taxpayer is already paying more, for administration, than Railtrack was asking for to keep going last year.

Byers dispossessed the Railtrack shareholders, and stunned the City, not so much, as some have suggested, because he used to be a Trot. It is true that 'Take back the track' used to be an old Trot slogan; but it is probably fair to say that Byers has self-lobotomised away his ideology. No, he did it because he thought it would be popular with the Labour back benches. In order to accomplish his aim, his conduct was far more serious in its implications than misleading the House over the non-sacking of Martin Sixsmith.

Before he could renationalise the company back in October, he had to make a case to the courts that Railtrack had no alternative source of income. That was not the case. Railtrack was not insolvent, at least in the sense that it was always open to Tom Winsor, the Rail regulator, to put more money into Railtrack by raising the rate charged to the train operating companies. The bill paid by the 25 TOCs would then be picked up by the taxpayer – so that, in a way, Winsor controlled the cash spigot from the taxpayer to Railtrack. Byers was aware of this; and to prevent Tom Winsor from saving Railtrack, he had recourse to threats. If Winsor exercised that power to bail out Railtrack, Byers warned him, he would simply force through legislation to countermand him. In other words, Byers was prepared to make an utter nonsense of the idea of an independent rail regulator.

Taxed on this question of whether he ever threatened the rail regulator, Byers has repeatedly denied it. No one – especially in the City – believes him. Had he not resigned, he would never be trusted again in any dealings with the private sector, because he might arbitrarily decide to change the regulatory framework.

Byers was a liar, trimmer, bungler, who made the final mistake of blurting the truth about the euro referendum. He had to go. Pity. I wonder whether there is anyone who wants to join the Protect Prescott campaign? Or since Mandy has said that he believes that he was 'put on earth to be a minister' (by what alien life forms he did not say), perhaps we should urge Blair to make him chancellor.

And I started to feel optimistic again.

We gave Blair a gong – and then the bubble burst

Sell. Get out now. Are you trying to offload some property? Flog it now, because this thing is going down the pan, and I can tell you now, with complete confidence, that the game is virtually up.

You don't need a canary in the mineshaft to foretell the coming collapse. You don't need to watch the flight of the birds, read the entrails of an ox or even to look at the numbers in the estate agents' windows.

I have found the key economic indicator, the one that tells you which way your house price is about to go. It is, I am afraid, the political fortunes of Tony and Cherie Blair.

Look back at the history of the British property market

over the past 10 years: compare the trajectory of New Labour, and shudder. Let us imagine that this couple, the Blairs, were an Islington town house, being brought to the market, as they figuratively were in 1994.

Handling the sale – initially to the Labour Party – are the thrusting firm of Campbell Millar, consisting of Alastair Campbell and his partner, Fiona Millar, among the most go-getting of all the go-getters in the world of Islington estate agents, which is saying something.

'We are delighted to offer this highly desirable conversion,' gushed Campbell Millar in their first particulars, 'which has the benefit of extensive modernisation throughout. The accommodation is deceptively spacious,' they said, which is of course estate agent speak for deceptive.

But never mind. The buyers, the Labour Party, were enraptured, and their investment proved fruitful. The housing market powered ahead between 1994 and 1997, and, symmetrically, the Blairs prospered mightily, the hottest political property Britain had seen for some years.

Tony axed Clause Four. He created New Labour. He won the 1997 election by a landslide – and then his market value really took off. He was Supertone; he seemed invincible.

He wobbled his chin emetically when Diana, Princess of Wales was killed, and everyone loved him. He bombed the Serbs, and was hailed the saviour of Kosovo. His poll ratings climbed to unprecedented heights for a sitting Prime Minister – and, in a quite eerie way, the housing market tracked his performance.

Tony and Cherie's initial popularity had been founded on genuine achievement. It was, on the whole, a good thing to kill off socialism and to destroy Old Labour. But after 1997, the attachment to Blair – and lust to invest in bricks and mortar – seemed to acquire an element of irrationality.

Nothing could quite deter the punters from buying

houses. Manufacturing industry began one of the longest recessions since the war. Gordon Brown brutally raided the nation's pensions. Britain slid slowly down the list of the world's most productive economies; and still the housing market was going gangbusters, with only the odd fit and start on the upward progression. And the story with the Blairs was much the same.

The Ecclestone scandal, the Hinduja passport business, the shameful and ludicrous Dome – affairs that would have chipped a good deal of paint off almost any other leader – left him unscathed.

By 2001, his poll ratings were so robust that he stormed through his second general election – and then, quite frankly, the housing market seemed to take leave of its senses. In 2001, it grew by some 30 per cent. Garages in Islington were going for a quarter of a million; gentlemen's conveniences in Chelsea were changing hands for the kind of money that, a mere three years earlier, might have bought you a house in Fulham or a chateau in the Loire.

The stock market was now a sea of red, and had been for ages, and still everyone poured into property with a gadarene mania. And so it was, alas, with the Blairs. Everyone could see that the economy was heading for the rocks, that Brown's borrowing figures were bound to go through the roof, that taxes were likely to go up with no tangible improvement in public services – and still people were ready to take a punt on Tony. In Europe, people started to wonder, in all seriousness, whether or not he might deign to accept a newly created post of president.

In a fit of madness, a group error for which I principally blame Frank Johnson, the jurors of *The Spectator* parliamentarian awards gave him not the wooden spoon, not the booby prize, but the Top Gong.

That moment, that award, will be seen by future historians as the occasion when the needle of approval teetered to its zenith. That was the instant before the value of Blair, as a property, began its rapid and inexorable decline. That was the sell indicator.

That told you everything you needed to know about the market in the Blairs: that they were grossly oversold. And then, as if to bear out my analysis exactly, the Blairs did something that precisely expressed how ludicrously inflated the housing market had become. They took £500,000, and blew it on two flats in Bristol, one for family purposes, and one as an investment. You only had to study the flats, with the funny wavy lines on the façades, to be reminded of all those exorbitantly over-priced Docklands flats that went into negative equity in 1992.

I don't know exactly in which respects Cherie lied. One feels rather sorry for her, in a way, being monstered by the *Daily Mail* for her friendship with a topless his 'n' hers massage-offering female Rasputin and her conman lover.

It is a bit off for the *Mail* to complain that she is interested in New Age crystals, when every day that paper invites its readers to believe that ancient fishgods built the pyramids, or that sunspots cure cellulite, or whatever.

Never mind. She lied. The Home Office is being forced to investigate any skulduggery surrounding the extradition of the slim-kit conman, and Tony has been forced into the ludicrous extreme of claiming that his wife spent the family fortune, on two flats, without telling him a word. Sell! Sell! Sell Blairs!

We end fifteen years of British politics with the Tories still
stuck on about thirty per cent in the polls. Blair may be
the victor in Iraq – but welfare is unreformed; the public
services are not better; the European issue is unresolved –
and his constitutional reforms are a mess.

Kylie's bottom shows the way ahead
for the Lords

Like finding a sixpence in a pudding, like watching a crouton float from the depths of some baffling minestrone, the world yesterday discovered a concrete policy in the primordial verbal soup that passes for the political discourse of Tony Blair. He took a stand.

After sitting on the fence for so long that some of us feared he would need to be surgically removed, he told us what he thought. While Robin Cook's brows bulged indignantly beside him, Blair gave his opinion about the future of the Upper House. Now before I tell you what he said, I am conscious that this subject, reform of the House of Lords, is not regarded as box office stuff. Some readers may wish that I could think of linking it, like so many other important articles in this paper, to Kylie Minogue's bottom.

All I can say is that I will do my best, over the next 900 words, to get her into the article. I know what the features editors want these days. I merely ask them to accept, before we come to the bit about Kylie Minogue's bottom, that this, too, is an issue of vital significance. There are many depressing ways in which this government has mucked about with people's legitimate expectations, and for which, frankly, they deserve to be sacked. One thinks of Railtrack, A-levels, and pensions. But there is something especially sickening and casual about the way they have decided to take the shears to our very constitution, hacking away like a drunken topiarist, and without the foggiest idea of what ultimate shape they want Parliament to have.

Next Tuesday, MPs will be asked to vote on a series of seven options on the future of the Lords. They are all bad, but it should go without saying that the one Tony plumped for yesterday is the most objectionable of the lot. He wants to expel the remaining hereditaries, and have a fully appointed Upper House. As soon as one imagines the Appointments Committee that will create this chamber, one sees how rank the whole operation will be.

Think of the lunches; the hackery; the behind-the-scenes schmoozing and fixing; the quiet words from the Government Chief Whip; the winking, the nose-tapping, the soft belching in the Savoy Grill Room, or Glyndebourne, or Ascot. It is a disgusting way to choose the revising chamber of a great and ancient legislature. That is why it attracts a machine politician and power freak like Blair, and that is why it repels Robin Cook, who still has something of the democrat about him. Like some thoughtful people on the Tory benches, Cookie wants a wholly elected second chamber.

The advantage of this is that it would protect the Upper House from jobbery, and the Prime Minister's desire to stuff it with his cronies. The disadvantages of popular election, alas, are almost as great as those of the appointive system. It would mean creating yet another cadre of busy-bodies calling on the electorate for their support, at a time when voters can barely be bothered to turn out for the general election, and when we have more elected politicians, per head, than at any time in our history. It would mean paying for these people – their salaries, their pensions, their housing allowances, their fuel discounts. But worst of all, it would mean that they could claim a democratic mandate. It is in the nature of things that the two Houses should disagree; but under Robin Cook's proposals there is no very obvious reason why the elected members of the House of Commons should prevail over the elected members of the Upper House. It is a recipe for gridlock and disaster.

That is why a great many Labour and Tory MPs reject this solution, and their arguments have force. So what does that leave?

On one point Blair was right yesterday: any hybrid system – part elected, part appointed – combines the vices of both, and has this extra disadvantage: that members would not be there on the same basis, and with the same authority. Some would swank around and claim popular support; some would always have the embarrassment of being a crony. Whatever we come up with, members of the reformed Upper House must have parity of legitimacy. We need something that combines the advantages of both – a dash of election, but no popular mandate – and I think I may have it. This is not one of the seven options for consideration on Tuesday, but it should be urgently taken up.

This solution is that the Lords themselves, almost 700 of them, should form the electoral college; and when any one of them dies or gives up, they should elect someone – whomever they choose from across the country – to fill his or her place.

One beauty of this idea is that, quite unlike the appointive system, it would confer great distinction and prestige on those elected to serve. It would be a fine thing to be judged worthy by your peers. It would be much harder to fix, much less open to governmental bullying and Buggins' turnery, than the appointive system; and yet it would not involve a new species of elected politician claiming a popular mandate.

It might perhaps be necessary to stipulate 10-year terms of office, and to draw up candidate lists to ensure the widest possible representation from groups and interests across the country. But that, frankly, would probably not be necessary.

Their lordships are already famed for their independence of mind; Labour and Tories are now almost level pegging, with the cross-benchers holding the balance of power, and they are the kind of people who would delight in bringing in everyone from all walks of life.

The two halves of Parliament would then be properly matched to allow the body politic to proceed, each House flawless in its own way, but each readily distinguishable from the other. It is a solution as beautiful, in fact, as the two halves, symmetrical but wholly anatomically distinct, of the rear end of Kylie Minogue.

Trust me, being sacked isn't all bad

Now that the plaster has stopped falling from the ceiling, and my latest prang has stopped ringing in my ears, it is time to admit that there is a certain surreal joy in being sacked.

It is meant as no disrespect to the man who sacked me when I say that the whole experience has unexpected advantages. There is the sudden sense of freedom. There is the feeling of broad horizons and the wind on your face, not just for me, but for the entire Tory front bench, which is no longer under the heavy obligation of having to agree with every word in *Spectator* editorials.

But mainly I'd recommend getting ignominiously sacked – and I want you to know that I insisted on my right to be sacked: 'Sack me,' I said, by way of an ultimatum, 'or sack me!' – because it is only by being sacked that you can truly engender sympathy. Nothing excites compassion, in friend and foe alike, as much as the sight of you ker-splonked on the Tarmac with your propeller buried six feet under. Nothing is so calculated to melt the hearts of your rivals. 'How are you?' they ask, clasping your hand with genuine solicitude, and when you mumble some halting words of thanks, they repeat: 'No, but how are you really?' And who could possibly grudge them their innocent Schadenfreude, their tender satisfaction in your plight? And the other great thing about being sacked in this way, from the opposition front bench, is that it is so economically painless. There is no compensation package. There is no redundo. There is no onerous system of formal warnings or industrial tribunals or suits for unfair dismissal. Why should there be? It was a good job, a job I was proud to do, but it was a Shadow Arts job, and carried no emoluments whatever. My family did not depend on the existence of this job, for the putting of bread on the table, and quite right, too. Not only was my extinction cosmically insignificant; it was also what the Treasury would call revenue-neutral.

The more one considers the position, the clearer it is that there were no grounds whatever for sympathising with me; and that is why I would like us to turn our thoughts to the tens of thousands across Britain who do now face the loss of their jobs, in circumstances far more serious than mine, and through no fault of their own.

It is agreed across the political spectrum that the public sector is growing at too fast a rate, and that this involves much waste. When we Tories discuss this subject, we invariably speak with brutal impersonality. We rave about the new public sector jobs that have been created since 1997, which we estimate at between 530,000 and 650,000. We wave copies of the *Guardian* appointments pages, where weird, politically correct non-jobs are advertised, week in, week out, often with very attractive salaries and perks.

Or we might cite Ross Clark's Job of the Week column

(in a magazine I dare not name), in which he picks the barmiest sits vacs, the waist-upwards gender awareness co-ordinators, the innumerable outreach and diversity officers, and we make the whole thing sound – as indeed it is – not just expensive but also ludicrous.

We point out that, from April 2003 to April 2004, the number of officials in Whitehall alone expanded by 12,280. That is bigger, my friends, than the entire population of Henley-on-Thames. It is bigger than Thame. If we Tories wished to reverse just one year's growth in Whitehall, we would have to sack the equivalent of the entire population of Ilfracombe, the seaside town in Devon!

And that is a problem about which we need to think more keenly, and not just because I am fond of Ilfracombe, and used to have a jacket that was made there. It may be that many of these 650,000 new jobs are 'non-jobs', in that they have been generated according to some demented politically correct algorithm. But we should also accept that the holders of these jobs are flesh and blood; they have families; they have mortgages; they have votes.

It is the most ingenious feature of Labour's public sector expansion that they have thereby created a clerisy of officials who depend for their livelihoods on a high-taxing, high-spending politically correct government; and therefore any incoming Tory administration must realise that shrinkage of that public sector will necessitate real courage, and will involve real pain.

It is true that the single fastest growing group within the public sector is the tax collectors, and no wonder, when you consider the rococo complications of Gordon Brownian government. This country is accumulating tax inspectors far faster than it is picking up doctors, nurses, or policemen.

It is also true that it would be a great boon to simplify the tax system again, as Nigel Lawson did, and to remove the need for so many of these people. But even tax collectors can feel pain, and that is why we must explain to them why their dismissal could be good not only for the economy as a whole, but also for themselves.

It should be explained, first, that the notion of weeding out some of the new public sector jobs is accepted across all parties, and the loss of some 80,000 posts is envisaged by Labour's Gershon review. It is also worth reiterating that many of these jobs are the result of reckless legislation and regulation: if you endlessly pass pointless health 'n' safety law, you will need pointless compliance officers, and so on. But the most important point is that these public sector jobs represent a huge transfer of wealth from the productive to the non-productive sectors of the economy, at a time when the private sector labour market is very tight, and skills are in short supply. There are other jobs waiting to be done and, if the coming shake-out directs people back on to the market, that will be no bad thing.

My friends, as I have discovered myself, there are no disasters, only opportunities. And, indeed, opportunities for fresh disasters.

Remember what happened to Scargill

I can remember exactly where I was when I experienced my first spasm of savage Right-wing indignation. It was 1984, at breakfast time – about 10.40 a.m. – and I had a spoonful of Harvest Crunch halfway to my lips. The place was the Junior Common Room of my college.

For the previous two decades I had viewed politics with a perfectly proper mixture of cynicism and apathy. Whatever I read under the bedclothes, it certainly wasn't Hansard. Like everyone at my school, I had undergone vague sensations of enthusiasm when the Falklands were recaptured, but otherwise, frankly, I did not give a monkey's.

Occasionally I would glance at the political columnists in the newspapers, and be amazed that anyone could pay them to write such tosh. I hadn't a clue who was in the Cabinet. The world was too beautiful to waste time on such questions.

So I was sitting there in a state of glorious indifference, hungover, probably lovesick, when something happened that caused a sudden streak of rage to course across my brain. Someone was rattling a tin in front of my nose.

I looked up. I stopped crunching my Harvest Crunch. It was one of the goateed Marxists, and he wanted me to cough up for the miners. Normally, I was as soft a touch as the next man for your right-on cause: debt relief, leprosy projects – count me in.

But, as I reached for my pocket, I found myself remembering some stuff I'd read about these miners, and the chaos they were causing with their illegal strike. Oi, I said to my fellow-student. No, I said. I won't give any dosh to these blasted strikers, because, as far as I can see, they are being execrably led, haven't had a proper ballot and are plainly trying to bring down the elected government of the country.

The bearded student Marxist (I think he's now at Goldman Sachs) looked so amazed that he almost jumped out of his donkey jacket, but I stuck to my ground. In fact, I became ever more indignant; and of course I think back now to that instinctive burst of middle-class outrage, as I look ahead, with mixed feelings, to the campaign of disobedience over hunting.

The other night I was ranting before an audience of about 200, about the monstrous illiberalism of the ban. There was much applause and hear-hearing, as I flayed

Blair for his cowardice. I said that I could understand the sense of betrayal in the countryside, and the desire of so many to raise the standard of revolt. As I spoke, a cry was taken up from table to table. 'Otis!' they called. 'Give us Otis!' Across England there are thousands of people yearning for someone to marshal them in rebellion. They need a Spartacus, a Wat Tyler, a Joan of Arc.

It may indeed be Otis, the son of Roxy Music's Bryan Ferry, or it may be someone else. In this week's *Spectator*, Charles Moore says that the Countryside Alliance has passed its Chamberlain period, and is now in need of a Churchill. Charles is far too modest to point out that he is himself ideally suited to the role, and that all his life has been but a preparation for this moment and this hour.

But if they cannot persuade Charles to serve, someone will be found over the next few weeks and months, and you can bet that the generalissimo will launch a serious and organised campaign. These people have innumerable Land Rovers. They have land. They have digging equipment, and bulldozers, and access to prodigious quantities of manure. They own the fields next to key strategic railways and motorways. They know all about burning bales of hay. There is no doubt that they could cause major economic disruption.

All my romantic instincts tell me that their cause is high and noble and just, and deserves support. But when they speak about 'bringing down Blair', I must confess that I fear for what will happen to them; and not just to them, but to every other cause with which they are associated.

Go back to that miners' strike, and the Scargillian revolt. Remember how people began with some feelings of sympathy for the rebels. We all heard their message; the threat to the communities, the Hovis ad pit villages, the way of life that would never return.

But suburban Britain was never likely to indulge Scargill

for long, and as soon as police were pictured with blood running down from under their helmets, the mood began to turn. Neil Darbyshire was spot-on in these pages yesterday, when he noted the basic apathy of suburbs on the question of hunting. Middle England may be interested in principle in the doctrine of liberty, but if the pro-hunt lobby starts impeding their liberty to use the motorway, or to get home for supper, then there will be hell to pay.

Scargill led his men to ruin. Defeat in the miners' strike meant not just the end of trade union militancy; it meant a wholesale rout for that kind of socialism. It was not just catastrophic for the National Union of Mineworkers; it was a disaster for trade unionism. The whole effort and enterprise was discredited, and membership has been on a steady downward path ever since.

And the miners' strike was a disaster not so much because of the aggressive tactics used, but because they failed, and Scargill was seen to have grossly misunderstood the public mood; and the tactics failed because, in the end, suburban Middle England looked at him and said no, stuff it, we don't want you to use bully-boy tactics to bring down the elected government.

That is why the coming leader of the countryside revolt must ponder his tactics hard. If they fail, it is a defeat by association for everything they stand for – shooting included. It may be possible to win, but the worst thing would be to pick a fight and lose.

What has it got to do with the Scots?

This newspaper's distinguished sketchwriter, Frank Johnson, once told me an amazing truth about his job.

Readers of his column will imagine that he sits in permanent vigil over the proceedings of the House of Commons, hunched over the gallery like a gargoyle at Notre Dame, motionless save for the polygraph skittering of his short-hand note. Frank's legions of fans can be forgiven for thinking that he drinks in every word, sifting each of our dud MP phrases for possible conceits.

'Oh no, old man,' Frank said. There were times, whole half-hours, when his mind went quite blank, and he found the parliamentary exchanges impossible to follow. Suddenly, he said, it was as if the entire place were speaking Swahili. He would try to apply himself; he would take the shears of logic to the sprouting hedge of verbiage; and he still didn't have a clue what was going on.

It was as if he were at a convention of Arab carpet-sellers, and someone had whisked off the headphones with the translation. At these moments, he confessed, he let his mind float above the Babel.

He would drift on the thermals of hot air like some bird of prey, until he heard a phrase to excite his interest, like the bleating of a sickly lamb in the pasture below. Then he would swoop.

And I was sitting in just the same Johnsonian coma of abstraction during the Hunting Bill debate the other day. The arguments had been chewed to the point of super-mastication.

Tory after Tory spoke for liberty; Labour MPs vied to be chippiest and most divisive. In spite of all my efforts, my eyelids were starting to droop, like one of those irritating lavatory seats that won't stay up – until at once I caught a phrase that made me stiffen my spine.

I rubbed my eyes, blinked, and began to seethe. A West Country Tory was explaining the sad consequences for Exford, and other places I know and love, when stag hunting is banned. Like many others, he spoke of jobs lost and the damage done to a way of life.

And as he was speaking he was heckled from the Labour benches by a Scottish voice. It belonged to a lolling figure of Hagridian proportions, a man who was clearly no stranger to the deep-fried Mars bar.

'What about the miners?' he said. 'You didn't care about the miners, did you?' At that moment I am afraid that I succumbed to a rare moment of rage. What did he mean?

Were we to take it that, in his view, this odious ban was a kind of revenge? He seemed to be saying that the destruction of livelihoods attached to hunting was in some way a fair requital for what Margaret Thatcher had done to the mining communities in the 1980s.

What a disgusting way to run a country: to visit an injustice on one group of (allegedly) well-heeled hunters, in return for the supposed injustice done to the miners. But that wasn't what made me see red. It wasn't so much what he said, as his accent.

He was from Scotland. He was about to ban hunting in England and Wales. And yet I, as an MP for an English seat, had no say whatever over the fate of hunting in Scotland.

In fact, to compound the absurdity, he, the Scottish MP, sitting in Westminster, had no say over the matter in Scotland, since hunting in Scotland is no longer part of the competence of the Commons, and has been devolved downwards to the Scottish Parliament.

It is a monstrous asymmetry. Under Labour's constitutional Horlicks (which is now far more than a bedtime drink, but an all-purpose word for events and policies occurring in Blair's second term), it happens time after time.

On Tuesday evening, 40 Scots voted with the Government for its imperfect plan for foundation hospitals, a good idea that has been vitiated by Treasury meddling. Labour's majority was only 35, which shows how important these Scots can be in a tight vote. But the key point is not the numbers of Scots voting for or against the Government.

The infamy is that they are allowed to vote on the matter at all.

Like foxhunting, health questions have been devolved completely to the Scottish Parliament. Scots members were voting on a question that was completely English, when English members had no such reciprocal rights over Scottish health questions; and when, to repeat the supreme absurdity, Scottish MPs themselves had no standing in the matter of healthcare for their own constituents.

It is an anomaly that was of course first recognised by Tam Dalyell, Father of the House and first poser of the West Lothian question, and he was not alone, among Labour Scottish MPs, in seeing that this was intolerable.

Who was the gingery Shadow Health spokesman, who, in 1992, said: 'Once we have a Scottish parliament handling health affairs in Scotland, it would not be possible for me to continue as minister for health administering health in England'? It was Robin Cook.

And how did he vote on Tuesday, in a giddy piece of intellectual dishonesty? He voted, as a Scot, in favour of an NHS reform that affected the English alone.

Our new Secretary of State for Health, John Reid, incarnates the very lunacy that Cookie foresaw. He sits for Hamilton North and Bellshill, and is now responsible for a department whose writ does not run north of the Tweed.

What is Labour's answer to this West Lothian question? That people should just stop asking it, while doing nothing to reduce the 72 MPs who make up the bloated Scottish contingent.

The most elegant answer is not to have an English parliament (we have quite enough politicians), but to have English votes on English laws; and to kick the Scots and Welsh out of the division lobbies on matters affecting England alone.

If and when a Tory government brings back hunting, I

don't want my Scottish chum allowed to heckle, let alone to vote.

End of Blair?

Blair dead in the water? No such luck.

I am all in favour of optimism, but this is ridiculous. There are people at Westminster, people I respect, people who have seen governments rise and fall, who now think that Tony Blair's political life is moving to its close.

If Cherie hasn't measured up the curtains for Dunspinnin, she had better get going, they say. It's all over for Blair, said a political commentator to me the other day. He's not just toast. He's crumbs. He's not just history. He's biology. He's physics.

Look, people keep saying to me, at the way he governs the country. He tells the entire Labour Party that he is not going to have a referendum on the European constitution, not over his dead body. No fewer than 319 Labour MPs are gestapoed through the lobbies to vote against such a consultation; and then Blair comes back from staring at the stars in Bermuda, and announces the most amazing U-turn since Emerson Fittipaldi skidded on an oil-slick at the Monaco hairpin.

He persuades his poor lobotomised backbenchers to support invasion of a Third World country on the ground that said country possesses WMD, capable of being fired at us within 45 minutes, and expects them to remain loyal to him when it turns out that (a) Saddam Hussein boasted no WMD more fearful than a tub of superannuated taramasalata, and (b) the CIA had expressly warned the British Government that the 45-minute claim was a load of old cobblers.

He presides over a total disintegration of the immigration and asylum system, and then makes a panicky speech, at the last minute, in which he seems belatedly to embrace Tory ideas about restricting access to benefits for those who are not really in fear of persecution. After seven years of massively expanding the public sector with form-fillers, clipboard-toters and quota-checkers, he holds an emergency summit to work out why 60 per cent of the population do not think public services have improved. Doh!

He's lost the plot, people tell me. He's drifting rudderless in the Wide Sargasso Sea of New Labour's ideological vacuum. According to no less an authority than Peter Oborne, political editor of *The Spectator*, the Prime Minister has been squinting at the calendar and wondering exactly when, this summer, he might suddenly disappear – poof – and reinvent himself as helmsman of, say, the European Commission.

Well, my friends, I am all for looking on the bright side of life. I have bet on the Grand National. I have put money into chocolate vending machines in Underground stations, even though this is a wholly academic exercise. Such is my congenital optimism that, the other day, I chained my bicycle to the railings outside one of our great stations, in the fond belief that, when I returned, it would still be there.

Of course I lost both wheels, but that act of credulity is nothing compared to the collective optimistic mania that is sweeping some sections of the Tory media. You're wrong, folks! Put away the obits. Get rid of the bunting.

Blair will not go this summer, and no, he will not go before the next general election. Here are at least three reasons. The first is that it is not in the nature of politicians to surrender their own political lives; they are like wasps in jam jars. They buzz on long after hope has gone. They go on because it is in their nature to do so, because all political careers must end in tears, and it is profoundly in the public interest that they should do so, in the sense that politicians will work hardest and best if they know that their only exit is to be terminated in the Darwinian struggle for popular affection and interest.

He will not go because there are scores of his back-benchers who know that they were not propelled to Westminster because their electorates fell in love with their own blue eyes. They know that Tony won their seats, because he offered Middle England a kind of Tory Lite party that seemed economically sensible without some of the nastiness that they had come to associate with my great party.

They also know that they have absolutely no practical way of disposing of Blair, because a leadership election would necessitate the votes of 80 MPs, a quarter of the parliamentary party, and there are not enough of them with the guts to trigger it.

And the third reason why Blair will stay and fight is of course that there is no one to take his place. He is New Labour, for better or worse. Straw? Pshaw. Blunkett? Junk it. As for Gordon Brown, and the idea that the baton could be smoothly passed to the Chancellor – cheated of his birthright for a mess of seared tuna at Granita – it is fanciful. Even if it were possible, technically, to effect such a transition, it would be an insult to democracy, not least because Brown, like so many other Labour members, sits for a Scottish seat, and is currently passing laws for England when English MPs have no say over those questions in Scotland, and above all when he, Gordon, has no say over those questions in Scotland. I would go so far as to say that the West Lothian question is now so acute that no sitting Scottish MP has a hope of becoming prime minister.

It is Blair, Blair and Blair alone who personifies New Labour, the gigantic neo-SDP envisaged by Roy Jenkins. That is why there is not the earthliest prospect of him going; and that is why he will soldier on, with his troops becoming ever more despairing. His strategy was triangulation: to push the Tories out to the Right, and to destroy Old Labour. He has ended up falling between two stools. His party has fallen out of love with him, and many are already mentally in opposition (so why not give them the extra satisfaction of formal opposition as well?); but they will keep him as their leader, and he will not go.

If I'm wrong, as I have pledged before, I will eat my hat. Joyfully.

What I should say sorry for

I am writing this in a cold, damp three-star hotel in Liverpool, and I have to admit I don't want to go out. Not only is it raining, there is also the chance that I will be beaten up. As everyone seems to know, I am on a mission to apologise to the people of this great city, and my heart is in my boots. The operation is bedevilled with difficulty, not least that no one seems to want to accept my apology. Local Tories have said that they intend to snub me. The Lib Dem officials who run the council have made a meeting all but impossible. The police have said they expect an enormous media circus which rules out a trip to the museums. There was a plan to sign a book of condolence for the late Ken Bigley, but we have reluctantly rejected it, on the grounds that it will look as if we are playing politics with a tragedy.

But what makes Operation Scouse-grovel even more depressing is that I am attacked by my own troops for embarking upon it. In the journalistic equivalent of the fragging that GIs used to perform upon their officer, Stephen Glover, our own media correspondent, has said that in coming to Liverpool I am letting down *The Spectator*. He claims in Tuesday's *Daily Mail* that in going to apologise, at the behest of Michael Howard, the Tory leader, I am acting like a whipped cur, and that I have compromised the integrity of the magazine. Not since the 18th century, says Glover, has the editor of a national publication been treated like the plaything of his political masters. It is a disgrace, says *The Spectator*'s media correspondent, and shows that I cannot simultaneously serve two leaders – Michael Howard and last week's editorial. He ends his piece with words of dark foreboding about the freedom of the press.

The first thing to say is that Glover's piece shows, of course, the fearless independence of all *Spectator* columnists. Not only does he beat up Michael Howard and the Tory party, he also administers a resounding kicking to his own editor – with whom he had lunch less than a week ago, at which companionable and bibulous ceremony he requested and was granted a sizeable rise! That's the spirit, Glover! If that isn't freedom of the press, I don't know what is. It is also in keeping with Stephen's reputation for detachment that before composing this remonstrance he actively decided not to call me to find out what I might actually be saying by way of apology to Liverpool. And finally, as with all Glover's excellent pieces, it must be conceded that he appears to have a good point.

It does look odd, on the face of it, that an editor should be making a penitential pilgrimage at the behest of a party leader. It is true that when the firestorm of hate began to engulf *The Spectator* last week, I immediately thought of travelling to the city to say sorry for the offence caused, and then vaguely shelved the plan on the grounds that it seemed unlikely to be taken seriously by the people of Liverpool. When Michael Howard rang on Saturday to suggest the same idea, I agreed that it might, on balance, do more good than harm. At that stage I had neither computed the implied Gloverian threat to editorial independence, nor did I foresee that Michael's brilliant spin doctors would present this as some sort of disciplinary procedure, in which the ideal headline was intended to be: 'SHAMED TORY BUFFOON JOHNSON IN LIVERPOOL GROVEL – IRON MIKE GETS TOUGH'. It is that impression, of an editor clicking his heels on the orders of a politician, that sticks in Glover's craw, and I can see why.

All I ask of my old friend is what exactly it is that he thinks Johnson the politician is doing that betrays the integrity of Johnson the journalist. In the course of his *Mail* piece, Glover attacks last week's *Spectator* editorial for its unwarranted slurs on the people of Liverpool. He says it was tasteless to drag in the Hillsborough tragedy, and that we should have got our facts right about this appalling event, in which 96 people died. He is right, and the only question is why he thinks it necessary to attack me for agreeing so exactly with his views. It may be that there are welfare-addicted Liverpudlians who answer to the characteristics we described in the leader but it was wounding and wrong to suggest that this stereotype could be applied to the city as a whole. It was sloppy to repeat the old canard that the Hillsborough tragedy was caused by drunken fans, when the inquiry report found no evidence for this whatever. To judge by the huge mail I have received, that mistake caused real offence and hurt. Faced with such anger, any editor would feel obliged to make amends, and that is what I do now.

It is true that if I were simply an editor, I would confine this apology to a short balanced letter. It is true that I am in Liverpool because I am additionally a politician; but my apology is different in scale, not in kind, from any other qualified editorial apology. Johnson the politician apologises for and refuses to apologise for exactly the same things as Johnson the journalist. Michael Howard, Stephen Glover and the people of Liverpool are quite right to object to parts of the article, but in so far as Michael Howard says the article is 'nonsense from beginning to end' I cannot agree. To do so would require me to perform a kind of auto-pre-frontal lobotomy.

Whatever its mistakes of facts and taste, for which I am sorry, last week's leading article made a good point: about bogus sentiment, self-pity, risk, and our refusal to see that we may sometimes be the authors of our misfortunes. The idea occurred to me when I was driving a child to a football match, and listening to the England–Wales game, where it was the intention to hold a minute's silence for Ken Bigley. I listened with mounting disbelief and disgust because instead of keeping silent the crowds started to jabber, swear, jeer and catcall. After a few seconds the referee gave up in embarrassment, and blew the whistle for the start of the match. The following day I could find nothing in the papers about this horrible event, and I brooded on the causes. How could people behave so thuggishly? The crowd's reaction showed that there was a falseness here: the ceremony required people to show an emotion that – manifestly, alas – they did not feel.

Suppose the crowd had been asked to hold a minute's silence for those who died in the war, or the victims of an IRA atrocity. That silence would have been interrupted by nothing more than a cough. So a large part of that crowd was in a sense rebelling against an imposed sentiment; and that made me think of an editorial on the culture of sentimentality in modern Britain, which is allied to the culture of victimhood, and I wanted a piece on it, not because I wanted to insult the people of Liverpool, but because I believe we have a serious problem in that we tend these days at every opportunity to blame the state, and to seek redress from the state, when things go wrong in our lives. Yes, it was tasteless to make this point in the context of Ken Bigley's death, and I am sorry for any hurt this has caused his family. But when a member of the late hostage's family said that the Prime Minister has Mr Bigley's 'blood on his hands' that was nonsense. Only those who killed Ken Bigley had blood on their hands, and it should not be taboo to say so.

It is important to make this point about our tendency to blame the state, because we live in an increasingly atomised society, where the state does more and more and where means-tested benefits multiply, and where good human emotions and affections that might once have been directed towards neighbours and family are now diverted into outbursts of sentimentality. We are in some ways as callous in our treatment of old people as any country in the world; and yet we are so sentimental about non-human beings, and so tyrannical in our sentimentality, that we are about to become the first outpost of civilisation to ban hunting.

We are so ready to see ourselves as victims that we have an increasingly hysterical health-and-safety compensation culture in which the chief culprits are scaremongering journalists, cowardly politicians and muddled judges who ought to throw out the attempts by lawyers to blame someone else – usually the state – for the misfortunes of their clients. Such are the views of *The Spectator*, its editor, and of Stephen Glover and, I bet, of Michael Howard as well. I heartily and sincerely apologise for the offence caused by last week's leader, and for the tasteless inaccuracies with which the point was made. But I cannot retract that point.

We need nuclear power and a new generation of boffins

It's enough to make you weep. Here we are, a nation that once led the world in scientific discovery. Who proposed the theory of gravity? A Briton. Who discovered the circulation of the blood? We did. Where did Faraday hang out, when he came up with the theory of electromagnetism? Right here in Britain.

We are responsible for just about every ground-breaking scientific advance, from the television to the computer to the hovercraft and the trouser press. We worked out DNA and we came up with antibiotics. There was a time when the upper reaches of the British Establishment were populated by scientists: J. B. S. Haldane, C. P. Snow, you name it.

Before she became a politician, it was Mrs Thatcher's proudest claim that she had revolutionised the composition of Mr Whippy ice cream, so that it contained more cold air bubbles per quart of vegetable fats. Above all, we were the nation that ushered in the dawn of the atomic age.

That was the subject of the first major essay I ever wrote, and I am happy to confess now, at a safe distance, that I plagiarised it entirely from a Ladybird book. It was called 'Atomic Power', I produced it at the age of nine, and in a spirit of unabashed and exuberant technological optimism I hymned the wonderful things that followed the fission of an atom of uranium-235.

I expect that there were thousands of children like me, who were amazed and enthralled by the pictures of Cockcroft and Walton in their Cambridge labs, and the eerie radioactive glow from their tubes and alembics, their hair slicked back, their faces rapt with the concentration of genius.

And who can forget the great Rutherford himself – I can see the illustration even now – and how he worked out that heavier isotopes must be more unstable by looking at a pile of falling books? This is the nation that split the atom and yet now, my friends, how fallen, how changed we are from that position of global eminence.

There is now a growing agreement that for the first time in a quarter of a century we must build nuclear reactors; there can be argument about how many, but they must be a part of the solution to our increasing energy problems.

But here is an awful truth, confided in me the other day by a deputation of engineers and scientists. 'If the Government decided to build a nuclear reactor today, there are only half a dozen people who have the experience to do it in this country, and they have all retired.' That's it, my friends: the birthplace of Newton and Boyle and J. J. Thomson – and we can't even build our own nukes any more!

The Government is desperately trying to remedy the problem with a £6.3 million nuclear science programme, aimed at keeping nuclear studies going for the next four years in seven universities, but in the short term it will make little difference. If we want a clean, green, nuclear source of energy, we will have to get the French, or the Japanese, or even the South Africans to equip us with the necessary technology.

Unless, of course, students and potential students see what a huge opportunity there is in this field, and start turning back to the subjects – in physics and engineering – that they have been spurning over the past 20 years. I hope I will not be seen as a boss-eyed, propeller-headed nukophile when I say that I hope they do, for all sorts of reasons. As I said on this page recently, I am far too terrified to dissent from the growing world creed of global warming.

But even if it turns out that the worry has been overdone (by the way, jolly nippy today, eh?), then there still seem to be overwhelming arguments for going nuclear. Look at the size of your gas bill; look at the extraordinary growth in the proportion of our energy needs that are now satisfied by gas. It was about five per cent in 1970, and it is about 45 per cent now.

It is terrifying to think that Mr Putin, or any less amenable successor, could have his thumbs on our gas feed-pipe; and it is terrifying to think that we could be perpetually vulnerable to the vagaries of some European gas cartel. We need an alternative, and one that doesn't just involve crucifying our landscape with wind farms which, even when they are in motion, would barely pull the skin off a rice pudding.

That is why I am reverting to my nine-year-old self's evangelism for nuclear power: because if there is an answer to global warming, then nukes must be part of the mix, and because we cannot afford to be dependent on foreign gas, and also, finally, because it would help to reinforce the crumbling science base of this country.

We are good at pharmaceuticals, and there are some of the spookier areas – such as the human genome and animal experimentation – where we are world leaders. But we have long since lost our lead in physics and engineering, and if what the engineers tell me is true, the problem begins at school.

We have too few physics graduates teaching physics; we have too few mathematicians teaching maths. The result is that far too much of the first year of university is spent on remedial mathematics, and the result is that it is quite hard to find people who want to be lecturers or tutors in the physical sciences – especially when they can earn double in the private sector.

That's why science departments have been closing – 30

per cent of physics departments gone in the past 15 years – and without science graduates you can't get good teachers, and the vicious circle continues. That is why the nuclear power programme – if and when it arrives – seems to offer hope.

It is not just that nuclear energy is environmentally friendly in itself: it offers a cheap way of producing the energy necessary to produce hydrogen, and therefore to produce hydrogen fuel cells, and heaven knows what else. It also offers the hope that we can restore British activity and prestige in the physical sciences, not just as an end in itself, but because if we have to rely endlessly on the Russians for our gas, and on the Arabs for our oil, then no nukes will be bad nukes.

Blair is not going to get yobs off the streets – you'll have to

It was like being drowned in molasses. It was like being hosed in treacle. I was lying in a state of after-lunch torpor while the eight-year-old was playing and replaying her favourite track, and through the door it stole, and up the bed and into my ear until it filled the fjords of my brain with such glutinous aspartame-flavoured schmaltz that at last I could take it no more and cried: 'Enough!' James Blunt, I thought, it's time to get a grip! Come on, man: stop being so indescribably wet. If she's so beautiful, stop standing there in your T-shirt and floppy fringe, and hush your hopeless falsetto crooning.

Go out and get her, is my advice, and if James Blunt seems drippy next to the rock stars of the good old days, he is positively macho by comparison with the Kaiser Chiefs. These are the weeds from Leeds whose hit single was 'I predict a riot', a tale about the bourgeois apprehension of a chap who tries to get a taxi on a Saturday night in the centre of town.

'Watching the people get lairy/It's not very pretty I tell thee./ Walking through town is quite scary/And not very sensible either,' sing these epic softies. Then the chap meets another chap in a tracksuit, who looks as though he might offer violence, but doesn't, and that's about it. It's pathetic!

When I was a nipper it was standard practice for a rock star to start the evening by biting the head off a pigeon and throwing the television out of the window before electrocuting his girlfriend in the bath and almost drowning in a cocktail of whisky, heroin and his own vomit. The self-respecting British punk rockers didn't get up on stage and start whimpering about how they predicted a riot. They incited riots. 'White riot, I want a riot, white riot, a riot of my own,' they sang, if my memory serves me correctly.

Let's face it, the rock star role models of yesterday were far more thuggish, brutal and in-yer-face than the rock stars of today, most of whom are almost embarrassing in their niceness; and if one thinks back to the 1970s and 1980s, it is clear that the riots were nastier, too. I make this elementary observation, because we are once again being invited to have hysterics about the yoof of today, and yob culture, and once again Tony Blair presents himself to us as the father of the nation, *pater patriae*, the man who is figuratively going to put the offending yobbos over his knee and give them a damn good hiding on behalf of us all.

And, of course, he is right, in this limited sense, that Britain has long boasted quite large numbers of ill-educated and ill-disciplined young people. He is right, too, that under Labour there are more and more families lost in the bottom 20 per cent of the heap, who are simultaneously over-taxed and over-dependent on welfare, and who do not always have a sense of social responsibility, to put it mildly. But there is something about Blair's solution that makes me ill, and it is not just the ghastly, patronising, mockney voice he adopts when he is saying something that he believes will have universal appeal on the estates of Britain.

What really depresses me is that these gimmicks probably will be immensely popular; and people will look at Blair blithering away about respect and say, yes, good on yer Tony, you tell them. Fine them! Send them to parenting classes! Confiscate their spray cans and send the whole family to the sin bin. Take their money away, even if it's only on suspicion that it may be ill-gotten.

Asbo-lutely right!

My objection is not just that these measures are centralising and authoritarian – an objection that is unlikely to cut much ice with people enduring anti-social behaviour. The trouble with this stuff is that it once again lulls people into the belief that the Government is really going to sort out their problems, when the reality is that the whole of the new anti-yobbo programme, parenting classes and all, will be about as much use to thug-plagued estates as Blair's doomed plan to march them to cashpoints for on-the-spot fines – i.e. no use whatever.

The police already have a panoply of powers to deal with these characters; they just don't have the resources to be everywhere at once and all Tony is doing is intensifying the illusion that he, Big Tone, is going to descend on your noisy neighbours and bang them away, or send them on parenting courses.

He would go up hugely in my estimation if he fixed us with his glittering eye and said, y'know, there wasn't a lot he could do, immediately, about the problem of these thugs, not with a million children being failed by schools.

But what about you, he should say, pointing at the public with a Kitchener-esque finger. What are you doing? I dislike his gimmicks because at every stage personal or communal responsibility is replaced by the state, and the more completely government assumes responsibility for problem kids, the less people will understand that part of civility is having the courage to reprimand someone for spitting on a granny, and not pass by on the other side. If we continue to treat comparatively small acts of thuggishness as matters purely for the Government, then we will never get thuggishness off our streets, and we the British public will never recover our individual and collective courage as long as we think that nanny Blair is going to deal with the problem himself.

The sad truth about Blair's 'announcements' is that they will play beautifully. Everyone will feel that someone is doing something about the problem, and everyone will slump back further into apathy and atomism. Mr Blair has obviously decided that his last months must be adorned with 'eye-catching initiatives' with which he can be personally associated, so that no one can say he is going gentle into that good night. But when the same old thugs and the same old families are causing the same old havoc, and the 'problem family sin bins' have gone the way of other eye-catching initiatives he has promised, it may be that people will decide enough is enough. At this rate I don't predict a dignified and glorious exit from Downing Street. I predict a rout.

Where would muddle-headed mugwumps be without Charlie?

In this season of goodwill and fellowship I am well aware, O kind and loyal readers, of the many calls there have already been on your charity, and I know how magnificently you respond. But I want today to draw your attention to the plight of a victim scarcely less deserving than the causes for which you recently rang *The Daily Telegraph* Christmas appeal.

He is far more winsome than the baby seals of the Canadian ice floes, with their voracious appetites for cod. He is more endangered than the Giant Panda, whose laid-back style he so brilliantly emulates. He is the red squirrel of British politics, a cheerful addition to a drab landscape, about to be ruthlessly extinguished by his grey-suited brethren.

Here he is, the fellow who actually increased the Lib Dems' representation in the Commons at the last election, and he is the victim of brutal briefings by 'unnamed' Liberal MPs. 'Charlie's gotta go,' say these nameless ones. 'He's in the last chance saloon,' they say, adding, 'ho, ho.'

Why are they so nervous of naming themselves, these unnamed Liberal MPs? It's not as though their names would be recognised by anyone else. The only distinctively named Lib Dem MP is my friend Lembit Opik, the brilliant asteroid spokesman, and he is one of the few to have had the guts to speak out for Charlie.

The rest are unnamed and brutal. It is pitiful to watch. And that is why I hereby declare myself the founding president of the Royal Society for the Protection of Charles Kennedy, and hope that as many of you as possible will feel moved to subscribe.

It is not just that Charlie is a thoroughly nice chap, which he is. It is not merely that he has been known to try to supplement his parliamentary rations with appearances on television quiz shows. My reasons for sympathy are partly that he is known to have a fondness for the gift of Dionysus, and that is to be defended.

We live in an age of easy, gifted telegenic politicians who never put a foot wrong or slur their words on *Newsnight*, and it is therefore magnificent that the Liberal Democrats continue to have a leader with a Churchillian ability to slot it away. But above all I am slapping a preservation order on Charlie Kennedy, and listing him as a Grade One landmark of our culture, because he, and he alone, represents a sizeable electoral minority.

To understand the modern Lib Dems, you have to understand a key feature of human psychology. The world is full of people who have pretty strong views about politics, and who are fairly sure where they stand on the spectrum. There are millions of people out there who want freedom, lower taxes, less regulation, less spin, the maintenance of Britain's democratic institutions, a culture of enterprise that encourages people to get on as far as they can, with decent public services and a net beneath which no one can fall. These tend to be Conservatives.

Then there is another huge group of people who seem to believe in higher taxes, more public spending, regulation, bossiness, control, surrendering the rebate to Brussels without any reform of the CAP and horrible bendy buses that crush cyclists. These people, by and large, vote Labour.

But there is a third group, a minority, but a minority that possesses a characteristic human psychological deformity. They can't stand the pettiness of intellectual consistency. They want it all ways, and are capable of holding two mutually contradictory positions at once. Their policy on cake is pro-having it and pro-eating it, and they need a party that reflects them and their politically schizophrenic personalities.

That is why it is so vital that we continue with Charlie Kennedy's Liberal Democrats and all their hilarious doublethink. There are not many Lib Dems in Parliament, but even in that tiny group they incarnate dozens of diametrically opposing positions. You want to know what the Lib Dem policy is on taxation, for instance, and you want to know whether they are for or against a 50 per cent tax rate. One half of your cerebrum thinks it is quite right that the rich should pay more; the other lobe thinks tax is quite high enough already. You are a perfect Lib Dem, a mass of contradictions, and your party supplies exactly what you are looking for.

Here is Chris Huhne MEP, their economics wallah, reported in this paper on 20 September 2005. 'The 50p top rate of tax is now looking in international terms quite uncompetitive . . . and there are alternative ways of being redistributive.'

And here is Sir Menzies Campbell, reported on the very same day in the same paper: 'I don't have any difficulty with a 50 per cent tax rate and I see no reason why those earning over £100,000 should not make a greater contribution.' Fantastic! Taken together, those policies cancel each other out and amount to babble, and the same goes for Lib Dem policies on the NHS. Nick Clegg MP says: 'I think breaking up the NHS is exactly what you need to do to make it a more responsive service . . . frankly the faults of the British health service compared to others still leaves much to be desired.'

And here is Evan Harris MP: 'Party spokesmen have to understand that the language we use when talking about reform is vital and talk of breaking it up is not helpful.' And so on. Vincent Cable wants to tax and spend. David Laws is against tax and spend. David Laws says let the market play a role in health. Steve Webb says don't. Only Charles Kennedy is capable of bubble-gumming this coalition together. It is now quite clear that if he were to go, he would be replaced by someone who might come perilously close to endorsing one position or the other, rather than keeping up the amazing Lib Dem strategy of endorsing both. The party would be taken over either by the likes of Mark Oaten and Nick Clegg, who seem in many ways to be very similar to David Cameron's Tories; or else it would go Left under Simon Hughes and the rest of the tofu-munching busybodies.

Like splitting the hydrogen atom, this microscopic party will be suddenly and violently resolved into a vaguely Tory proton, and a vaguely Labour electron. And where will that leave the muddle-headed mugwumps who want high tax and low tax at once? A huge minority, the politically schizoid, will be deprived of representation. It is not fair.

Save Charlie Kennedy this Christmas.

Cameron

Cameron knows how to balance compassion with Conservatism.

Over the past few months I have lost count of the number of people who have asked me – satirically – why I am not standing in the current Tory leadership contest; and after I have bumbled out some reply, they have always said, oh well, who are you backing? 'David Cameron,' I have said, quick as a flash, and for the most part this answer has so far drawn a look of anxious blankness, the look you see when people are sure that they ought to have read some classic work, and are in two minds whether to bluff it out or admit ignorance. 'Oh yes,' they say, mentally noting that they ought to get to grips with the subject of David Cameron, along with Stephen Hawking's *Brief History of Time* and *Midnight's Children* by Salman Rushdie.

Well, I hope that if there was anybody out there still ignorant of the merits of Cameron, that ignorance was dispelled this week. You may not want to go quite as far as Bruce Anderson, whose essay on Cameron in this week's *Spectator* is a kind of tear-sodden nunc dimittis. Like old Simeon in the temple, Brucie has seen our salvation, and though you may not be prepared to agree with him that Cameron is our saviour and a light to lighten the gentiles, and the glory of the Tory party, most dispassionate commentators would surely have to concede that it has been the 38-year-old's week.

Cameron is the one who has made up the most ground. Cameron is the contender on whom the odds have shortened most dramatically. Before they get any shorter, I urge you all to go out and have a tremendous punt, and as for my colleagues in Parliament who are still toying with other options, I say this. David Davis and Ken Clarke are both great men, in many ways; but be good to yourselves, my friends, and think it possible that now is the moment to hitch yourselves to the Cameron bandwagon for the entirely cynical and self-serving reason that he is not only the best candidate, but that he is going to win.

Cameron has come closest to finding the language we need if we are to make the meaning of Conservatism clear to a new generation. I like this stuff about there being a 'we as well as a me' in politics. I like his constant repetition of 'we're all in this together'; indeed, I am vain enough to have a feeling that he nicked it from me. It is a simple idea, but it bears explication. It means that Toryism is not about one section of society grinding the faces of another section of society, with Tory politicians getting off on the sheer ideological purity and savagery of it all.

It means recognising that there will always be winners and losers, and if we want to encourage people to win – as we do – then we must also be prepared to look after the losers. We're all in this together because if people at the bottom feel shut out and lost, then they are more likely to turn to crime and despair, and make life worse for everyone, including themselves.

I like Cameron's pitch, because he understands the vital importance of optimism in politics, and stressing that the Tories are the party of energy and opportunity, whereas Gordon Brown's Labour Party, whichever way you cut it, will always be rooted in the politics of chippiness and envy and spite. In fact, I found nothing to dislike at all in what he had to say, and much to admire, so I will end with only a couple of notes of caution to my fellow 'modernisers'. The first is that I am not at all sure what the hell we mean by 'modernising'.

If I were a punter I would be heartily sick of hearing the Tories whiffle on about whether they are nice or nasty, gay or straight, does my bum look big in this and all the rest of it. And what is all this stuff about 'change'? Unless my ears were deceiving me, someone up there on the platform said that we Tories had to change the way we walked, the way we talked, our sexual composition. Well, I don't think we should aggravate the woes of the NHS with thousands of Tory thrusters queueing up for speech therapy and gender reassignment. From the point of view of the electors this obsession with changing our appearance is also dull, narcissistic, and completely irrelevant to their problems. No one gives a monkey's whether we wear ties or not, or whether we have baseball caps or breakdance down Blackpool promenade.

What they do care about – and this is the second point – is how they are governed; and while we Tories must articulate a new compassionate Conservatism, we should never forget that in asking people to vote for us we are essentially asking to take charge of taxation and spending, and that our prime duty is to bring a new and more sensible – and more Conservative – style of economic management. We are likely to face Gordon Brown at a time when his record looks increasingly vulnerable. Inflation is on the rise, retailing is in difficulties, and he has not cut a single one of the 84,000 jobs he promised to lose in the public sector. That means the public sector is continuing to expand, and Brown is taking ever more money from the private sector to fund this expansion, and therefore preventing its use in wealth creation or the generation of new jobs, and all without the reform that would deliver real improvements in those public services.

It would of course be wrong to go into the next election promising a huge purge of public sector jobs, and it would be electorally foolish, since the 800,000 new officials Gordon has created not only have jobs and families; they have votes. But the Tories must never forget that millions of people are looking to them to save them from the depredations of the taxman – and those millions are by no means the richest in society, but the very poorest who pay grotesque proportions of their income in tax.

Of course the Tories must rediscover compassionate Conservatism; but the trick of the next few years will be to show that you can have compassionate policies that are for the benefit of business and enterprise, and that you can gradually bear down on spending and taxation in a way that is good for everyone. That is the connection we must demonstrate. That is the job for Cameron, and Cameron is the man for the job.

WHO ARE THE BRITISH?

Never have the British felt more under threat. Scarcely a month goes by without some new elegy by Roger Scruton or Peter Hitchens, called something like 'The Death of Britain', and mourning the vanishing of our ancient nation. Whence this menace? There is the EU, with its insatiable love to harmonise national differences. There are Labour's constitutional reforms, which have split the country up and provoked English nationalism. There are the moves to do away with things most redolent of Britain: foxhunting, the hereditary peerage, corporal punishment. And then there is the general rise of political correctness and touchy-feely American sitcom values, most sensationally displayed after the death of the Princess of Wales. The country has changed, become more diverse and more tolerant. Which can't be altogether a bad thing.

Mind you, the most ludicrous laws often turn out to be British.

Congratulations! It's a Belgian

Mr Howard, Home Secretary, you have a reputation as a Euro-sceptic, justified or not. Allow me to suggest to you another reason why it is nonsense to suppose Britain is now at the 'heart of Europe'. We British can live here on the continent. Under basic EEC principles, we can work here. But if we are so foolish as to have our children here, in the continent's broadly excellent maternity hospitals we run the risk of forfeiting, by your laws, what is most precious in their inheritance. When I look into the faded-denim-blue eyes of my seven-week-old daughter, Lara Lettice, the injustice almost chokes me up. Home Secretary, my daughter is a Belgian.

When this shattering truth emerged at the British Embassy's swish, new velour-and-pine quarters on Rue d'Arlon, Brussels the edge was, at first, taken off my indignation by the charm of my informant. 'I'm very sorry,' said Mme Michelle Roelly, a largish Belgian with octagonal reading glasses and plenty of jewels. Had it been one of those chalky British officials, breaking off from his crossword to tell me my girl was not British, I think I might have started yammering at the attack-proof glass like a drunk in a benefit office.

At the next window, a Hong Kong Chinese called Mr Tang and his two small pudding-basin-haired sons were in similar perplexity. 'Wha-ha-happened?' Mr Tang asked the embassy official, also a Belgian, fanning out three apparently identical maroon British passports against the glass. How could it be that one of his sons was fully British and one was not? 'Wha-ha-we-gotta-do?' he demanded, politely, hopelessly.

Further down the line, a runaway Tamil was trying to get a message to his folks in Streatham that he was OK. At once, it was as if one was on Ellis Island. Is this what they feel like, those poor, huddled masses that we read about, longing to burst into Europe from the Mediterranean littoral or eastern Europe in a tidal wave?

It had come to this. After four years of plugging away in Brussels, reporting on British interests in the European Community, for a largely British readership, had I *gone native*? Were we *foreign*, then, Marina, my wife, and I?

Call me an idiot if you like – and some of my relatives have – but it did not occur to me, *ante partum*, that the issue of two freeborn British citizens could be foreign. 'Oh, but he or she can,' said Michelle. 'The child may not be British,' she added finally, surveying our various birth certificates. The reason is Willie Whitelaw's 1981 British Nationality Act, which came into effect in January 1983.

A Home Office man was quite candid about its target. The Tories were determined to slam the last bolt against immigrants from the Caribbean and the Indian subcontinent. 'Your sin,' he said jovially, meaning Marina's and my sin, 'is that you were both born abroad.' True, we were. But had our fathers in 1964 been working in what the Home Secretary has been pleased to define in Note K as 'Crown Service' within the meaning of the Act, for instance, the War Graves Commission or the European Patent Office, all would be well.

As it was, they were merely employed by the BBC and the World Bank. In consequence, we suffer the shaming sheep-and-goats separation of Willie Whitelaw's 1981 Act. No matter how British our antecedents, the fact of our nativity in Berlin and New York means that we are merely 'British by descent'; while all you blessed readers who were born in the UK to British parents are, in the prissy, topsyturvy locution of Whitehall, 'British otherwise than by descent'; for which read, True Brit, Jolly British, No Question About It.

And the essence of belonging to this second-class category, 'British by descent', is that you cannot, while abroad, transmit your nationality to your children. The object, says the Home Office, is to prevent large families in, say, Calcutta disseminating British citizenship down the generations, without setting foot in the UK, and then arriving in one of those aforementioned tidal waves.

By default then, as the Belgian Interior Ministry glumly admitted, we have a bonny Belgian baby. She does not even get dual nationality, unless you count Walloon and Fleming.

Never mind the worrying practical disadvantages: her dubious eligibility for British local authority education grants, the cancelled right to play cricket for England, to join the Foreign Office, to stand for parliament, to become head of MI5. What concerns me now is the *principle*. She is just *not* Belgian. It is no consolation to say, as the chirpy Home Office man said, that she would have 'the same colour passport' as a Briton.

So, Mr Howard, let me put it to you straight. Do you really wish Lara Lettice to be loyal to Baudouin and Fabiola, rather than Her Majesty? Do you wish to see her claimed by a nation which refused to sell us ammunition in the Gulf war? Shall she scamper, her face gleaming with chips and mayonnaise, as thousands of Bruxellois did the other day, to watch the National Day firework display, her heart beating at the sight of the black-red-yellow flags?

Remedies exist. We could apply to you, Mr Howard, enclosing a non-refundable £85, asking you to review her case. But, as Michelle points out, no one has been successful in this for at least two years. Myself, I am tempted by the Zola Budd option. Even at seven weeks, it is possible to discern how she could do an adoptive country some service in the track and field events. Why not waive the rules, Home Secretary, with an eye to the 2012 Olympics?

But the best course, Marina, an EEC lawyer, tells me, is to go to Luxembourg, to the European Court of Justice. Of course, it goes against the grain to invoke this slayer of British national sovereignty. Yet the British Nationality Act seems in conflict with EEC law, restricting workers' rights to move freely and settle in another member state, by depriving them of the right to pass on nationality to their children. 'Looking at jurisprudence such as the Choquet ruling in 1974, you would have a 50 per cent chance of success,' says an EEC legal expert. We can go with that.

You may say that there is an element of the Rees-Mogg about such a court case. But, as he has discovered, in the face of government stupidity on this scale litigation is the only answer.

A theory about our schizoid approach to Europe.

Revelation on the road from Hastings to Maastricht

If you have not seen it before, you walk in a sort of stupor down the darkened corridor in Normandy, listening to the narrative on the headphones and taking in the blue, ochre and rust-coloured wool that is scarcely faded for being more than 900 years old. You perceive the little jokes, the cooking techniques, the dainty hands and the etiolated early medieval bodies swaying at the hips and neck. In this 70 metre strip cartoon you see also a morality tale justifying the Norman invasion.

The Bayeux tapestry ranks with the Pyramids and the

Parthenon as one of the wonders of the world. Perhaps it was the magic of this work of art. Perhaps it was the effect of a flagon of Norman cider. But the experience prompted in me a sort of revelation, an interruption of my almost incessant meditations on Britain's place in Europe.

It is regularly said that Britain is special in Europe, in that she was never conquered in modern times; and that this makes her reluctant to hand over sovereignty to Brussels. All the other European countries, the argument runs, were subjugated. Their political classes were discredited during the Second World War, their institutions destroyed. By contrast, it is observed, Britain has not been invaded, or at least, people will add, not since 1066.

I have always felt this analysis left something unsaid. What of the Norman invasion itself? What was the effect of the conquest? I will lay my cards on the table. I have long been troubled by the political significance of the Battle of Hastings.

Et fuga verterunt Angli, says the last line of the Latin commentary, as the Norman knights charge on their heavy steeds. And the English turned in flight, the weeds. England was captured by the people the tapestry calls 'Franci', the French. Oh, the shame of those words. Perhaps it is important to Britain that it has not been invaded since. But it is also important, surely, that in 1066 it *was* invaded, and how.

You could argue that the conquest was a good thing, good for the construction industry, for instance. And it would be an exaggeration to say that patriotic Englishmen hang their heads today if you mention the Battle of Hastings. A silence does not fall in pubs if you say 'Pevensey' or 'Tostig'. But for the English who were then alive, Hastings was a disaster.

It was more than just one in the eye for Harold. It was our battle of Sedan, our Aegospotami; and worse. It was not just a defeat, followed by proconsular rule by an occupying power. The events of 1066 were, in the words of the historian John Gillingham, 'a catastrophe for the English. No other conquest has been followed by so total an elimination of the Ancien Regime.' What became of them, these house-carls of Harold, those whose corpses are not shown nude and dismembered at the bottom of the tapestry? The entire aristocracy was dispossessed or expelled. Their language was adulterated. They fled to Scotland, Denmark, Russia. Some turned up in the imperial guard of Byzantium. As William of Malmesbury wrote in 1125, 'England today is the home of foreigners and the domain of aliens'. The country became *Outremer*, the term the French government now uses for Guadeloupe or Martinique, an overseas dominion.

Almost everything was pillaged from a country that was regarded as a northern Eldorado. The Normans were robbers, says Orderic Vitalis, the Anglo-Saxon chronicler. The Norman monk Guitmund told William the Conqueror to his face that 'the whole of England was like the hugest robbery'. Sir Richard Southern summed up the conquest: 'No country in Europe, between the rise of the barbarian kingdoms and the twentieth century, has undergone so radical a change in so short a time as England experienced after 1066.'

And the insight I had, whether fuelled by cider or not, was that it might be politically important that we were conquered. Come off it, I hear you say. Talk about an old story. And what do you mean 'we' lost the battle? Are the English not now a happy melange of the combatants?

Well, remember that by 1075, when all the Normans had crossed, they were a tiny minority: perhaps 10–20,000, of a population of 1.5 million. Therefore the genetic inheritance of the modern Englishman is overwhelmingly non-Norman. Ask your friends: Who won the Battle of Hastings, them or us? and I'll wager the answer is 'them'.

What interests me is the consequent national myth, and national consciousness.

My suggestion is that the memory of the conquest is one of those many things that puts us in two minds, about whether to rejoice in our links with the continent, or whether to be dismayed. The dispute over the conquest was alive in the 17th century, and it flared up for the Victorians, in their search for national identity. Some popular historians, such as Edward Freeman, emphasised England's splendid isolation and thought the conquest an assault by foreigners. 'We Englishmen,' he wrote, 'live in an island and have always moved in a world of our own.'

Thomas Carlyle, on the other hand, was thoroughly in favour of the takeover, on the ground that Britain was inhabited by a 'gluttonous race of Jutes and Angles, capable of no great combinations; lumbering about in pot-bellied equanimity'. Carlyle's point is debatable. Most modern historians would say that in music, dance, literature, embroidery and other artwork, pre-conquest England was at least as civilised as Normandy. The tapestry itself is of Anglo-Saxon work, and probably survived only because, unusually, it was not made of gold or silver thread.

The central point, though, is that the controversy lives, at all levels. The schism is in the essence of the country. Everything is a compromise between two inheritances. Our language is the confluence of two mighty streams (which is why it is so uniquely rich in puns). It is not stretching things too much to note that Mr Major compromises between the Little-Englanders in the Tory Party, and those who have no hangups about integration with a continental system of Government. I do not say that all pro-Europeans are of Norman stock, and vice versa, though I note that Budgen, Marlow, Shepherd sound fairly convincing Anglo-Saxon names.

Now the two tendencies in the national psyche are preparing to do battle in the next Treaty-changing conferences, the preparations for which will start in June. Last week the European Commission proposed plans for more qualified majority voting, ending Britain's right of veto.

If you want a first clue as to how the political classes will react, think of the most famous date in English history. When the Tory party splits over the 'Son of Maastricht' reforms and the single currency, think of Hastings. We never got over it.

You may have forgotten Cool Britannia. Apologies for bringing it up again.

Britain: so cool it's baaad

Man alive, I've just seen the hippest, most jiving place on earth. I've been mingling with the baddest dudes and the grooviest chicks in suits and spectacles and shoes with buckles and all kinds of crazy gear ... and guess where they were? Right here in my office in Canary Wharf!

I've just been out to buy my trendy Prêt à Manger sandwich 'with no obscure chemicals' – only famous ones – and, having greeted the editor, 'Chuck' Moore, with the usual high five, I sat down to write in the blissful certainty that I am where it's seriously at: in the funkiest office, in the funkiest town on the planet.

It says so, here in *Time* magazine; and it's all thanks to Tony Blair. It even has a picture of our office, on the contents page of *Time*: 'Tower Power: Canary Wharf reflects the new Britain'.

'Renewed Britannia', says the cover of the international news magazine. 'With a fresh government, a sturdy economy and a confident mood, Britain bounces back.' Zowee. Inside, Blair explains to *Time*'s Atlantic editor, deputy Atlantic editor and London bureau chief how he proposes to 'rebrand' the country.

'When I see pageantry in Britain, I think that's great, but it does not define what Britain is today,' says the PM. This Friday in Edinburgh, while 2,000 delegates assemble for the Commonwealth Conference, the redefining begins, a new identity for us all. A video called *Britain: The Young Country* will be shown, made by Spectrum Communications.

No bagpipes, no brass bands, none of that *traditional* old codswallop. This video shows stunning images of the best of British: brash young designers, advertising whiz-kids, hot young chefs from Sir Terence Conran's Mezzo restaurant, cool young Liam and Noel in their Kangol finery, and, of course, the Dear Leader himself.

Yes, Britain is undergoing nothing less than a product relaunch, says 10 Downing Street, and not before time. According to the think-tank Demos, which has had a big influence on Blair through his adviser Geoff Mulgan, we have a serious image problem abroad. We're fusty, crusty, and musty. 'Britain is seen as a backward-looking country with bad weather, poor food and arrogant, unfriendly people,' says Demos. The very word British is so embarrassing that companies such as British Telecom and British Home Stores now prefer acronyms. Blushing British Airways has axed the Union flag from the tailfin. And can you blame them? Seventy-two per cent of the world's largest companies see national identity as crucial to buying products, and the very word Britain connotes strikes, draughty houses, dreams of empire, snobbery – or so says Demos.

Now Blair can hardly abolish the word Britain – not yet. But he can change the associations of the name. Hence

Operation Rebrand, which *Time* calls *Britannia redempta*. Hence the Young Country video, the celebration of new sunrise talent.

You will have spotted at once the staggering hypocrisy. After decades of raging at the Conservatives, for allegedly promoting useless service industries at the expense of good old heavy manufacturing, Labour now hails these luvvies as a great British triumph. It was the Tories who produced the conditions that allowed this flowering. These restaurants and outrageously expensive artists with their pickled animals are indirectly funded by the Tory financial boom, the reforms which meant that London-based firms manage 60 per cent of the turnover in internationally traded equities. It was just that the poor old Conservatives couldn't articulate the mood. When Saatchi and Saatchi said 'Britain is booming' during the last election campaign, everyone tittered. When Michael Heseltine made speeches about 'Cool Britannia', no one listened. John Major's idea of a popular hero was Colin Cowdrey.

Barely six months later, everyone seems to attribute the British revival to Tony Blair. It's an affront to the intellect, but never mind. Let us pass on, grinding our teeth, and consider what on earth Labour means by a Young Country. Mr Blair cannot mean it literally. Britain's population is the sixth oldest in the World, with 15 per cent over 65. If Tony Blair wants to rule a really young country, he should go to Côte d'Ivoire, where 50 per cent of the population is under 15.

The phrase must be metaphorical and, for some Blairites, one suspects that the rebranding of Britannia is really a smokescreen for destruction. As Mark Leonard says in his ground-breaking Demos pamphlet, *Britain TM*, it is time to review 'stamps, letter-heads and official documents'. That's right: it's off with the Queen's head, off the stamps, anyway. Young Country means abolishing the Old

Country: the House of Lords, foxhunting, weevilled old notions such as parliamentary sovereignty and the union of 1707. It means tilting at windmills like 'the culture of deference' – which hardly exists any more – and pulling down Oxbridge from its eminence.

In so far as it has substance, the move to create a 'Young Country' is likely to be damaging. As a PR stunt, it seems unlikely to work. People don't invest in Britain because Tony Blair has glamorous parties for footballers at Number 10 or can play a Fender Stratocaster. They invest here because Britain still has a flexible highly educated labour force, now likely to become less flexible through Labour's decision to sign the Social Chapter and inflict a minimum wage.

Whenever British prime ministers try to capture the genius of the nation, they always seem to be groping and missing. Stanley Baldwin spoke in 1924 of 'The sounds of England, the tinkle of the hammer on the anvil in the country smithy, the corncrake on a dewy morning, the sound of the scythe against the whetstone, the sight of a plough team coming over a hill, the sight that has been in England since England was a land, and may be seen in England long after the Empire has perished and every works in England has ceased to function, for centuries the one eternal sight of England'.

Well, when did you last see a plough team coming over the brow of a hill, let alone hear the tinkle of hammer on anvil? Baldwin's vision was irrelevant within 30 years. John Major's vision, from Orwell, of 'long shadows on county grounds, warm beer, invincible green suburbs and old maids cycling to holy communion through the morning mist', was laughed to scorn by Blair's assistants.

Will Tony Blair's vision of 'The Young Country' fare any better? Lots of young designers specialising in buttock exposure, a few loutish and derivative Britpop stars, multi-millionaire restaurateurs who charge you £5 for a bun? It catches the taste of the moment, all right. After a few years of this boosterism, though, I wager we will all be crying out for the old Majoresque understated, tongue-tied self-effacement.

And in my experience, that is the feature of the British that foreigners prize the highest.

Blair's devolution 'project' begins to irritate.

Cry grows for England and St George

You see it on taxis. It flutters from the roofs of pubs, the flag that only 10 years ago seemed to be of purely anti-quarian interest. Yes, amid the crashing chords of *Jerusalem*, and the baying of the red and white warpainted terraces, and with a faint aroma of beef, Bisto, custard and socks, the new nationalism is at hand.

Dared and goaded by the prospect of Scottish autonomy, wound-up by Welsh whingeing, recoiling from regionalism, baulking at Brussels, and sensing that the end of 'Britain' may be inevitable, a forgotten sentiment is occurring to the one people in this island who, says Alan Ford, never get a fair suck of the sauce bottle.

And the murmur grows to a chant, and the chant to a roar, and, to the horror of the politically correct and to the joy of some romantic Right-wingers, the cry is England! Eng-er-land! Cry God for England and St George, whose day falls at the end of this week.

Simon Heffer has written their manifesto, *Nor Shall My Sword*, just published by Weidenfeld, and now the BBC has found Alan Ford, whose *Counterblast* programme is broadcast tomorrow. 'I want my country back, and that is the bottom line, and I am not on my own,' says Ford, a Lincolnshire father of two.

Mr Ford was raging in comparative obscurity until an article by Sir Peregrine Worsthorne sent him utterly ballistic. Sir Perry was saying that Scottish and Welsh nationalisms were perfectly lovely, he said, but that 'the English mustn't have it because it turns us into football hooligans and fascists. I took exception to that and I whacked down a letter to *The Spectator*.'

Mr Ford, a sales manager for a publishing firm, says he received overwhelming support, including a very handsome offer from the BBC to give him a platform. You can see him denounce the PC jobsworths who refused to give an Essex landlady a special licence for St George's Day, while St Patrick's Day was nodded through.

He has uncovered the absurdity of the ban on *Land of Hope and Glory* from Gillingham football club; and the monstrous intrusion of the Leicester police, who confiscated a woman's collection of porcelain pigs, breaking some of them, because their position in her front window gave offence to Muslims.

The media, says Mr Ford, are skewed against those of Anglo-Saxon origin. 'The news presenters are not English. They're Irish, Scots, Indian or African. When they go out into the supermarkets to interview the public, they interview anyone but the English.'

He thinks our schools are failing to teach English history, while Welsh, Scottish and other cultural identities are sedulously encouraged. 'If we can't teach them history, they'll have no respect, and if they don't have any respect, they won't care. If you can't give these kids some sense of the history of their country, you can't expect any loyalty; and you can't live here, and be protected by the state here, and say, "My loyalty is to Bangalore" or wherever.'

But Mr Ford, I say, aren't you being a little bit paranoid

about this threat to English 'culture'? English is the language of global commerce, the Internet, air traffic control. Whence this insecurity?

'As a nation which represents 84 per cent of the people on these islands, we are being marginalised, because a third of the Cabinet are Scottish, and our institutions are paralysed about offending minorities.

'I have no guilt complex about the Empire, but I find the history of my country is being undermined so that six per cent are not offended.

'The overall *modus operandi* is that the English must be controlled. We are demeaned,' he says, citing an ad for Ikea that has the slogan: 'Don't be so English.'

Yes, but what do you mean by English? 'Fundamentally, our culture is Anglo-Saxon white European. It is ethically Protestant, even if most of them don't go to church. We are pagan more than anything else. The thing that has made me English is several thousand years of accumulated culture. If you take a group of white Anglo-Saxon Englishmen, we can trace our roots back 6,000 years.'

You can't be black and English, says Mr Ford. You can't be Indian. Can you be Jewish and English? He hesitates. 'Quite possibly, because of the eastern European background, and as my wife's partly it, yes. They've suffered enough. Cromwell, who was a hero of mine, let them back in.'

So there we are. That's the point. 'Englishness' is about race, or 'culture', whichever you prefer.

Mr Ford wants to stop all nonwhite immigration. There is no doubt that the English pay through the nose for Scotland, and if the Scots are so foolish as to break away, the English taxpayer can expect to do well. But if we then experience English nationalism like that of Mr Ford's, and we lose the term 'British', we may be throwing away a protective catch-all identity.

Mr Ford will doubtless think me a wet, but wouldn't it be better for people to think themselves 'British', than to think themselves either English or foreign?

'We're told we're a nation of racists. My retort to people who say that is, "If that's what you think, why don't you leave?"'

Ancient ways under threat in the new era.

Yes, I did feel lucky

'OK, punk,' I breathed to the bird, sighting that sucker down the polished barrel of the Beretta 12 bore as it flew fast and dark and hard, and the heart knocked in the ribs.

'Are you going to get lucky?' I hissed like Clint as the creature attained its maximum speed, of maybe 40 knots, high and clear against the stark silhouettes of the trees, and I covered the thing with the barrels, comme il faut.

Blam. Yup. It was going to get lucky. But hey, punk, did I fire one or did I fire two? And blam I fired two; and the pheasant lolloped on, untroubled by the vast penumbra of lead we were pumping into the sky.

And I turned to look at Bill Mitchell, and he looked at me sorrowfully from under his tweed cap adorned with badges of game and sport, and he said the inevitable words which I still found somehow unbelievable.

'You were well behind there sorr.' Behind! Teufel! Unless one of these punks went right ahead and made my day, we were in for humiliation here. There I was, dressed like a mixture between Lord Emsworth and Otto von Bismarck, equipped with the finest ordnance, schooled, cajoled and instantly reloaded by the most thoughtful

112

shooting tutor in Scotland – and wasting pounds of pellets on the desert air.

In spite of the cold, so cold that I was wearing pyjamas underneath, a flush was mantling the back of the neck. There seemed to be some misapprehension about us Telegraph folk, perhaps because of the reputation of editors past and present who like to hold leader conference by mobile phone from the moors, while churning the ether with lead.

'I can't believe you've never been shooting before,' said Cazzy, aka the Countess of Derby, at dinner in Dalmeny Castle the night before. Well, ahem, I sort of never got round to it, having aged 13 failed something called the Empire Test, which involved safely cleaning, loading and firing one of the Lee Enfield 303s used at the battle of Mons.

In fact, the closest we ever came to field sports was when my brother shot me with an airgun, I explained to the astounded Countess, who will be familiar to many as the girl who used to go out with Prince Andrew. That was it, until the previous afternoon, when Bill and Harry Dalmeny gave me a session with the clay pigeons.

Intended to buck up morale, the result was ambiguous. To put it mildly. One by one the orange clays floated in a dreamy autumnal arc from the machine through my field of fire, until they landed virgin, intact, in a growing mound on the turf. After watching me blaze away for a while, Nicky the nice German count, who was staying at Dalmeny in exchange for maintaining some of the furniture, said: 'I'll go and move the cars a bit further away.'

Finally, when they had lugged the machine up a hill so that it was whanging them directly at us, one of the clays virtually alighted on the end of the gun like an exhausted snowflake, and I gave it what for. Pow. But as Bill pointed out, in the first paradox of shooting, you don't go for the ones like that. 'You only shoot the sporrrting birds,' he said.

Before daybreak, as I stared through the curtains at the darkling lawn, and the shapes of the slumbering pheasants, the brain fizzed with whisky-induced paranoia. Was that bird fated to die by my incompetent hand? What if it embodied, on the Hoddle doctrine, the soul of one of my more sinful ancestors?

Worse, what if I failed to hit a thing? Harry, aka Lord Dalmeny, 31, had issued me with one of the favourite sets of tweeds of the sixth earl. As I came into the breakfast room, the most extraordinary sight seemed to me to be the panoramic view over the golf course of the Firth of Forth. Oh no, said everyone else, sniggering, the best thing was the sixth earl's plus fours.

You could have fitted a pheasant or two down the seat, apparently. 'The Sixth Earl must have been a bit of a lardarse,' said someone, and they all rocked over their bacon and mushroom. 'What fun,' said someone else, looking at my purple and white games socks. Then we were off.

We stood outside the castle, a seriously crenellated grey coadestone affair built in 1815 by the fourth earl on an estate occupied by the Rosebery bunch since the days of Charles I. Harry Dalmeny, son and heir of the Earl of Rosebery, gave us our instructions, including the numbers of the pegs we were to stand at on the first drive.

'We're moving off in five seconds, shooting pheasant, pigeons and woodcock if you see them' . . . Or if you have the faintest idea what they look like. Then it dawned that the chicks were coming too; not only was this humiliation time, I was to be outgunned by the gorgeous Tamsin Lennox-Boyd, and Harry's wife, the divine Caroline, aka Lady Dalmeny, the one-time Portillo policy wonk whose 30th birthday we would celebrate that night. 'Tamsin only shoots to kill,' said Ted Lennox-Boyd, as we got into the 4 × 4s.

And now we were standing at our pegs, straining our eyes at the trees like GIs looking for Vietcong. From somewhere over the horizon Joe Oliver, the head keeper who has been here since 1974, blew an old British Rail platform horn to announce the start.

Nothing happened. Then there was a vague racket in the wood on the top of the hill and you could see the dogs and men rootling around. 'They'll be coming fast and furious, sorr,' said Bill. Still nothing happened, and the moment of judgment drew closer, and the words of Harry Dalmeny from yesterday tea-time echoed in the soul.

'It's all about *cojones*,' he said. Deep down it's a primal act that expresses your virility; and when you contract the fever it can become a necessary part of you. The sixth earl, Harry's grandfather, whose glutei so magnificently filled the rear compartments of this suit, used to be wheeled out in advanced old age, mounted upright and a gun fixed diagonally in his grip: and still he hit them.

That is the hormone, the jaegerlust, which drives these heroic toffs to keep the thing going, in spite of the financial haemorrhage and the oppressions of the modern age. Lord Rosebery, who does not shoot, but who entertains the corporate visitors to Dalmeny with spotlit mini-tattoos from the battlements, explained that Labour had done some dastardly thing with tax.

This means, as I understand it, that it is no longer possible to offset losses from shooting against profits from the estate as a whole. Then, as Harry Dalmeny put it, 'public acceptance of shooting is on more of a knife-edge.' The Scotsman won't even let them advertise, he said. And the butchers won't buy the birds in case someone breaks a tooth on the shot, and they are sued.

If things don't look up, they said, the Dalmeny shoot,

115

where birds have been blasted from the heavens since the first fowling-piece was invented, will close. Never! I vowed, and had some more tea.

'Are you a crumpet person, Basil?' asked Lady Rosebery. And suddenly this reverie was interrupted. Just as I was pondering the cojones question, there was a flapping to my left and Woah! a bird whizzed past at shoulder height.

'No,' said Bill as the hands scrabbled feebly with the safety catch. 'You don't shoot those ones.' Of course. The Dalmeny pheasant is not as other pheasants, being a dynamic breed called the Scandinavian or blueback.

Since it is the slow, fat ones, which, by refusing to become airborne, have the higher life expectancy, your British pheasant is evolving towards slowness and fatness. But these Scandinavian or bluebacks, whether through athleticism or stupidity, are still determined to fly and – and here they were coming now: one, two over to the right, and the palpitations resumed . . .

But no, curses, they kept swinging away the wrong side of the beech tree, suicidally aiming for Harry and pow pow, the lovely streamlined missiles were transformed into moulting cartwheeling feather dusters, and Harry's dog Ben ran in, like Lord Cranborne. And then another dark shape appeared against the grey sky. OK, baby, you're mine. Time for Operation Cojones. The gun was lined up. Blam, blam. We stared. The bird sailed on. And – blam blam – it happened again. 'You need to follow through more,' said Bill. 'You need to aim eight or 10 feet ahead,' and the prickling fear began.

The topography of Dalmeny is ideal to assist the bird escape the gun. There are woods on steep hills, so that they are quite high overhead by the time they reach you. This is thought by shooters to be a good thing. Then huge efforts are made to ensure that they are as frisky and elusive as possible.

This batch of kamikaze bluebacks had come from Shrewsbury at the age of seven weeks, and then had a lovely early autumn in the woods, with drinkers and managers and wire to keep the foxes out. 'The art of pheasant shooting is to breed them in one wood, feed them in another wood, and shoot them in a third,' said Harry, obscurely.

Whatever the secret was, the pheasants seemed to regard my 45 degree sector as a kind of safe haven, beating their wings between 12 and 20 times, as pheasants do, and then just gliding insolently as the triple A burst around them.

OK, so this wasn't going to be a pheasant hitting day. But there was the pageantry to enjoy, the sheer ritual. Soon, after the second or third drive, it would be time for the consomme with chili sherry and the vast Thermos full of sausages with marmalade. There was the sight of the 18 beaters, stops and picker-uppers, one aged only three, like something out of Tolkien or Hardy with their amazing green tweed kit, all with purposeful flaps and pockets and double lapels.

There were the dogs, the romantic language, the walking across fields of winter barley and always the expectant adrenalin-filled standing and staring at the trees. 'Yes, Bruno,' said Lady Rosebery, my hostess, who used to work in the theatre. 'I've set the stage and I've designed the setting, and everyone comes and does their own little turn. It's the thrill of school plays. There's a light in the eyes of the people taking part.' And she was right, of course, even if that part was to be the buffoon who couldn't hit a barn door.

Such were my reflections when, hey, another one, high, fast – and it was a miracle. It was like the feeling when you catch a cricket ball right over the top of your head, and you can hardly see it. I looked at Bill and his eyes were wide with delight, and I realised he was mirroring my own expression. 'That was a sporrrting bird!' he cried.

Yes, I gave that bird the gift of death, as Hemingway puts it: one of those things, to judge by the bird's response, which it is more blessed to give than to receive. Then Bill was unscrewing a flask full of something he called 'hare's blood', a mixture of whisky, Drambuie and cherry brandy, and a feeling of elation flooded through.

Hey, what was going on now? He was approaching with the pheasant and daubing blood on my forehead. 'It's bad luck to take it off,' he said. So the day was saved from ignominy, and after the first drive we went to look at the bag, tied up in rows on a trailer pulled by an ancient Massey-Ferguson 35X.

The pathos of those closed eyes, the invisible wounds, the shimmering blue ruff, the red, the green, the black. Thou wast not born for death immortal bird, said Keats. But in your case, alas, I am forced to make an exception.

The day went on, up hill and down dale, and as my tally mounted to four, my cockiness rose, like an Osaka shipping tycoon on the moors for the first time. Enough of Blitish way! What this job needed was a bigger and more powerful gun. Give me bazooka!

Ah, what did I understand? When Teddy Derby said 'the birds were flying very nicely', he didn't mean they were easy to hit. He meant they were high, difficult, *sporting*. We were told of a man called Cunningham Reid, who is such a dead-eye dick that he uses some kind of rusty old popgun. Lunch came: chicken pie followed by blackberry and apple crumble, with bits of Kit-kat thoughtfully broken up and added to the fruit bowl; and after lunch the wine and the confidence took their toll.

'Och, how can you miss that?' asked Bill sadly as yet another bird taunted our muzzle. 'Well,' said Harry at the end, 'you definitely killed five birds.' Hang on . . . Bill and I had put the tally at the eight. Eight going on nine.

Still, the awful truth was that Harry had put me in the best possible stands, and I'd expended huge boxes of cartridges.

Harry had himself shot 35 of a total of 106. Both the girls had left me for dead. Lennox-Boyd, my next door neighbour, had overhauled me after a slow start. As he put it, 'I couldn't hit a sausage all day, and then I could hit – a sausage!'

It seemed there was a Czech cosmetics tycoon who had been at Dalmeny the other day who had shot worse. He had a wooden leg and glass eye and various other infirmities. At the end I went down to the sounding sea, in a state of apres-shoot euphoria, and reflected like Fotherington-Thomas on the dead birds.

Their last sight, before death folded them in his wings, was of Dalbougle castle and the Firth of Forth. A great way to go. Did I feel guilt? No, though I had felt no particular blood-lust either. These pheasants had done nothing to me.

It was pure competition. That night was wassail and celebration and bagpipes on the stairs, and, as the eyes closed, I could see the birds coming fast from the skeletal woods, one and then another: high, free and above all safe from harm.

I bet they voted New Labour.

Huh, I thought. Double Income, No Kids. That's what we have here. Bastards.

The plane was full of middle-class Brits, tanned by the alpine sun, fit, in so far as the chalet diet allows it, and the charter company had made the usual balls-up. Every time you turn up with a load of children, they decide for some reason that you are to be dispersed as widely as possible throughout the flight.

So when my wife, baby and one child had installed themselves in row one, seats A and B, and I had installed myself and two other children in row 20, I turned to my neighbours. Usually one might ask a stewardess to help out, but I decided to trust my own powers of charm. The plane was still stationary. The flight was still at the gate and would be for about ten more minutes. 'I wonder,' I began in the most cordial and winning way to the husband-and-wife team seated on my right, 'I wonder whether I could persuade you. . . .' What I was about to ask was whether they might be able to see their way round to swapping seats with my wife and her section of the children.

As far as I could see, this was a win-win situation for the lucky couple. They would extricate themselves from the company of myself and my two children and find themselves in the front row: the coveted position from which they would be the first out of the plane. As for us, the manoeuvre would enable us all to be together, and share the joys and sorrows that go with taking four children on an aeroplane. As I say, it is a piece of trivial diplomacy which I have comfortably pulled off several times.

So you can imagine that I was astonished when the man, sitting furthest from me, by the window, did not allow me to complete the sentence. 'No,' he snarled. 'For Christ's sake, the flight only lasts an hour and a quarter. What are you staring at?' I realised that I must have been gazing dumbly at him, and muttered something about not meaning to stare. 'What are you staring at?' he repeated, more belligerently. 'You asked me a question and I've given you an answer; now what are you staring at?' I must have appealed mutely to his wife (she had a wedding and engagement ring), but she rolled her eyes, looked away and said that 'it had been a bad day'.

Well, I dare say it had been a bad day. We had all been struggling back from the slushy passes, looking for gloves under beds, waiting in our coaches in interminable traffic-jams in Bourg St Maurice and all the rest of it. But nothing, or so it seemed to me, could conceivably justify this sheer downright nastiness. As my wife pointed out later, she would have given the couple what for. She would have said something snappy, like 'I'm staring because I've never come across anyone so rude and unpleasant in all my life.'

Alas, I didn't have the nerve. I quivered, like a puppy unexpectedly kicked. I had one brief, feeble moment of retaliation, when one child said he wanted very badly to be sick, so I said in a voice loud enough to be heard for several rows, 'Why don't you come and be sick on this chap here?' But mainly I sat there, seething and brooding. And my thoughts turned to a fragment of the newspaper that I had come across, soggy and sat-upon in the chalet, about some bishop who had been laying into those who elect, for one reason or another, not to have children.

Yeah, I sneered to myself, as I sneaked a good look at them both. They were in their early thirties, plainly married and pretty well-off. He had a watch by Tag Heuer, designer spectacles and – though his face was buried in the window in an effort to avoid meeting my eye, and though my memory may be contaminated by loathing – it seemed to me that he looked very much like a priggish, puffy, pathetic squashed tomato. She was reading *Tatler*. In fact, to compound my distress, she was buried in an article by our own Toby Young, one of his ones about dressing up as a girl or going to bed with supermodels or something. Huh, I thought. Double Income, No Kids. That's what we have here. Bastards.

As if sensing my gaze, the couple started huddling away

from me and twining their hands together, and he was rubbing her hair with his hands as if to say it's all going to be all right, darling. Yuk, I thought, and stoked my rage with half-remembered fragments of the bishop's remarks. It was 'selfish' not to have children, the bishop said. Yoh! Marriage was all about having children, and those who opted out were frauds, he said. Right on, bro. Only people who didn't understand what it was all about could behave like that, I told myself, and sat fizzing and popping until, for such is our training, my intellectual faculties demanded a change, and I began to argue in the adversative.

Hang on a mo, I thought. Why the hell should the childless couple always be expected to defer to other people's snotty little kids, the product of nothing but their selfish desire to replicate their genes? Wasn't it grim enough already for the childless mother – and Heaven knows why she might be childless – without being forced to abase herself before the noisy, smelly, inconsiderate fecundity of other people? Why did I think I had a divine right to shove people about an aeroplane, just because we'd gone to the trouble to have a 'family'? Family schmamily.

Good for old Tag Heuer, I started to think; perhaps, after all, he was evincing nothing but that old-fashioned Anglo-Saxon bolshiness so admired by Rudyard Kipling. Perhaps, in refusing to budge from row 20 to row one, he was showing the same mulishness which defeated Hitler . . .

I think I must have been lost in meditation because at that point one of the children spilt his water and it was necessary to mop it up, and the other one wanted to go to the lavatory, and I knocked my coffee over; and I thought how much handier and jollier it would have been if we were all together, and my incontinent rage returned, against Tag Heuer and his wife.

Remember this, Mr and Mrs Tag Heuer, if you are sensible enough to have jacked *Tatler* in favour of *The Spectator*: you may be paying for the absurd child benefit that mounts up in our children's bank accounts, but when you are old and frail, and in need of state-subsidised nursing and medicine, it will be our children who are paying, out of their earnings, to keep you alive.

So next time you face a bashful, sheepish request to swap places for the sake of the kiddies, I suggest you leap to attention; or else it won't be long before some smart political party pledges, as part of its pro-family crusade, that it will be illegal for indolent charter companies to separate children and parents on planes, and anyone making any trouble will be put off at Geneva airport.

Jack Straw suggests a feeble means of putting the toothpaste back in the tube.

One Nation

The world of football was rocked the other day when Jack Straw had an idea. I know, he said, let's have a British football team. England, Scotland, Wales, Northern Ireland, all united to produce a band of superstars. His proposal was not greeted with joy on the terraces, and there was much snickering by men in sheepskin coats. The wretched Straw was forced to go on television and issue a retraction; and yet there was a logic in his thinking with which many of us will sympathise. The Home Secretary has to deal with the lawlessness of our inner-city estates, instantiated in the feral murder of Damilola Taylor, a ten-year-old Nigerian immigrant.

Thoughtful Labour figures have for some years been brooding on why Peckham, and other such areas, are so much nastier than, say, the Nigerian suburb from which Damilola originated. The answer, they think, is to do with the anomie of the inhabitants, a sense that they have no stake in their society. They take their benefits from the state, but feel no particular loyalty in return. In areas where primary immigration is still taking place on a large scale, there is only the vaguest sense of belonging. To what do they belong? The Afro-Caribbean community? The Vietnamese community? The answer is often unclear, and this has psychological consequences. There seems no reason to behave respectfully towards that little old woman coming out of the Post Office if you feel that she belongs to a culture that is alien from your own. That feeling of alienation will be all the stronger if you suspect that she, for her part, looks down on you. Why not piss against the wall if you feel that it is not really your wall, but part of a foreign country?

One response to this problem is just to call, in Enochian fashion, for a hauling-up of the drawbridge. That is unattractive, not least because there is a strong moral and economic case for allowing limited immigration for those who want to work, and who will not just be a burden on the state. Jack Straw's solution is different, and involves borrowing (yet again) an old Tory idea. Labour ministers hope to create that vital sense of belonging by building up 'Britishness', and asserting the virtues of Britain as a country with which all its inhabitants can identify. Gordon Brown and other ministers have studied America, and the strong civic sense that is inculcated in immigrants. American children are all made to pledge allegiance to the flag. It is still necessary, for all citizens, to have some basic knowledge of the constitution. When people immigrate to America, it is because they want to be American, and they puff with pride when they succeed. Can anyone honestly say, surveying the arrivals in our inner cities, that they

124

have come here because they want to glory in the name of Briton?

Labour ministers have been groping desperately for the symbols of Britishness that will create this sense of belonging, which will in turn produce responsibility. The irony, of course, is that while Mr Straw babbles about British football teams, there are plenty of institutions which have served to unite a disparate people for hundreds of years. To enumerate them would make a sensitive New Labour soul wince, so here goes: the crown; the flag; the rule of law; the British army; and parliamentary democracy, the image of Big Ben with which Britain is still identified across the planet. How weird, how whacky, that Mr Straw should call for loyalty to a British football team, when Labour has done more than any other government to break Britain up. It is utterly absurd that Labour should be calling on us all to remember the value of that inclusive word 'British', when it is the government's own devolution programme which has fomented the rising sense of Scottishness, and Englishness.

As for the other symbols of Britishness, one can see why the government finds it difficult to appeal to them. The crown, the flag, the army – they're all victims, one way or another, of Cool Britannia. It is hard, finally, for Labour to ask the people to rally round our national heritage of parliamentary democracy, when this week the government is busy undermining Parliament at Nice, and slowly turning self-government into a nonsense. If they want us all to feel loyal to British institutions, they could start by not destroying them.

The Tories used to have a good slogan. 'Labour says he's black. We say he's British.' It's possible to be anti-racist, and against the race relations industry.

'Am I guilty of racial prejudice? We all are'

Am I a racist? I jolly well shouldn't be. Look at my life. House in some Islington media gulch. Kiddies romping around in the minimalist basement. A couple of snowball-head Aryans and then one with fairly olive skin and one in between. They are the produce, within the space of four generations, of India, Turkey, France, Germany, Russia, international Jewry, Wales and England.

In fact, I like to think my instincts, in this respect, are as blameless as those of the average Guardian reader; and the thing is, I am guilty none the less. Not of racism, I hope, but of spasms of incorrectitude, soon over, soon regretted. When I shamble round the park in my running gear late at night, and I come across that bunch of black kids, shrieking in the spooky corner by the disused gents, I would love to pretend that I don't turn a hair.

Now you might tell me not to be such a wuss. You might say that I am at no more risk than if I had come across a bunch of winos. But somehow or other a little beeper goes off in my brain. I'm not sure what triggers it (the sayings of Sir Paul Condon? The *Evening Standard*?), but I put on a pathetic turn of speed. You might tell me that when they shout their cheery catcalls, I should smile and wave. And, you know, maybe a big girl's blouse like me would break into an equally rapid lollop if it were a gang of white kids.

Quite possibly. The trouble is, I'm not sure. I cannot rule out that I have suffered from a tiny fit of prejudice. I have prejudged this group on the basis of press reports, possibly in right-wing newspapers, about the greater likelihood of being mugged by young black males than by any other group. And if that is racial prejudice, then I am guilty.

And so are you, baby. So are we all. If there is anyone reading this who has never experienced the same disgraceful reflex, then – well, I just don't believe you. It is common ground among both right-wingers and left-wingers that racism is 'natural', in that it seems to arise organically, in all civilisations. It is as natural as sewage. We all agree that it is disgusting, a byproduct of humanity's imperfect evolution. The question is, what to do with the effluent? It seems to me that today's solutions are almost as wrong as those of Enoch Powell 30 years ago.

One of the features of conservative cant is the assertion that 'Enoch did not have a racist bone in his body'. Oh no, say my friends the Powellites. He was simply pointing out that other people – the benighted folk of Wolverhampton – could not be expected to show the same restraint. It is all very well for the Hampstead liberals to be tolerant; but what of the urban poor, those at the sharp end? Powell himself was not a racist, say the Powellites, but he spoke for those whose baser feelings were too sorely taxed by their neighbours. He was not a racist; he was merely the prophet of racism. Well, even if you accept the distinction, you have to admit that, as a prophet, Powell got it crashingly wrong.

Where is the foaming river of blood? Call me a media milquetoast, but I don't see a race war; I see innumerable examples of colour-blind cooperation. On questions of race, the man to listen to is not Enoch Powell, but WF Deedes, who served in the same Tory cabinet, and who thinks our record in this country is as good as anywhere in the world. Powell got it wrong, by underestimating the tolerance of the British, and by conjuring up a racist genie that proved not nearly as vile as imagined. And the same

127

mistake, of course, is being made by the race relations industry today.

Heaven knows why Macpherson made his weird recommendation, that the law might be changed so as to allow prosecution for racist language or behaviour 'other than in a public place'. I can't understand how this sober old buzzard was prevailed upon to say that a racist incident might be so defined in the view of the victim 'or any other person'. This is Orwellian stuff.

Not even under the law of Ceausescu's Romania, could you be prosecuted for what you said in your own kitchen. No wonder the police are already whingeing that they cannot make any arrests in London. No wonder the CPS groans with anti-discrimination units, while making a balls-up of so many cases.

Suppose a racist phrase or incident were really defined entirely according to the perception of some third party. Here's the Guardian's own Gary Younge, on the subject of Ali G. 'Imagine the tables were turned, and a black comedian created a white Jewish character, who made jokes about being a tight-fisted, highly ambitious mummy's boy.'

Of course Mr Younge was using this ugly stereotype to show that some people could take offence at the comic's portrayal of black men as 'stupid, sexist, drug-taking layabouts', but isn't it possible that someone might have taken offence at Gary's own words?

If the Macpherson report had been implemented in full, you might not get away with that, Gary. And that would be crazy, wouldn't it? Where the left, the Guardian, Macpherson and the whole PC brigade are just as wrong as Powell, is in thinking that we should endlessly hunt for evidence of one of humanity's worst features, tease it out, legislate for it, bang on about it, create thousands of jobs financially dependent on discovering it.

In reality, provided we have a reasonable legal framework for minimising the problem – like the infrastructure used to remove sewage – we could probably achieve the same results, if not better, if we axed large chunks of the anti-racism industry, stopped taxing so many people with the threat of legal action, and left a bit more of the struggle against racism to tolerance and good manners.

This is an abridged version of the Keith Joseph Memorial Lecture delivered to the Centre for Policy Studies on 25 March 2004.

The Queen fights back

My father's father's father was a romantic Turkish politician who ran a small but distinguished conservative magazine, and whose career ended in a series of judgments that were romantic and certainly conservative, but unwise and sometimes reckless.

Most reckless of all was when my ancestor took it upon himself, as interior minister in the government of the last sultan, to sign the arrest warrant for Ataturk, now acknowledged to be the father of modern Turkey, and whose visage adorns almost every municipal building in the country. A short while later, my great-grandfather was having a shave in a place called Izmit when he was beaten to death and stuck in a tree. That is why my paternal grandfather, who was born Osman Ali, arrived in this country in search of what would now be called asylum.

I say all this to demonstrate that although I am of course British, and have far more English than Turkish blood, I have a predisposition to be sympathetic to those who have come to this country, in fear of their lives or not, with the intention of making a new start.

129

The reason we worry about the scale and pace of immigration today is that, bluntly, the present influx does not seem to be assimilating in quite the same way as their predecessors did. According to Andrew Green of Migrationwatch, the net inflow of immigrants to Britain is now about 170,000 per year, a figure which takes no account of failed asylum-seekers who do not leave the country, and other illegals. We are apparently expecting an extra two million non-EU immigrants per decade and, pro-immigrant though I am, that strikes me as a legitimate subject for political discussion. Never one for being outflanked on the Right, David Blunkett has already warned that people feel swamped. More significantly, it now appears to be acceptable, in left-wing circles, to call attention to the threat posed by immigration to the British way of life.

A couple of Harvard economists, Messrs Alesina and Glaeser, have produced a fascinating explanation for the different willingness, in Europe and America, to take money from the rich and spend it on the poor. Government spending in America is about 30 per cent of GDP, and in Europe it is about 45 per cent of GDP, and one important explanation for the difference, say the economists, is race. It seems that people are more likely to support welfare if they live close to recipients of their own race, and they are more likely to be antipathetic to it if they live close to citizens of another race. This insight has been seized on by the Left, and provoked an anguished article by David Goodhart in *Prospect*, called 'Too Diverse?', in which he says that if we have a society that is too diverse, too multicultural, too Balkanised into immigrant groups, then we will lose that sense of reciprocity and mutuality and community that we need to maintain people's commitment to the welfare state.

So at the beginning of the 21st century, amid general

paranoia about globalisation and immigration, nationalism is being invoked by the Left for the salvation of socialism in one country. Now you or I might think there were plenty of other good reasons for wanting to preserve a spirit of reciprocity and community, beyond the Goodhartian ambition of protecting the pristine integrity of our 1948 welfare settlement. But there is one underlying assumption in the discourse of Goodhart, Blunkett and Green, and that is the reality of racism. It now seems to be accepted on the Left – when it was never accepted before – that racism is endemic in the species.

I don't want my taxes wasted on scroungers of any colour; but it seems to be common ground that people's resentment is accentuated if they feel the money is going on foreigners, and particularly on foreigners of a different colour. That strikes me as being sad but probably unavoidable; and in that sense racism is like sewage: something that a civilised society will manage and channel. The question is how.

The most obvious answer is to prevent huge numbers of unassimilated people arriving in such a way as to perturb the indigenous people; and if you are in favour of immigration, which I am, then you should be in favour of people who come here to work, and you should not so disastrously mismanage the asylum system that hundreds of thousands of illegals are left in limbo, technically forbidden to be economically active and a continual irritation, therefore, to the taxpayer. But given the scale and pace of the immigration already under way, that is not enough; and here we come to the second and most amazing volte-face by the Left.

Almost seven years after New Labour came to power, vowing to do away with Old Britain, they have rediscovered the vitality of old symbols in a way that is hilarious and also rather moving. On 26 February this year,

131

members of the Hatterjee family became British citizens in a ceremony described by Ferdinand Mount in a recent issue of *The Spectator*. They were serenaded by the national anthem and they shook hands with the Prince of Wales. And all these people, thousands a month, are not only swearing or affirming their allegiance to the Queen, her heirs and successors. There is now a new pledge, which one might call the Tipton Taleban clause. 'I will give my loyalty to the UK, and respect its rights and freedoms,' says the pledge. 'I will uphold its democratic values. I will observe its laws faithfully and fulfil my duties and obligations as a British citizen.'

Consider the astonishing implications of those words – astonishing, that is, for this country to demand. 'I will give my loyalty to the UK.' Ten years ago Norman Tebbit suggested that immigrants should pass the cricket test: that third- or fourth-generation UK citizens, sitting in the crowd at Lord's, should on the whole requite the benefits they have received in this country by cheering for England.

At the time this feline observation was denounced – across the political spectrum – as quite irresponsibly provocative. And now a Labour government explicitly demands loyalty to the UK. If you accept, as seems reasonable, that loyalty to the UK is logically indivisible from sporting allegiance, then Norman Tebbit's cricket test has been given ceremonial form by David Blunkett. Early reports suggest that the naturalised immigrants love these ceremonies; they love the Union flag there – the very flag that is banned from the lockers in the workplace on the grounds that it is intimidatingly racist – and the government loves them, too. That is because there has long been a recognition that Britain will not work if it is just what Philip Bobbitt called a market state.

You could in theory construct a polity in which no one had any particular romantic attachment to the nation itself;

and we could all live wherever we happened to be in the same spirit of emotional detachment, paying our taxes, and in return receiving certain services and protections. Of course it would be a rather dismal sort of place; and it would also be impractical. Because the key feature of nation states is that they do demand of their citizens the willingness to make sacrifices for the general good, and on the whole people will make those sacrifices only if they feel a basic loyalty to the nation. It is as if the government is appalled at the fissiparous effect of multiculturalism, and is suddenly reaching for the glue.

That is the meaning of these citizenship ceremonies. Left-wingers have finally grasped that if this country is to succeed, if it is to be cohesive, we must have a basic and shared understanding of what it means to be British. It would be fair to say that Labour has ended up, in 2004, with a rather different interpretation of being British from that with which it began in 1997.

For much of its seven years in power, Labour has mounted an assault on what it conceives of as the institutions of Old Britain. You remember Cool Britannia, and the moronic and ahistorical Dome, and Cherie's refusal to curtsy, and Bob Ayling's preposterous and commercially disastrous removal of the flag from the tailfins of BA jets. It was just the beginning of a New Labour project to reconfigure what it meant to be British, and the agenda was spelt out by Gordon Brown in a speech in April 1999, only four years ago. 'Old Britain is going,' announced Gordon, who still likes to give two fingers to tradition by turning up in a suit for the Lord Mayor's banquet. 'The old order of unreformed institutions is passing into history.'

It was pretty clear that by these institutions he meant the union between England and Scotland, the doctrine of parliamentary sovereignty and, sotto voce, the monarchy. He pointed with excitement to a poll showing that the public didn't think much of the House of Commons as an emblem of Britishness. It was old-fashioned to think that power had to be centred on London, he said, and extolled the genius and dynamism of the coming regional governments. He cited Professor Linda Colley, to the effect that the institutions of a united Britain were really the creation of empire and external peril; and those things having been removed, the tired old crenellated institutions of Britain could be broken up and reformed, and sovereignty could be pooled with Europe. No, he said, what really united the nation was not Parliament but the NHS, chosen by 71 per cent as the thing most representative of Britain.

One can see why this might be appealing to a Labour politician who has so vastly expanded the public sector – though not necessarily front-line staff – and entrenched the position of the NHS as the biggest state employer this side of the Urals. But when you are stuck in some foreign hell-hole, and thinking green thoughts of home, do you necessarily think of the NHS, with all its beauties and advantages? Do you pine, like Rupert Brooke in the first world war, and wish you were in some NHS ward? I'm not sure.

And if it wasn't the NHS that united the nation, said Gordon Brown, it was the BBC; and again one can see why the idea of 20,000 taxpayer-funded journalists of preponderantly leftish views might have seemed congenial to Gordon then, if not now. Then he told us that being British meant that everyone who can work has the right and responsibility to do so. This strikes me as a little glib, to say the least. There is nothing particularly unBritish about a wife who stays at home to look after the children, or stays at home to watch the television, or indeed a belted earl who has never done a day's work in his life. But these things, at any rate, were the aspects of Britishness that Labour chose to extol: the NHS, the BBC, and the Gordon

Brownian obsession with work; and the other tired old symbols of Britishness they set about to deprecate or destroy.

The Crown was removed from the Treasury letterhead. I remember being amazed, sitting on some Police Bill, when we just nodded through a clause changing the oath of loyalty sworn by police constables so as to remove a specific reference to the Queen. I went into the Lobby, found Chris Moncrieff of the Press Association, issued a torrential statement of denunciation, and heard no more about it.

The government will shortly agree a new constitution for this country, hammered out in unintelligible negotiations with other European countries, and will not even give us a vote on it. The absurdity of regional government continues, in the sense that gravel pits can be dug or houses built in south Oxfordshire, on the say-so of some Guildford bureaucrat. We now have a devolved system of government in which measures can be imposed on England by Scottish MPs, when I as an English MP have no say over those questions in Scotland and – the final absurdity – they, sitting for Scottish seats, have no say themselves. The hereditaries have been banned, or will be shortly; and still the Kulturkampf goes on.

If you are staying in the Marriott Kampala and you meet someone in the Windsor Suite, where the hotel managers will have gone to great trouble to find some British-style prints to put on the walls, what will you see? It is a dime to a dollar that those pictures – intended by the globalised hotel business to connote Britain – will show scenes of fox-hunting, a sport that is to be banned by Labour not for reasons of cruelty, but because of chippiness and class war, and because fox-hunting is so deeply redolent of Old Britain.

Only last month the government announced, for no

reason at all other than a vague teenage republicanism, that they were going to remove the reference to the Crown from the Crown Prosecution Service. And yet this is the very government which now asks newcomers not just to swear an oath of loyalty to the Crown, but also to the United Kingdom. This resentful adolescent Labour government, after six years of spite and vindictiveness, has just installed a ceremony in which the Union flag is prominently displayed and everyone sings 'God Save the Queen'. What is going on? The answer is that we are witnessing a screeching and undignified U-turn, at least by one part of the government.

When immigrants come here, they instantly see the point of symbols like flags, and anthems, and the Queen, whose DNA incarnates British history in a way that people understand all over the world. For 20 years the Labour party was completely wrong in the main economic arguments. It is now dawning on them – not fast enough – that they may also have been wrong in the cultural arguments, and that their adherence to the doctrine of multiculturalism has been a mistake, because it produces a segregated market state where people insist on their rights, but have no sense of common loyalty or purpose. If you want to engender that loyalty, it is no use appealing to the NHS, or the BBC, or our common desire to work, as Gordon Brown suggests. You have to go back to the things that really resonate in people's hearts; and while Conservatives have no monopoly on those institutions, it is certainly a conservative insight that they should not be lightly cast aside.

This is a turning point: we have to fly the flag for Britishness again

I have already had enough about how perfectly normal these young men were, and what charming fellows they were, and how there was nothing they loved more than serving in dad's chip shop or helping an old lady across the street or a good game of cricket in the park.

'All he wanted to do was have a laugh,' said one of the neighbours last night, about one of the sick quartet responsible for killing themselves and at least 52 others in London. 'He was sound as a pound.' Yeah, right. If these four young men were perfectly normal Yorkshiremen, then what the hell is happening to this country? Of all the shattering revelations of the past few days, the worst has been that these suicide bombers were British.

They were our very own. They were as British as a wet Bank Holiday. They were as British as Tizer, and queues and Y-fronts and the Changing of the Guard, and the chips that made them what they were. They were born in British maternity wards, and attended by every comfort that the state could give.

They went to British primary schools and learnt about Britain from British teachers, and when they murdered so many of their fellow Britons it was the British emergency services who tried to save what lives they could.

That shocking fact of their Britishness tells us something frightening about them and about us, because, as suicide bombers go, they are unusual. When the Palestinian bombers attack Jerusalem or Tel Aviv, they usually come from miserable lives in Nablus or Hebron. When the 19 suicide bombers destroyed the Twin Towers they originated, without exception, from the Arab world, mainly Saudi Arabia.

137

We seem to have pulled off the rare feat of breeding suicide bombers determined to attack the very society that incubated them; and the question is why. Why does America import its suicide bombers, while we produce our own?

Last summer we had a magnificent holiday driving around America, and for a cynical Brit it was astonishing to see the way the Americans fly that flag of theirs. On every porch, on every flagpole, on every bumper: there were the stars and stripes, unabashed, exuberant, proud. Contrast our treatment of the Union Flag, which is endlessly being cited in racial harassment cases, on the ground that it is provocative merely – for instance – to stick it on your locker. Remember Bob Ayling, the Labour-supporting businessman who succeeded the late, great Lord King at British Airways, and decided that the Union Flag was so embarrassing that he stripped it from the tailfins of his planes.

The Americans would be mystified by our approach to a national symbol. For them the flag is a vital agent of integration, a way of asserting that, in that vast immigrant country, each person is not only American but equally American, and has an equal stake in society. That is why American children still begin their day at school by pledging allegiance to the flag, and that is why the Americans show a patriotism and a simple enthusiasm for their own country that our jaded British sensibilities find childish.

Well, if you consider what is taught in British schools – and when you think that one of the killers was actually a primary school teacher – it is hard to deny that in their assessment of what a nation needs to stick together, the Americans are right, and we are tragically wrong. It is not just that most British children no longer know much about British history (13 per cent of 16- to 24-year-olds think the Armada was defeated by Hornblower, and 6 per cent ascribe the great naval victory to Gandalf). The disaster is that we no longer make any real demands of loyalty upon those who are immigrants or the children of immigrants. There are many culprits, and foremost among them is Enoch Powell. As Bill Deedes has pointed out over the years, the problem was not so much his catastrophic 1968 tirade against immigration, but the way he made it impossible for any serious politician to discuss the consequences of immigration, and how a multiracial society ought to work.

In the wake of Powell's racist foray, no one had the guts to talk about Britishness, or whether it was a good thing to insist – as the Americans do so successfully – on the basic loyalty of immigrants to the country of immigration.

So we have drifted on over the intervening decades, and created a multi-cultural society that has many beauties and attractions, but in which too many Britons have absolutely no sense of allegiance to this country or its institutions. It is a cultural calamity that will take decades to reverse, and we must begin now with what I call in this morning's *Spectator* the re-Britannification of Britain.

That means insisting, in a way that is cheery and polite, on certain values that we identify as British. If that means the end of spouting hate in mosques, and treating women as second-class citizens, then so be it. We need to acculturate the second-generation Muslim communities to our way of life, and end the obvious alienation that they feel.

That means the imams will have to change their tune, and it is no use the Muslim Council of Great Britain endlessly saying that 'the problem is not Islam', when it is blindingly obvious that in far too many mosques you can find sermons of hate, and literature glorifying 9/11 and vilifying Jews.

We have reached a turning point in the relations between the Muslim community and the rest of us, and it is time

139

for the moderates to show real leadership. That is why I want to end with the words of my Labour colleague Shahid Malik, MP for Dewsbury, who said yesterday: 'The challenge is straightforward – that those voices that we have tolerated will no longer be tolerated, whether they be on the streets, in the schools, in the youth clubs, in the mosque, in a corner, in a house. We need to go beyond condemning. We need to confront.'

Well said, Shahid; and it is time for the imams to follow.

The end of part of England

As soon as I see Bertha's rear end backing down the tailgate towards me, I think there has been some mistake. They told me they would find a nice quiet mare, given that I have never been riding before. Advancing upon me are the towering bay buttocks of the biggest horse I have ever seen.

In a daze, I mount the stool, held for me by Di Grisselle, joint master, shove one foot in the stirrup and try to swing myself over. Bertha chooses that moment to reverse, and I begin my first day's hunting, in the last week of that ancient custom, by slowly and dreamily falling to the concrete farmyard floor.

So let us leave me there, between the stirrup and the ground, and review the reasons for this desperate act. 'You're very brave,' everyone keeps saying, 'not to say foolhardy.' In fact, by the time I come to grips with Bertha I have been made – I suspect deliberately – apprehensive. 'When I took up hunting again in 1997,' said my host Charles Moore as we drove to the meet, 'I hadn't done it for 25 years, and I didn't sleep a wink the night before.' Really? I said, as it dawned that I had slept last night in the tranquillity of ignorance.

We passed a single magpie, and I could not help noticing Charles's long mumbling prayer of propitiation, all about 'say hello to Mrs Magpie . . . give her my best . . . my name is Charles Moore,' and so on at such length that I became seriously rattled. Charles is a veteran, a pro. He is entitled to the pink, green-collared jacket of the East Sussex and Romney Marsh. He is never happier than when he is hurtling from the saddle, collarbone first, towards some dry-stone wall or briar patch, and if he was so spooked about events ahead that he was doing magpie prayers, what hope was there for me?

Apart from an hour on a camel in Egypt, and a few hours on an elephant in India, I had never been properly transported on a large mammal, and though I have done some things that are arguably brave, such as attending the births of four children and driving at 160 mph on the M40, I have never ridden a horse at speed. My father and grandfather were known to have hunted with the Devon and Somerset staghounds, but somehow the option never cropped up for me.

There was only one reason for doing it now, and that was to show my anger and my support; though I speak as one who has never had any particular urge to kill animals. Indeed, when the stag hunt used to appear in our valley, and ring the basin of the hills like Sioux, our overwhelming feeling, as children, was for the deer. When they came through the yard, with the glutinous grins that all hunting folk bestow on civilians, we would rush out and scream, 'He went that way! He went that way!' like French peasants trying to save an airman from the Gestapo, and the hunt would grin their glutinous grins and ignore us. And as anybody who has seen it will know, there is scarcely anything more terrible and pathetic than the sight of a deer brought to bay – facing the music, as they say, of the hounds.

To say that the final stages of a hunt are not in some sense cruel is to talk nonsense; but that is not the point. The extinction of hunting will lift scarcely a pebble from the mountain of British cruelty to animals. This is not about cruelty. It is a Marxian attack on something Labour absurdly believes to be a class interest. It is a selfish attempt by the Prime Minister to repay his lobotomised back-benchers for their acceptance of the war in Iraq. It is an utterly contemptible way to govern a country. I may have secretly backed the deer against the hunt, but I still want deer running through our valley on Exmoor; and if – as all the evidence suggests that it will – the deer population dwindles when there is no hunt, and the farmers shoot them to extinction, then I will hold this Labour government and all its supporters in a cold immortal resentment and hound them until I die; because they will have killed off something that is part of England for no other reason than spite.

That is the anger that impels me to turn out now, in borrowed gear, and to haul myself again aboard Bertha. 'He looks very pale,' says a woman. 'Here,' says a man going around with a flagon of yellow liquid, 'have some Dutch courage.' Charles introduces me to the other master, Tom Arthur, red as a letterbox, who shakes with his left hand since his right has been freshly trodden on by a horse. I try to stay on, as Bertha backs randomly through the meet, and notice that the burst capillaries in the cheeks of my fellow hunters have turned not so much purple as black.

I notice how fine the hunt looks, in their black coats and white stocks (Charles, a stickler, says the correct term is 'hunting tie'), but mainly I think how tiny we are, as a group. There are plenty of irritatingly proficient Thelwell-style children, but the East Sussex and Romney Marsh has only 50 full subscribers, and it occurs to me how cowardly it is of Labour to pick this minority off. Before I can defend them properly, however, I feel I must understand what they do, and that is why I am now having a crash course in riding from a sweet blonde called Jenny.

Normally Jenny Yeo likes a vigorous day of bouncing in the saddle and leaping five-bar gates, but she has agreed to help, and frankly, I need it. I have taken to kissing Bertha's aromatic neck and saying, 'There, there, darling, you don't want to kill me, do you?', but before I can master the rudiments of steering, a man parps a horn and we are off, down the farmyard, through the thin crowd, for the beginning of the hunt.

For the first few hundred yards Bertha is led on a rope by a groom called Zoe, but by the time we have reached the end of the first field she is so spattered with mud that it seems inhumane to ask her to continue. So then Jenny takes the rope in her spare hand, and I know, with dread and rapture, that I am sooner or later going to have to manage on my own. But for now I am able to follow Jenny, like some clapped-out first world war general, and try to grasp what is going on. It is quite mysterious. It is like war, in that there are long periods of inaction, followed by terrifying exertion and ludicrous bravery. Detachments of horses seem to get trapped in the wrong field, and wheel and curvet in the sodden grass.

Jenny and I come to rest opposite a wooded escarpment, where the dogs can be seen writhing in the undergrowth. 'The hounds are speaking well,' says Jenny. 'They are giving good tongue,' she says, and they are certainly making a noise. Then Jenny and a nice lady called Polly talk about how they are looking forward to being locked up before we inexplicably move on, through the waterlogged kale and the Brussels sprouts, to another part of the same wood.

'It's really all about jumping, isn't it?' I say to Charles as he returns, painted with mud, from surmounting some obstacle. 'No, it's not,' he says. 'It's about hunting.' That,

I am afraid is true. We are kidding ourselves if we think the joy of hunting is just to do with mucking about in the open air, or comradeship, or pageantry. At the heart of the thing is the death of the fox. It is possible simply to have a great time on a horse, as I do, even if it is initially painful.

Trotting, for instance, proves – how shall I say – wearing on the goolies, and when I gasp my distress to Jenny she laughs richly and points out that she has no goolies herself. Such is our exhilaration that we both find this tremendously funny. Then a bystander shortens the stirrups and before you know it Bertha and I are trotting and bobbing in unison. And then there is the glorious moment when the whole hunt is heading uphill towards a distant council estate; a pale sun is shining on the windmill; the earth is starting to grumble under the accelerating hooves; the hounds are giving heaps of tongue in an adjoining copse; Bertha and I are trot-bobbing like crazy, and any second now I know that my beast is going to break into a canter, and then Jenny gives a little cry of 'here we go', and we do.

Doing my best to hide the sick rictus on my face I hang on to the neck-strap as Bertha attains a speed of – oh – 20 mph, but it feels like 90, and it is yeehah thunder thunder thunder all the way from one magnificent end of the field to the other; and by the end of the afternoon I have formed my own aesthetic of hunting. It is like skiing, in that you are personally tracing, at speed, the contour of the landscape, and then there is the added interest of the weird semi-sexual relation with the horse, in which you have the illusion of understanding and control. There is the military-style pleasure of wheeling and charging as one, the emulative fun of a pseudo-campaign.

As the day goes on, I begin to pick up inklings of the etiquette, the elaborate courtesy about gates, and the need to shout 'Ware hole!' (or Warhol!, as Charles puts it, perhaps in honour of the artist) if you see a hole. Out of the corner of my eye I am continually watching the sun, and as it sinks and gilds the soggy fields of Sussex I know that I have virtually attained my goal, which is survival.

But everyone else has a different understanding of the objectives, as they continually point out. 'I'm sorry you haven't seen a fox,' says Di Grisselle, the joint master. 'I'm afraid we haven't shown you much sport yet,' says someone else. 'Bit of a slow day,' says Tom the other master, when we get back to the boxes in the dusk. According to Charles, the hunt did kill four foxes ('two brace', he speedily corrects himself), but they died at the hands of the terriermen; they weren't properly chased, and this, it seems, is a disappointment.

My friends, there is no getting round it: the chasing and killing of foxes is what this is all about. And does that make it wrong? As it happens, I have already seen a dead fox this morning, on the A20 near Sidcup, so chopped up by traffic as to resemble sodden grey cardboard. Ten times as many foxes die on the roads as are killed by the hunts, and unlike the hunted fox they have a truly cruel and lingering death, haemorrhaging from glancing blows. Is the Labour government going to ban cars?

Therefore it must be that Labour objects to the mental state of the hunting people, the fact of the bloodlust. Well, let us leave on one side the disgusting impudence of a government passing judgment on our mental states, when we are all asked to tolerate deviancy of one kind or another. In banning this trivial and ritual expression of bloodlust, they are doing something literally immoral. They are going against the grain of human nature, and using legislation to suppress an instinct as old as man. And yet the real reasons for the ban have nothing to with cruelty or bloodlust.

This ban arises from hatred, Labour's hatred of what they think of as 'Old Britain'. It is an attempt to exterminate a section of our culture; not just the hunt, but everything that goes with it, the hunt balls, the hunt suppers, the Jilly Cooperesque brayings and fumblings, and the dependent livelihoods of the men and women in green tweed and badges, like characters from *Lord of the Rings*, who see to the hounds and the foxes and the horses and whose pride it is to ensure that we have a day's 'sport'.

It is a brutal and pointless liquidation of a way of life. They ban it just because they can; and the people I really despair of are those idiots who say that they 'don't care much one way or another'. About five or six years ago I went to see Blair, and asked him why he was banning hunting. 'Oh, I'm not one of those who would go hunting on a Saturday, nor would I go out protesting,' he said. Is it not therefore doubly revolting that he has imposed this tyrannical measure, and voted for it himself?

I loved my day with the hunt, and hope they have the courage and organisation to keep going for ever. They are going out with the hounds this Saturday, and if the hounds pick up a fox, so be it. How will the poor cops prove *mens rea*? And will they not have to produce a fox in evidence? I hope that the hunt holds up the ban to the ridicule it deserves, that they defy the police and the magistrates and the government, until a new government can rescue an old tradition and restore it for the sake of freedom and freedom alone.

The best way to cure ourselves of Islamophobia is to have a laugh

Among the disasters of my early journalistic career was the time I was sent by the newsdesk to Walsingham in Norfolk, to report on what was promised to be a major religious bust-up. There were these Anglo-Catholics, the news editor explained, and they wanted to march with an image of the Virgin towards a shrine; and then there were these evangelical Protestants. It was gonna be a real ding-dong, said the news editor. He wanted action, colour, quotes, personality. He wanted ecclesiastical fisticuffs with lashings of sectarian abuse. He wanted the Gaza Strip comes to Norfolk.

As far as I can remember, the clash of denominations was a bit disappointing. It was steaming hot, and the evangelicals obliged by shouting a few anti-papist slogans, while the Anglo-Catholics psalmed away sweetly. And then God caused the whole lot of us – just and unjust alike – to be drenched in a summer downpour, and I fled to a café to phone over my account; and no sooner did it hit the apathetic streets of Britain than the protests began.

In thrashing my brains to think of a way of describing the image of Our Lady of Walsingham, I had come up with the phrase 'bobbing doll'. This seemed fair, because the statuette had lovely rosy porcelain cheeks, and she did indeed bob as she was carried on the shoulders of the celebrants.

But according to the many people who rang and wrote in, these were very far from the mots justes. I was told that I was crass, idiotic, grossly insensitive and mortally offensive. One man managed to find me in the phone book late at night and gave me such an ear-wigging that I almost felt like making my own pilgrimage to the shrine, on my knees, and scourging myself with a copy of the offending piece.

And yet when I look back now, the remarkable thing is not how much fuss they made, but how little, especially if you think what we have come to expect from some Muslims. I have in mind not just the murders of Pim Fortuyn and Theo van Gogh, but the trembling refusal of a noted Islamic scholar to write an article for *The Spectator*. 'You don't understand,' he said. 'These people will kill me if I say what I really think. I mean kill me.'

What makes modern Islam so politically troublesome is that some Muslims can be induced to take offence not just at an insult to Islam, but at any injustice suffered by one of their co-religionists, and it is this deep personal sense of outrage – scarcely explicable to our post-enlightenment souls – that helps the whacko imams to warp the alienated young men into becoming suicide bombers; and that is why we are now so desperately using new law to trammel what non-Muslims can say about Islam, and what Muslims can say about their own religion.

Much of what Charles Clarke is proposing is surely right: we should of course crack down on the hate-spouting mullahs. Take away their benefits; kick 'em out, and if their arrival is not conducive to the public good, stop them coming in. Let us make much better use of the existing law against any incitement to murder and terror. But I am less convinced by the new restrictions on free speech.

The proposed ban on incitement to 'religious hatred' makes no sense unless it involves a ban on the Koran itself; and that would be pretty absurd, when you consider that the Bill's intention is to fight Islamophobia. As for the measures Clarke announced yesterday, to stop people 'glorifying or condoning' acts of terrorism, they seem to trap us in a semantic convolvulus. What is 'condoning' an act of terror?

The *Daily Mail* yesterday denounced the evil mullahs who 'blame us' for the bombings, in the sense that we were co-invaders of Iraq. But, er, it was surely the same *Daily Mail* that, two weeks ago, printed an article by Sir Max Hastings, saying that the chief provocation for the bombings was Britain's role in the Iraq war. Are we proposing to bang up Sir Max, George Galloway and all the millions of Britons who make the same point as the evil mullah?

These bans are likely to cause confusion and disappointment, since they will be impossible to operate; and in any case they are just tip-toeing round the real problem, which is fear of Islam; not Islamophobia, but fear of discussing the good and bad in that religion without giving offence. It should be part of the general long-term programme of winning back disaffected British Muslims that they no longer feel that it is Islam which exclusively defines them, and therefore that any insult to Islam is an insult to their whole being.

That is why we need to begin the re-Britannification I mentioned last week; and part of being British is recognising that this is a free country, in which people can have frank views about religion. Militant Islam has been shielded from proper discussion by cowardice, political correctness and a racist assumption that we should privilege the beliefs of a minority, even when they appear to be mediaeval. It is time the discussion was opened up not just to reason, but to reason's greatest ally, humour. Instead of banning the discussion of the 72 virgins of paradise, the alleged meed of the suicide bomber, would it not be much more efficient to make fun of this ludicrous claim?

When is *Little Britain* going to do a sketch, starring Matt Lucas as one of the virgins? Islam will only be truly acculturated to our way of life when you could expect a Bradford audience to roll in the aisles at Monty Python's *Life of Mohammed*; and when an unintentionally offensive newspaper article about Islam is requited not with death threats but with the exasperated but essentially kindly letters one might expect from Christians.

We have a long way to go, but the first step is to stop treating this subject as so terrifying that it cannot be satirised. Some things may be sacred, but they are no less sacred for being made the object of good-natured humour; and if that is frivolity, it is frivolity with a deeply serious intent.

Naturam expellas furca, tamen usque recurret: Though you may drive out nature with a pitchfork, she will always come back; inborn character is ineradicable. Horace (65–8 BC)

Lefty thinking

A little while ago I was being ferried in to make a speech at a university, and my handlers warned me that things were not looking good. There was going to be a riot at the front door, they said. They couldn't guarantee my safety. It seemed that some of the scholars took issue with my views about higher education finance, and they were armed with eggs.

'These guys are nasty,' said one of my minders. 'We're talking Seattle protester-type stuff. We'd better go in the back.' So we scooted pathetically through the kitchens, and into the venue through the fire exit, and against a background of near-continuous monkey-house screeching and pant-hooting I tried to make my speech. This proved impossible, and after someone had kindly refreshed me by pouring a pint of bitter over me, I did what all politicians do in such circumstances.

I made a bee-line to the oppo, swaying and chanting under banners saying 'Bog off, Boris!' and put on my best Cecil Parkinson beam. 'Hell-air!' I said, thrusting out my hand to the nearest Left-wing agitator; and to my amazement it was taken, and shaken warmly. I looked more closely at my adversaries, and under the slogans and the agitprop I saw nothing but a charming collection of basi-cally middle-class kids, with some really rather reasonable concerns about debt.

They weren't crusty; they didn't have matted dreadlocks or medicine bottles stuck through their lower lips; they weren't invoking Gramsci or spouting neo-anarcho-syndicalist slogans. They were nice, decent, hard-working bourgeois people, and in 25 years I am sure they will all be QCs or the heads of News and Current Affairs at the BBC or the next Tory leader. What, I thought to myself, has happened to the old Left? Where are the Trots? Where are the headbangers?

It was all very different in my day, I reflected; and that is a point that has occurred, perhaps unsurprisingly, to all the former crypto-communists who now run the BBC. There is a new series which started last night on BBC4 called Lefties, and it is an elegy, a lament, for a vanished species. The thesis is that the old beret-sporting Left-wingers are disappearing from these islands. They are being driven from their ancient reservations on the shop floor and in the polytechnics, and have fled to a few remote hiding-places: the odd senior common room, Parliament, the leader conferences of some of the liberal papers. They are like those poor fishermen in the Andaman Islands, overwhelmed by the 21st century, clinging to their old language and customs, but basically outmanoeuvred and humiliated by history.

One has only to think back to the 1970s or 1980s, when the landscape heaved with Lefties, to see how sudden has been their extinction. It wasn't just Scargill: every time you turned on the TV, there would be someone using a phrase such as 'the aspirations of my members'. People would listen to Eric Hobsbawm droning on about 'the contradic-tions of capitalism', and every member of the Labour Party carried a personal commitment in his or her wallet to the nationalisation of the commanding heights of the British economy.

They would drive around in Citroën 2 CVs with bumper stickers opposing nuclear power; they said the rich were bloodsuckers and they wanted to consign the Royal Family and other emblems of privilege to history – or herstory, as they called it, in deference to feminist dogma. Yesterday in the House of Commons a Labour MP stood up and hailed the 100th anniversary of the foundation of the Parliamentary Labour Party. They all cheered and waved their order papers; and yet how utterly divorced the present lot of Labour MPs are from their pioneering predecessors. These creatures no longer emanate from the bowels of the British workforce: they aren't dockers or miners or fitters, or precious few of them. They are PR people, and pressure group frontpersons, and journalists. To paraphrase the Bible, they may spin, but they haven't done much toil. All of which we on the so-called Right of the argument have taken to be a huge compliment. It is a commonplace of political analysis that Tony Blair is the ultimate creation of Margaret Thatcher, and that the Lefties of the world were ideologically incinerated in the crucible of 1980s Britain.

'We won,' say the Right. We trounced them and thrashed them and left them for dead. They believed in socialism; they believed in punitive taxation; they believed in the public ownership of industry; and all their useless ideas derived a deep unspoken legitimation from the continued existence of Soviet communism; and then that went belly-up, the Berlin Wall fell, Labour ditched Clause Four and Eric Hobsbawm has been, frankly, looking pretty idiotic ever since. That is what we Conservatives say, and in our long triumph we have become dangerously smug.

We are right; of course we are right. But you cannot destroy the Lefty instinct; you cannot defeat it by argument. As Gilbert and Sullivan point out, it is an essential part of human nature. Every little boy and girl/That's born into this world alive/ Is either a little liberal/ Or a little conservative.

It is my firm belief that we could plot a vast binomial curve of political affinity, with the bulk of the population being somewhere in the middle, but with large numbers still on the extreme Left or Right. The Lefty instinct hasn't gone away: it has just mutated. Once they discovered they had lost the big economic arguments, Lefties decided there was no longer any need to own large chunks of industry. They could achieve their objectives through regulation, and the tyranny of political correctness. Lefties are fundamentally interested in coercion and control, and across British society you can see the huge progress they are now making in achieving their objectives: in the erosions of free speech and civil liberties that are taking place under this government, in the ever more elaborate regulation of the workplace, the bans on hunting, smacking, smoking, the demented rules about the numbers of children you may take in a swimming pool, the proposed plan to tag your car to see where you have been, Prescott's mad spy satellites to see if you have built an unauthorised conservatory.

The Lefties aren't dead, my friends; they have simply adapted brilliantly and smoothly to new circumstances. *Naturam expellas furca*, as we say in Henley, *tamen usque recurret*.

LITERARY HEROES

In so far as I have learned how to produce half-readable English, it is thanks to the sub-editors of the Daily Telegraph. Whenever I slipped in an adjective, they cut it out. Whenever I tried a joke, they carefully edited it so as to remove the punchline. They always improved things. Here are some of my other heroes, though for balance we should have had articles about Homer, Shakespeare, Milton, Evelyn Waugh and the rest of the usual suspects. I still quite enjoy reading PG Wodehouse, though these days it's a bit like listening to Van Morrison: more than half an hour and you overdose.

An interview with the cat in the hat

This was no time for play.
This was no time for fun.
This was no time for games.
There was work to be done.
There was deep,
Deep, deep gloom.
There was gloom in my room.

All week I was hunting
By phone and by fax.
I used all the tricks
That are known to us hacks.
I rang the PR girls.
I looked low, I looked high.
I was hunting a cat
And shall I say why?

This cat is a weird cat.
This cat has a HAT.
This cat is a winner.
He's the champ, he's the best.
His books have sold more
Than all of the rest.

Take a two and two zeroes.
Add three zeroes more,
Then three zeroes again.
Watch them go out the door!
His sales are so big
They would go round the planet.
He is much, much, much bigger
Than *Peter* or *Janet*!

And he's 40 today,
40 years of success.
I needed to talk to him.
I could not. What a mess!
Did he answer my calls?
Did he phone? Did he heck!
I just sat in my office
And I felt like a wreck.

So there I was
Moping like that
When who should come in
But the CAT IN THE HAT!
'Relax,' said the Cat.
'I like hax to relax.
I don't like to see
Some poor hack get the sack.'
Yikes, Cat! I said
And I sank back in my chair.
Cat seems an odd name
For what we have here.
To be blunt your old face
Looks more like an ape
And as for your nose –
It could be a grape!

'Well the kids seem to like it,'
Laughed the Cat as he sat.
'They like me like this,'
said the Cat in the Hat.
My name is Ted Geisel
But I'm called Dr Seuss
(You can say it like "juice",
Though I say it like "voice").'

Why, Cat! You great thing,
You taught me to read!
How can I thank you
For such a good deed?
'Good deed?' laughed the Cat
'My my my, what a hoot!
I'm a tinseltown adman.
I did it for loot.
From *Green Eggs And Ham*

And other such bosh
The money rolled in
With a great slosh of dosh!'
But why did it work, Cat?
What tricks did you do?
To make us kids like
A Hat Cat like you?
'Do tricks?' laughed the Cat,
'I should say I did lots.
I drew funny pictures.
I wrote funny plots.
I ate cake in the bath.
I turned the house pink.
A big long pink cat ring!
It looked like pink ink!

'And did the kids like it?
Well, what do you think?
I like kids to have fun
When their mother is out.
The mess they can make!
The things they can shout!
I took off in the 60s,'
said the Cat. 'It was cool.
If the rule was a bother
You just broke the rule.'

And then I went VOOM
Inside of my head.
I was struck with a thought.
Hey, Cat, I said,
That hat on your head,
I have seen it before
On the head of the guy
Who says, 'Go to war!'

That hat is a spoof!
It's like Uncle Sam!
Say, Cat, was your theme
Against Vietnam?
'Hey, hey, hey,' laughed the Cat,
'don't think me rude,
But you kind of sound
Like a bit of a pseud.
My work is not art!
That stuff is for the birds.
I just keep my vocab
To 225 words.
Here's a tip,' said the Cat.
'I've read some of your stuff.
You use lots of Latin!
Get rid of that guff!
Keep your words short.
One vowel sound will do.
Then people might read you
All the way through!'

Gee, thanks, Cat, I said,
I'll scrap that old junk!
I'll axe that long tosh!
... but that Cat did a bunk!

The case for Hornblower

Oh, the paeans of praise for Patrick O'Brian. Never was
an author so showered with fashionable testimonials. Max
Hastings throws banquets for him. William Waldegrave
writes scholarly monographs on the fascinating coincidence between the life of Captain Jack Aubrey and his
great-great grandfather aboard HMS Thetis.

And how snooty everyone is about the hero of my own childhood. Wooden, lifeless: that's what *le tout Londres* says about Horatio Hornblower. Not a patch on O'Brian, they say; and, for those of us who spent their nights with a torch under the bedclothes reading of the salt-spumed scourge of the French fleet, it is all dimly insulting.

That is why, after an interval of some years, I have risen early and read 100 pages of each, C.S. Forester and O'Brian; and I say now to the Hornblower-knockers: belay there, splice your futtocks lads, and stand by to go about.

Patrick O'Brian's Post Captain gets under way on page seven, and one is grateful for this head start. Come on, one feels like muttering at Aubrey and Maturin, as they play endless games of piquet and talk about their love lives: Engage the Enemy More Closely!

I will grant that O'Brian is a man of delightful erudition, subtly playing on Jane Austen, who never mentions the Napoleonic Wars, by plonking his characters in the middle of an Austen-style set-up, complete with bustling mother, and daughters darting glances at black-curled officers.

OK, so he is chock-full of gags about 18th-century medicine and diet. He has a wonderful ear for dialogue. But, as our heroes fritter their time in inconclusive boudoir assignations, one longs for the crack of the timbers beneath the roaring carronade, the raking of focsles with red-hot grape. Look at Hornblower's amazing 100-pages of derring-do.

We've hardly left Spithead before he's beaten off Simpson, the awful bully, and scandalised the navy with a duel. By page 21, Mr Midshipman Hornblower has been promoted to an exciting frigate, called the Indefatigable, prowling the Channel in search of Frenchies to duff up.

By page 40, it's ahoy, top-gallants athwart and let go the halliards, a ship in view. 'I don't like the cut of her jib, Sir. It's a Frenchie.' In next to no time, Hornblower, a mere 17, is in charge of the prize, the Marie Galante.

A few pages later, to his shame, his prize sinks beneath him, as a hole beneath the waterline causes the cargo of rice to expand; and I remember, as a child, meditating on the weight of that dreadful risotto. Next, he's captured by a French privateer. Then he sets fire to the ship, and the French are captured. Then they capture another French ship because Hornblower masters the icy pit of fear in his stomach and runs along the yard, 100 feet up, without any foot-rope.

Soon after, Hornblower breaks up a hideous game in which a man called Styles kills rats with his teeth. Then he helps French counter-revolutionaries blow up a bridge, witnesses a guillotine in action, and, at the bit I've got up to, things are obviously about to turn nasty . . .

Talk about action, eh? At a comparable stage in O'Brian's narrative, Aubrey and Maturin are still saying things such as 'By God, I wish I were in Bath' and 'You do look miserably hipped', and taking about two pages to walk up a hill and notice a rabbit.

They say Hornblower has no character; and it is true that he is described in nothing like the ornate detail of Aubrey, the hard-living Tory rake, and Maturin, the saturnine spy and man of medicine. But Hornblower has always seemed so economically limned by Forester.

Seasick and yet a burgeoning naval wizard; skinny, pale, froglike, youthful and yet authoritative: an Octavian figure. We are told he reads Gibbon, and that this inclines him to atheism. He has a keen sense of honour. He says things 'icily'. He is tone deaf. If that isn't characterisation, I don't know what is.

The more you set O'Brian side by side with Forester, the more obvious it is who is the true master of the genre. Forester saw first the dramatic potential of the wooden universe which was a ship of the line; and O'Brian has simply lifted motifs, such as the interesting dodges for getting a ship out of trouble. Which is not to detract from O'Brian's literary achievement, only to say that it is an evolution, not a revolution.

In defence of Wodehouse

If anyone thinks P.G. Wodehouse was a Nazi collaborator or, as the *Independent* described him last Friday, 'a sinister character with extreme right-wing views and even Nazi sympathies', then that is a comment on the catastrophic illiteracy of the age. There can scarcely have been a more devastating portrait of a fascist than in Wodehouse's *Code of the Woosters*. You will recall the figure of Spode, the would-be dictator, whose eye could open an oyster at 50 paces, and whose followers went around in black shorts ('You mean footer bags?' cried Bertie. 'How perfectly foul').

In the magnificent climax of this work, Bertie rounds on Spode, who has been behaving in an overweening fashion in the matter of the silver cow-creamer. Yes, for once in his career of masterly inactivity, Bertie Wooster lets another man have a piece of his mind. 'The trouble with you, Spode,' he says, 'is that because you have succeeded in inducing a handful of halfwits to disfigure the London scene by going about in black shorts, you think you're someone.

'You hear them shouting "*Heil Spode!*", and you imagine it is the Voice of the People. That is where you make your bloomer. What the Voice of the People is saying is: "Look at that frightful ass Spode swanking about in footer bags! Did you ever in your puff see such a perfect perisher?"'

It is to Wodehouse's eternal credit that this satire of Mosley and fascism, and all their hysterical pomposity, appeared in 1938; which was the year of Appeasement, and the Oxford by-election. In that election there appeared on the pro-Appeasement ticket one Quintin Hogg, who in 1941 was to disgrace his family name by accusing Wodehouse of 'treason'.

The charges against Wodehouse are so feeble, so deformed by spite, that they are worth repeating only for the light they cast not on Wodehouse, but on his enemies. In a nutshell, Wodehouse was at Le Touquet in 1940, trying to finish a Jeeves novel called *Joy in the Morning*. He had four chapters to go, and it seemed inconceivable to him – as it did to the British High Command – that the Germans would reach him before he had reached his lovingly plotted conclusion. As it was, and here, perhaps, are the real culprits in the whole business, the French folded in record time. Wodehouse was captured, and imprisoned in Loos, Liège, and later in a place called Tost, about which he made some jokes. He spent the war in captivity, and that was why he had to chase up royalties from neutral countries such as Sweden and Spain. This money was paid through the German foreign office; and, we now learn from the Public Record Office, this wholly innocent procedure put MI5, and now the *Independent*, in something of a state.

On being transported to Berlin, he was prevailed upon to give some light-hearted talks on German radio about camp life: how they made a cricket ball out of a nut with string round it, and what it was like to be given a shower by a French warder ('You come out of it a finer, deeper, graver man') – that kind of thing. 'Of course,' he wrote in a letter to a friend on 11 May 1942, from Berlin, 'I ought to have had the sense to see that it was a loony thing to do to use the German radio for even the most harmless stuff, but I didn't. I suppose prison life saps the intellect.'

If anyone's moral compass was scrambled by the episode, though, it was that of Hogg and everyone else in Britain who was moved to persecute him. As George Orwell pointed out in his essay 'In Defence of P.G. Wodehouse', the Left saw it as a 'chance to expose a wealthy parasite'; which, as anyone who has studied his modest life and indefatigable working methods – he produced five novels in prison, and ten short stories – will know is about as far from the truth as the *Independent*'s cretinous assertion that he was 'extremely right-wing' or had 'Nazi sympathies'.

Some of his assailants were authors, like A.A. Milne. For some of us, the doings of Christopher Robin become yet more emetic, when we remember how his creator behaved. Worst of all, the government started to take a hand. Duff Cooper, the Minister of Information, incited the BBC to do Wodehouse down, to sneer at his name, and to call him a 'playboy'. Soon the letters column of the *Daily Telegraph* was full of bile, and Quintin Hogg compared him to Lord Haw-Haw.

There used to be on my reading-list at school a book by one Wolf-Trotter, called *The Herd Instinct in Peace and War*, which explained how the Athenians were incited to turn against Socrates during the Peloponnesian war. Nothing is uglier than the whipping-up of prejudice, by demagogues, against those who are for some reason believed not to share the correct spirit of the age. It is a skill, of course, in which this government excels.

We caught a taste of it during the Kosovo crisis, during which the impartial reporting of John Simpson from Belgrade was denigrated by Alastair Campbell, and the patriotism of other reporters impugned; or one might mention the way the Prime Minister joined the mob in baying for the blood of Glenn Hoddle, who has some curious but harmless views on reincarnation. Wodehouse, in his own way, was as innocent as both. It was not as if he was some holy fool, who failed to understand the moral dimension of his predicament. As others who listened to his broadcasts appreciated, he saw the Nazis for what they were. His broadcasts were used throughout the war, at the American intelligence school at Camp Ritchie, as models of anti-Nazi propaganda.

He made fun of his captors, as he gently and lethally satirised Spode, who 'looked as if Nature had intended to make a gorilla, and had changed its mind at the last moment'. His only failure was in not seeing how, as the mood of the country changed in 1941, his actions could be seized upon by the bullies and creeps who still, unfortunately, have so large a role in public life. Like Spode, whose dark secret it was to be the proprietor of 'Eulalie', a lingerie store, they will get their comeuppance. They have their dark secrets, too. Campbell has his Eulalie.

Iron Tongue

Lines Not By Ted Hughes, Poet Laureate, on the Occasion of the Piercing of Zara Phillips's Tongue with a Metal Stud and the 98th Birthday of Her Majesty The Queen Mother.

I sit in the cavern where
Jaws eat and are finished
Shut wombed in a dark shed of mouth.

A big trout muscle I dart
And writhe through oceans of speech
or tirelessly piranha

The gulleyed chinks between the
Skull-rooted tombstones in search of
Spinach, cornflakes, spaghetti

Al Vongole, anything else that gets
Stuck ... The light breaks from
the gibbet-hung tattoo parlour.

They see me. I try to get up
And run. 'It's him. It's him.'
A freezing hand catches me by the

Blind root and comes the drilling
Pain and flesh twirled like
Dry bark bits and blood in

The loud tunnel. In goes old stud,
Deep in otter gaffed by welding cold
Fish fur fang fowl fox ow ow ow.

It'th frankly jolly unthightly
and maketh it hard to thpeak.
Happy 98th Birthday, Your Majesty.

Virgil's message for the Middle East

It was the custom for many centuries, and in some places
it still is the custom, to mark any great crisis by consulting
Virgil. You flip open the collected works of the greatest
Roman poet, close your eyes and jab; so that, for instance,
if your finger lights on *equo ne credite, Teucri* (trust not
the horse, Trojans, *Aen.* II 47), you don't bet on the 4.15
at Doncaster. The habit seems to date from early Christian

166

times, because the Fourth Eclogue, published in about 40 BC, was found to contain some stunning stuff about the birth of a saviour-child, not to mention a virgin. 'This chap Virgil,' said the early Christians, 'he must have been a prophet.'

King Charles tried the *sortes Virgilianae* on the eve of the battle of Naseby and, if you read Virgil, you can dimly see why. Perhaps it is the elevated diction, the poetic compression. It may be that his words, which, as he said, he licked into shape like bear-cubs, can bear a multiplicity of meanings. Or it might be that he truly was a marvel, that he understood human nature in some deep and universal way.

I have never been so amazed by his gifts for prophecy as I was one summer, while languishing on a kibbutz in Israel. The invasion of Lebanon had recently taken place, and the massacres of Sabra and Chatilla. The name of Ariel Sharon, who is now Prime Minister, was already the object of international vilification. I was trying in my undergraduate way to apportion right and wrong, while mugging up on the *Aeneid*, when suddenly the words seemed to swim. I saw the hidden meaning of the text. And the vatic truth of Virgil is all the more useful now when the Middle Eastern conflict seems so bitter, and uncontrolled, and has spilled on to the letters pages of this magazine.

What is the second half of the *Aeneid*, which tells of the foundation of Rome, but an extraordinary allegory, 2,000 years in advance, of the postwar foundation of Israel and the cruel struggle with the indigenous Palestinians? Do you remember it? Do you hear your Latin O-level tolling from the depths, like the church bell of some sea-drowned village? You don't? Then let me remind you.

At the end of the Trojan war the city is in ruins, the population massacred. There is a small band of survivors, led by Aeneas, and they have no choice but to flee overseas in search of a new homeland. Throughout the voyage they are persecuted by Juno, queen of the gods, with a bias and vengefulness that border on the irrational. Finally, they come to their destined land in Italy. Now when I say it is destined, I mean just that. Throughout the poem, we are told that Italy is the location marked out by fate, a special place, reserved by the gods, for the survivors of the Trojan massacre. Virgil goes to some lengths to contrive a link between Troy and the site of the future Rome. We are informed that a very long time ago a shadowy hero called Dardanus had left Italy and made his way to Troy.

In other words, it is important to Virgil that we should think of the Trojans as having some right of return to this land, some link with it sanctioned by myth (though you will agree that the Trojans had a much less impressive territorial claim to Italy than the Jews had to Palestine). And, of course, when Aeneas and co. arrive there are people already there, indigenous people, and they view the newcomers with fear.

Aeneas and the Trojans find themselves sucked into war with Turnus and the Italians, the Latins. Ostensibly it is a struggle for the hand of the beautiful Lavinia, but her name also connotes the geographical area around Lavinium. This is a struggle for land and for mastery. The Latins live in Latium. The Trojans want to live there. One or other will have to give ground. Latium, incidentally, is on the West Bank of the Tiber. For the last six books of the poem, this means *bella, horrida bella*: war, bristling war.

Who is in the right? With whom should we expect Virgil to side? For a lesser poet, that question might have been easy. The *Aeneid* is a political poem, written to please the emperor Augustus. It is an epic that glorifies the foundation of Rome. Virgil was a Roman. He could have demonised all those who stood in the way of Rome's greatness. He could have blackened Turnus, so that Aeneas might shine the more brightly. And what does he do instead?

Respectfully, I say to all those who have strong feelings on the Arab-Israeli question that they could do worse than read the climax of the poem, in Book XII, to see how Rome's best poet dealt with the tragic dilemma.

Here is Turnus, fleeing for his life before the wrathful Aeneas. He has no weapon but a stone and, as he tries to throw it, his blood freezes and his limbs fail, and he falters in fear. And there is Aeneas, infinitely better armed, his spear and sword newly forged by Vulcan. Does he stay his hand? Does he show mercy to the underdog? He does not.

He hurls that spear like a black hurricane, and it passes through the outer circle of the sevenfold shield, and through the cuirass, and into Turnus's thigh. Then, as Aeneas stands over him, the stricken Latin holds up his hands in the universal, eternal gesture of surrender. For a second or two, as we enter the last 20 lines of the epic, the Trojan hesitates. He lets fall his sword arm, until his eye is caught by a trophy on Turnus's shoulder, the baldric of Pallas, another Trojan whom Turnus has killed.

Then, on fire with fury, and terrible in his rage, Aeneas gives way to vengeance, and he butchers Turnus. Boiling with anger, he buries his sword in the chest of his adversary, and, as the poet tells us, 'his limbs relaxed and chilled, and his life fled moaning and resentful to the Shades'. And that's it. That's the end.

You put down the *Aeneid*, as they used to say on the back of blockbusters, breathless and stunned. No one can read it without being aghast at the sudden brutality of Aeneas. No one can fail to feel pity for Turnus. That is what makes the poem, and the greatness of Virgil. He has been venerated down the ages because he has the moral depth and poetic sensibility to see tragedy on both sides.

It wasn't the fault of Aeneas that he was to found a new homeland in Italy. It was an act preordained by the gods. And, in any event, where else were the Trojans to live, harried as they were over land and sea by the hatred of Juno? And it wasn't the fault of the poor Latins that they should be living in the exact spot which fate had marked out for the new nation.

I remember munching my felafel back in the kibbutz, and preparing for another 12-hour session of washing-up, and thinking, by gum, yes, Virgil is right. That is how to look at Israel and the displaced Palestinian peoples. It is possible to support Israel's right to exist, and to believe in the destiny of Israel as passionately as Virgil believed in the destiny of Rome, and still to feel moved by the sufferings of those who were forced to make way.

With Virgil in your hand, you begin, too, to see the enemies of Israel with new eyes. There is a trace of Juno, surely, in the blistering fury, the implacability, of some of the recent correspondents to *The Spectator*. I think of Juno's raging speech in Book X, where she denounces the Trojans and their illegal settlements. 'They take up the pitchy firebrand and violently assault the Latins, they lay a heavy yoke on farmlands not their own and drive off their plunder,' she froths, furious with Jupiter for letting it happen. And there, I think, speak Ian Gilmour and his kind, as they call attention to the breaches of UN declarations, the shootings, the disproportionate Arab casualties.

They have a point; they have a view. But it is a partial view and one wonders whether deep down they accept the hard, fated necessity of Israel to exist. Lord Gilmour has elsewhere analogised between the Israeli occupation of the West Bank and the Nazi occupation of France, as well as the Soviet occupations of Hungary or Afghanistan. These do not strike me as happy or accurate comparisons. For all its faults, Israel is the only democracy in the region;

and it seems to me that critics of Israel pay insufficient attention to another aspect of the Palestinian tragedy: the mad way in which young Arabs are manipulated into violence by their leaders.

But then you will find all that in Virgil, too, if you look. You will find how the virus of madness, *furor*, infects the Latins, when a peace might have been attained. You will also find a prophecy that one day, after Turnus is dead, '*paribus se legibus ambae invictae gentes aeterna in foedera mittant*' (both peoples, unconquered, will join with equal laws in an everlasting pact). In the days when MPs could quote Latin they used to say this about Ireland with such blissful persistence that O'Connell had to beg them to stop.

I know it sounds optimistic to talk now about a pact between Arabs and Israelis. You may also say that they haven't much call for Virgil these days, the suffering peoples of Nablus and Hebron and Jerusalem. To which I would say that nothing much else seems to have worked. Virgil the prophet has not always been wrong, and he understood the tragic symmetry of a war between predestined settlers and displaced natives. Read him, Gilmour, and see the position of Juno for what it is.

WHAT HOUSE?
WHAT CAR?
WHAT THE HELL?

It was the end of the Cold War, and the consequent univer-sal spread of free market capitalism, which, as I say, was the pivotal moment of the last fifteen years. Here we con-sider just some of the glories which our consumerist society has been spreading across the planet: fast cars, porn, post-ironic game-shows, expensive children's toys, luxury bodyguards, house market speculation and, joy of joys, a privatised railway system.

London house prices

There used to be an iron law of economics, I think, that when the crocuses were out, or possibly the daffodils, then, first in ones and twos and then in joyous, colourful clumps, the 'For Sale' signs would sprout in the streets of London. Clearly, this has not been true these last few years. As one in search of a house, who has pushed buzzers and admired rockeries across the nation's capital for two months, my guess is that this year the choice and availability will be little better.

'It'll pick up,' say the estate agents, the hounds of spring, snuffling and chivvying. At this stage, surely, any such optimism will make matters worse. It sows hope, the hope that, if owners will just wait, it is only a matter of time before prices once again take off. For the English owner-occupier, the hope is more dangerous than the despair. My guess is that he or she could have further shocks in store.

Let me at once say that these are merely the observations of a provincial oaf, a bumpkin, stuck away in Brussels for five years, without the benefit of countless dinner-party symposia on the housing market, the immense learning on the subject shared by most *Spectator* readers.

But I can say with authority that the mind-set of the London vendor is to be found nowhere else in western Europe. Speaking as a would-be buyer (buyor, I almost said), the assumptions seem as demented as ever.

Despite the punishment of the last four years, the middle classes cling to the superstition that the natural trajectory of their houses' value is vertiginously upwards. So strong is this belief that, as far as I can see, instead of dropping their sights, they would rather sit in a dim, cold property, progressively selling off the furniture and eating Kit-e-Kat, waiting, waiting for the market to turn and for the mass mania to begin again.

In consequence, very little habitable property seems to be for sale, and almost nothing central and affordable. I know that some of the potential sellers, in fact, 2 million across the country, are in the negative equity trap, the mortgage being worth more than the value of the property.

One feels the pathos of these debt desperadoes, the DIY fiends who have spent tens of thousands wrecking a perfectly good house with peach-coloured fitted wardrobes and walk-in mirrored bathrooms, all half-built because they ran out of money.

Then there are the other, equally frantic reasons why

some want to sell: the young couple in an intensifying hell of noise and perfumed nappy bags; the wife of the musician suddenly stricken by a disabling illness. Take your time, they say, as one tears one's eyes away from the fascinating self-analytical jottings on the bedside table; as one speculates, how unfairly, about their lives; the pitiful testimony of the built-in chopping board, scored with 20 years of devotion to Mrs Beeton, now to be abandoned; the cats, that sure index of unsatisfied human cravings – the flaps, the scratching-posts, the multi-storey cat-baskets.

One almost flinches at how obviously the owner, usually the wife, has made an effort with her appearance, doubtless on the advice of some hectoring property supplement – lipstick, haircut, necklace – and how she has laid out photographs of the minuscule yorkstone patio in the summer when the creepers are in full leaf.

And then, after they have been anxiously watching from the corner of their eye, one hears the painful gush, almost of relief, when they detect that one is not likely to be a taker for the place where they have occasionally been so happy. 'Oh, I think it will be far too small for you, with your baby' etc. One feels so intrusive, so callous.

And yet, however much the heart bleeds for them, these people are fundamentally deluded. The asking prices are still crazy.

I had always thought Notting Hill was meant to be a vaguely bohemian area. Marina and I would be very happy in this house here near Ladbroke Grove, for example, amid the ulcerated stucco of what appears to be a disused international ganja exchange. But Mr Faron Sutaria is asking us to pay £395,000 for the privilege.

Laugh, if you like, at my naïvety; but is it not frightening that my generation is expected to go into debt to the tune of hundreds of thousands of pounds to live within a long cricket ball's throw of the west end of the Portobello Road?

175

Am I alone in finding it strange that one's parents, not, *mutatis mutandis*, appreciably better off than ourselves at comparable moments in their lives, were able to buy great schlosses in central London?

As for the present meagre market, some of the more reasonably priced items are acquiring landmark status. Almost every estate agent in London seems to be offering 'this rare opportunity to purchase' a house in Sebastian Street, EC1, which appears to be freshly mortar-bombed. Just pour in another couple of hundred thousand grand, the implication is, just add a roof and, hey presto, a bargain!

We did make an offer on what seemed to be a pricy but just manageable terraced house off Highbury Fields, and the vendors said snap at once. It was only later that a rival agent told us that the Channel Tunnel's underground rail link to St Pancras would require a ventilation shaft and escape hatch somewhere near the kitchen.

The rest of the offerings are dominated by people pitching the price at what they fondly imagine their home should 'achieve' in two years' time. If anybody is interested I could show him a small house in Brook Green, darkest Hammersmith. All right, so it has polished stripped-pine floors and a sunken bath; but it costs £350,000! *Donnez-moi un break*, as we say in Brussels. On the day we saw it, Michael Frayn, the prognathous *farceur*, was in the kitchen. Maybe that's it. Maybe it's an extra £30,000, just for being the kind of house in which Michael Frayn might have his hands wrapped around a mug of tea, polishing his epigrams on a Saturday afternoon.

And if, in the next couple of years, people did come to think nothing of paying that kind of money, the price rise would be treated as the most tremendous piece of good news, front-page in all the papers, pure Martyn Lewis; whereas, as the Bundesbank president, Herr Hans Tietmeyer, once pointed out, in Germany and elsewhere it would be a bad sign. It has suddenly struck me, coming from Brussels, why the British middle classes will never wear a single European currency, whatever Sir Leon Brittan may say in his new book. It would be like the ERM, only worse. It would be the end of house-price inflation.

Going on *Have I Got News For You*

Walking down the Holloway Road the other night. Feeling a bit low. On my way to buy some beer from the corner shop. Man goes by on a bike. 'Oi, you,' he cries, 'you chinless tosser.' For some reason this enrages me and I make to pursue him, but he has the advantage of wheels. I don't mind being called a tosser, but I draw the line at chinless, since I have a fine selection of chins.

As I wander disconsolately on, I wonder what has inspired his wrath, and conclude that it must be this TV gameshow I keep going on. A lot of people say an MP should not go on a show like that. They say it is not commensurate with the dignity of the office.

Think of the great statesmen of the past, they say. Would Winston Churchill have gone on *Have I Got News For You*? Would Pericles? Look here, they say. If you go on a show like that, it is like going into a ring with Mike Tyson, pointing your chin at him, folding your hands behind your back and saying, come on then you big gold-toothed wuss. Of course you are going to be decked. You are there to be made a fool of, a prat, a berk, a buffoon.

You must be utterly mad, say my many critics, to try to match the dice-n-slice wits of Merton, Hislop, Deayton. One man told me, a few years ago, that I was barely more articulate than the tub of lard they once put in the place of

Roy Hattersley. Another compared my performance unfavourably with that of the late Paula Yates, who called Ian Hislop the spawn of the devil before bursting into tears.

The very nice woman who runs the *Telegraph* executive dining room once told me, as if to cheer me up, that I came across as being marginally less shifty than Neil and Christine Hamilton. If you remember, they were handed brown paper envelopes at the end of the show.

In fact, there has been so much criticism, over the years, for my three appearances, that I feel obliged to defend my motives in going on. Because I know that there will be some who read this page – high, sacerdotal intellects – who feel that the hot seat of *Have I Got News For You* is not the place for an *homme serieux*. Is that what you feel? If you do, I must respectfully disagree.

As one of the many doe-eyed producer girls told me, an invitation to appear on the programme – now in its 11th year – is by no means a rare or exclusive thing. I happen to know that they have recently invited Max Hastings, one of my journalistic heroes. And why did he turn them down? Was it because he thought the whole thing was beneath him? Possibly.

But might it not also have been that he was afflicted by an unwonted spasm of self-doubt? I do not know whether the Liberator of Port Stanley went all yellow-bellied as he contemplated an hour of tart rejoinders from Ian Hislop. I do not know whether his knees knock. Only the great war reporter can tell us if he secretly trembles at the idea of coming off second best to Paul Merton. But does he not owe it to us to prove our suspicions unfounded, pick up the phone, and accept the gameshow's challenge?

The first and best reason for going on, is that it is rank cowardice not to. And I could go further, and elaborate some political reasons, as well.

They say that the House of Commons is not what it was. They say that MPs are losing out in the Darwinian struggle for power. They are being constitutionally eclipsed by the media, by Brussels, by inventive judges. Well, is that not all the more reason for us to lever ourselves off the green benches and take the fight into the enemy camp? Why should the tribunes of the people not pop up on the big vernacular TV shows, and not just the thing after midnight with Andrew Neil?

If I understood the producer girl rightly, the last Tory MP they had on the show was my fellow Euro-sceptic Teddy Taylor, and that was five years ago. It is not for want of invitations.

And then there is a final and by no means unimportant consideration. They give you a thousand pounds. That means you can take approximately two children skiing. That's worth quite a lot of TV humiliation, in my view. And if you are still not convinced, if you still think it's all infra dig, then I give up. But I have only one question. What are you doing, at 9pm on Friday, and 10pm at the weekend, watching the thing in the first place? That is the real scandal of *Have I Got News For You* – that so many people watch it.

I am stunned by how many intelligent and educated people seem to have nothing better to do than watch this programme. They could be taking their loved ones out to dinner, or to a play, or flying by Easyjet to Nice, or taking some other measures to boost the British economy and stop us all sliding into recession. They could be reading a book – a rip-roaring account of the last election campaign, for instance, modestly priced at £14.99, published by Harper-Collins. They could be learning the piano. They could be knocking out a play. Instead, they sit like the prisoners in Plato's cave, watching the flickering images before them and mistaking them for reality. That is the shocker: not that people are so foolish as to appear on TV, but that people are so idle as to watch it.

And that, of course, is the best way to protect yourself from shame, if you do go on it. Don't watch it. I haven't . . . yet.

The iron-on lady

'OK', I said. 'Groovy', I said. Every so often the style gurus and stunt merchants of the *GQ* car department come up with a real snorter of an idea, and the only course is to snap to attention.

'It's gonna be brilliant,' said Tim Lewis, the automobile supremo. 'We get this new Mini Cooper S, a fantastic car, a real monster car, and we superimpose a picture on the roof!'

'Tremendous, Tim', I exclaimed, because it is important to humour one's bosses, 'and whose image are you proposing? Saddam Hussein?'

'Close,' said Lewis, 'but no cigar. You're going down to the Tory party conference, aren't you? Well, you are about to be the most popular MP there. You will find blue-rinse matrons blubbing and patting your flanks. Acnoid Tory boys with sterling-silver "Keep The Pound" badges are going to be licking your hubcaps, Boris. Because we are going to decorate your car in glorious, pouting Technicolor with a six-foot, two-and-a-half times life-size rotogravure photo-image of . . . Margaret Thatcher!'

'Tim,' I said weakly, closing my eyes to steady my nerves, 'that is one hell of a wheeze.' And over the next few days, as I waited for the car to arrive, I tried to persuade myself that it would, indeed, be a cinch to carry it off.

'Yeah, well?' I would say, if anyone asked me what the hell I thought I was doing with a picture of Maggie on the roof. Why shouldn't a British car pay homage to the woman who revived our motor industry, by the wise expedient of flogging it off to the Japanese and the Germans? Maybe Tim was right. Maybe it was about time we Tories started sticking up for Maggie and her legacy, and stopped leaving Blair to lay claim to all that was best in her inheritance.

I had just about persuaded myself that it was a runner, when She arrived. 'Fantastic!' I stammered, as Tim unveiled the Mini Thatcher.

She was in her *Gloriana Imperatrix* mode, in a deep-indigo dress, hands folded royally in her lap and covered with bling-bling. Her hair was immaculately bouffed, not its normal pineapple chunks colour, but more marmalade-ish, like bronze-lacquered strands of shredded wheat.

She looked terrific. In terms of motor car iconography, she was a major statement. But could she really be risked in public? If you went on *Question Time*, and said Maggie Thatcher had done a lot of good for the country, the audience would howl and curse, scratching and hooting like flea-ridden gibbons. Oh, Maggie, baby, I thought once Tim had left, how can I do this to you? They'll scratch you with key rings. They'll shake their fists.

Across Britain, sour-faced, taxpayer-funded politics lecturers are teaching the young that Thatcher was a vile shrew, who encouraged selfishness and greed, who destroyed our manufacturing industry, who denied the very existence of society. Of course it is all lies, but what do they know, the youth of today? Overcome by funk, I decided to do something I had never done before. I disobeyed Tim.

I hid the Maggiemobile in an underground car park in London's Russell Square, and went to Bournemouth by train. That night, though, something spooky happened. As I lay in my hotel, I thought I heard a voice calling in the dark, a low, breathy contralto. 'It's a funny old world,' said the Maggiemobile from the dark of the garage. 'They all betrayed me. Heseltine, Hurd, Patten – and now you, too, Boris. Why won't you drive me? Are you frightened? Are you frit?' It went on for hours, and after two nights, I could take it no longer.

I returned to London and rushed to the garage. She was all right. No one had touched her or scraped her. I caressed her shiny hindquarters, as cerulean blue as a Tory conference platform. And was it my imagination, or did her smile look especially regal tonight? I turned her on, and she barked her approval, with that splendid, full-throated noise that so embarrassed and frightened Howe, Gilmour, Pym and the Wets. Soon we were heading to Bournemouth, with all the British-made vigour and confidence of the Task Force heading for the Falklands.

My date was a black-tie awards dinner for 600 tax-collectors (I get some pretty hot gigs, you have to admit), and I was seriously late. But, boy, can that Maggiemobile shift. It seemed incredible, as she whanged and weaved through the rush-hour traffic, that she had only a 1.6-litre engine. I discovered that she had six forward gears, and at one point I was doing 70 in second, not entirely by mistake.

Heaven knows how fast we were going, when, somewhere along the M25, we hurtled round a corner into a wall of cars. There were red tail lights everywhere. It was brake or die. And the Maggiemachine showed the gift for self-preservation that kept her in power for an amazing 11 years. We halted. We waited. Soon I was beginning to get worried. I was meant to be the keynote speaker, and I had a sermon all ready about the joy of tax-collecting, or something of that kind.

Should I jink off at the next turning, and try to find another way to Bournemouth? And then the voice came on again in my head, as the mighty car spoke. 'You turn if you want to', said the car, feminine and yet brimming with conviction, 'the Lady's not for turning until the junction after next!' As so often, she was right. Soon the traffic cleared: we reached the M23, turned right, and hummed down to the coast.

It was interesting, as we cruised the streets, swarming with students, to see how the world reacted to the re-emergence of Margaret Hilda Thatcher. They craned their necks to make out the picture, and then they broke out in broad grins. 'Bring back Maggie!' someone shouted and he seemed neither old nor insane.

The following morning, having discharged my oration, I was back in London to return the car. A cowled-up black kid, not much older than eight or nine, came by on his way to school. Who's that? we asked him, pointing to the roof.

'That's the Queen,' he said, and beamed.

Two wheels good, four wheels bad

'I know what,' I told my publisher the other day, as a light went ping in my head. 'I've got just the book for you.' And I outlined my wheeze for a blockbusting international super-seller called *I Don't Know How He Does It* or possibly *Men Who Do Too Much*. It's gonna be huge, I told her: aimed straight at the growing market of stressed-out career-juggling husbands. Someone needs to speak for the kind of guy who stands up to make a speech in the board-room, or in the House of Commons, reaches for the notes in his breast pocket, and pulls out the eight-year-old's homework.

Surely, I told her, there were zillions of have-it-all-males desperately trying to cope with the multiple roles demanded by the 21st century: husband, father, cook, cleaner, go-getting executive, and so on? To be honest, a slightly glazed look came over my publisher's face. I had the impression that she thought sales would be limited; and so I have put the project on the back burner.

In this article, I have a more modest ambition, which is to satisfy the vague curiosity of those who have worked out that I am not only a hard-pressed MP, but also editor of *The Spectator*. 'I Don't Know How You Do It,' they say. To all of them I reply, I will tell you how I do it. I do it with a bicycle.

For the careerist nappy-changing MP-cum-journalist-cum-house-husband, a bicycle is the indispensable tool of survival. I can get from Holborn to the Division Lobbies within 11 minutes. No single piece of technology – not even the mobile – is so vital.

In four years of pretty solid cycling around London, I have fallen off only once, and that was admittedly while negotiating the Palio of Trafalgar Square while talking on a mobile phone. I therefore feel able to offer a few small pieces of advice to my fellow jugglers. Here are some of the Dos and Don'ts of cycling in London, arranged alphabetically.

A is for ABUSE, which you must, frankly, learn to accept. You will get it from people driving lorries, cars, rubbish vans or, indeed, any other type of four-wheeled vehicle. Motorists will scream at you if you so much as twang their wing mirror or leave the teensiest scuff in their paintwork, the kind of thing that would easily vanish with a good rub or, failing that, a dab of Humbrol model paint. If you are a Tory MP, you will also be told, repeatedly, by people you have never clapped eyes on before, that you are a 'Tory tosser'.

B is for BOLLOCKS, which is the most vigorous rejoinder

you are permitted, preferably under your breath. No matter how grave the provocation, you should never scream back, since it jars everyone's nerves and adds to the general air of incivility in our streets. You may, at a pinch, mutter BALLS or BELT UP.

C is for CRASH HELMET. I urge you to wear one, though in disobedience to Kant's Categorical Imperative I don't myself. My explanation (and I admit that it is feeble) is that I don't like to be lured into any false sense of security. They made helmets mandatory in Australia, and so many people stopped cycling that doctors reported a surge in CORPULENCE, one of the problems a bike can help you fight.

D is for DEATH. Every successful bicycle journey should be counted a triumph over this.

E is for EXERTION and ENDORPHINS and ECSTASY, the first producing the next, which produces the next, as you whizz through London's lovely streets, and you look at the play of light through the plane trees, and you inhale the open air, and you think of the suckers stuck in the taxis, the cars, the buses and, God help them, the Tube.

F is for FREEDOM. With no other means of transport, except possibly skiing, can you determine so exactly the path you intend to follow, and arrive there so quickly. The beauty of cycling is that you can decide, from a distance of ten yards, that your front tyre is going to trace a course six inches to the right of that manhole cover and a foot to the left of that broken beer bottle. And you do it! It's about autonomy, man.

G is for GEARS. At the risk of heresy, I have never seen the point of the very high gears. Why sit and pump like a maniac when it is so much easier to stand up and grunt? Once my bike was nicked, but because my children had been fiddling with the gears I was easily able to overtake the thief on foot.

H is for HANDLEBARS. The key thing about handlebars is not to shoot over them. No matter how spongy your grip is, a lot of cycling will produce a HORNINESS in your HANDS.

I is for INDICATE, which I suggest you do with all the extravagance, beaming, waving and eyebrow-waggling of Simon Rattle bringing in the wind section.

J is for JELLY. This is what you become, psychologically and perhaps also physically, if you forget to indicate, shoot over the handlebars, and bite the asphalt of Trafalgar Square.

K is for KLAXON. Mine fell off, and I don't really recommend them. Time spent parping a horn or ringing a bell would be much better employed braking, weaving or just screaming.

L is for LIGHTS. Gotta have 'em. They will greatly reduce your chances, at night, of being squashed by a LORRY.

M is for MUDGUARDS. Get 'em. Otherwise road spray will produce embarrassing and ambiguous trouser stains, even when it isn't raining.

N is for NO-HANDS. What I like to do late at night, down a dark, deserted street in Islington, when I have had a couple of pints and am feeling moderately invincible.

OIL is what you get on your hands after executing the manoeuvre above, coming a cropper, and being forced to spend ages putting the chain back on in the dark.

P is for PHONE. I see no reason why you should not treat your bike as your office. Provided you hug the kerb, as St Paul's ship hugged the coast of the Mediterranean, you should be entitled to make telephone calls. It is probably safer to use a hands-free gizmo, but to all those who want to ban the use of mobiles on bikes, I say this: there are plenty of one-armed people in the world. Are we so cruel and discriminatory as to forbid them from using a bicycle? We are not. What is a mobile-phone user but a cyclist who has, effectively, only one arm? I rest my case. P is also for PAVEMENT, which you should only mount in the most extreme circumstances (e.g., if you are driven off the road by one of Ken Livingstone's demented new single-deckers, so long that they can't turn corners); and P is also for the PARADOX of the ramps for the disabled which have been installed, at such colossal expense, on every pavement in London. They, of course, make it vastly easier for cyclists to ascend the pavement at high speed, greatly increasing the risk that they will collide with, and permanently disable, pedestrians.

Q is for QUEUE, as in queues of cars, throbbing, panting, waiting. Tee-hee.

R is for RIDGEBACK, the make of my bike, suggestive of a racist Rhodesian dog. I have seldom felt cooler than when passing a bunch of toughs, and one shouted to his mates, 'Oi! Look! Ridgeback Cyclone!'

S is for SADDLE. I have had five bikes stolen in the last four years, which is a pretty devastating comment on law and order in Blair's Britain, and the modern concept of *meum* and *tuum*. But the most traumatic moment was coming out of the cinema to find someone had taken my saddle. Why? To what perverted end?

T is for THIEVES, who are everywhere and who will at last be tackled with Sharia ruthlessness when I and other Tories come to power (Hon Membs: Hear hear, waving of Order Papers). T is also for TYRES. Don't bother with the knobbles. Don't get all that heavy-tread mountain-bike stuff. London is full of tarmac. Get tyres of Kojakian baldness and smoothness, and you'll shave ten minutes off a 45-minute trip.

U is for UMBRELLA, perhaps the only advantage a pedestrian has over a cyclist when it is raining. I have a kind of red rubber burka, but sometimes it covers my eyes and is frankly dangerous.

V is for V-SIGN. Permitted, but only under the grossest provocation.

W is for WOMEN CYCLISTS, who are indistinguishable, in manners and morals, from male cyclists. Some are charming and after-you-Claude. Some are extremely aggressive and judgmental.

X is for XAVIERA Hollander, who has no place in this guide except that she is, or was, a bit of a bicycle in her own way.

Y is for YELLOW LIGHT, and the ancient dilemma. When you spot one of these 20 yards out, do you give it some welly, and scoot across just before the first motorbike can knock you over? Or do you play safe, and rest your left foot on the kerb, and have a breather?

Z is for ZOOM, which is what you had better do if you decide to go for it, and I cannot, in all conscience, recommend that you do. Be safe, my friends.

You can with this Nissan

10.30 a.m. It's a dull, cold morning and it is also – though I don't know it yet – the day on which I will experience what we politicians call 'a little local difficulty'. I have no idea, as I step out onto the Camden street, that the clock is ticking and that in only a few hours I will cease to glory in my role as Shadow Minister for the Arts.

But I know that my enemies are starting to close in on me, and my hungover eyes scope out the terrain. He's there. Of course he is.

The *News Of The World* snapper is waiting for me in his hilarious, tint-windowed, mod-conned Land Rover, with bull bars and about 12 headlights, some of them mounted as if for lamping rabbits, and – doubtless – a rabbit is how he thinks I feel. But no. Not today. Not I. I am not going to give in easily, because at this critical juncture in my life story I have been given a Nissan to drive: a 350Z, the most exhilaratingly sporty Nissan ever made.

As I unlock it, I see the reporter do a double take and then scamper back to his Land Rover. He can't believe it's my car.

'Tee, hee,' I say, and start the engine, not any old engine but the awesome 3.5-litre V6, hailed by *Ward's Auto World* – every year for the last 11 years – as one of the world's ten best. Arum, goes the engine, arum arum arum araaaah, and the car snouts from the parking spot like a questing panther. 'Right, you tabloid buggers,' I think, 'I'm going to give you the slip.'

10.35 a.m. Alas, I forget that I am in a one-way street, and by the time I sort it out, I find the cocky little bastard is on my tail.

10.35.00001 a.m. Turn into Mornington Crescent and put the machine through warp-factor six.

10.35.00002 a.m. *Teufel*! The Land Rover is still on my tail, and in traffic like this there's nothing much to be done about it.

10.59 a.m. I pick up a companion from Notting Hill and explain the problem. She looks at the snapper, who has parked up on a double yellow next to her house. We can see him through the tint windows. He is cheerfully blazing away, and then down comes the window and out comes a telephoto lens the size of a milk churn.

The camera mews like an impudent seagull. I want to punch his lights out. I walk towards the Land Rover, grimacing strangely.

'I'm really sorry,' says the snapper, lowering his camera. 'They told me to follow you all day. I am only doing my job,' he says.

'Oh all right,' I say. I still want to punch his lights out, but I am overcome by a sudden and ignoble feeling of solidarity with a fellow newspaperman despatched by his desk – as all of us sometimes are – to cover some godawful story. And anyway, I have a better idea.

'Come on,' I say to my companion, 'let's shake him off.' I select first gear. I rev up. I note that the engine can achieve a peak torque figure of 363Nm at 4,000 rpm.

At the very moment when the traffic lights on the corner of Elgin Crescent and Ladbroke Grove are turning from amber to red I howl out of my parking place in a pall of rubber, turn left through the lights, and lean back my head in a rich, easy laugh of triumph.

11.00 a.m. Hell and damnation. He's still there! This is turning into a struggle between two of the greatest commercial empires of the 21st century – Nissan and News International.

I can't believe the adhesive quality of this Murdoch-owned Land Rover. But my Nissan can do 0–62 mph in just 5.9 seconds, and here in Notting Hill, I have an advantage. I grew up here, from age 15 to 18. I know the roads. Or at least I think I do. 'Hold on,' I say to my companion and she gives a yelp as we lurch left . . .

11.01 a.m. . . . down Arundel Gardens, cocooned by the multi-link suspension's amniotic fluid effect . . .

11.01.34 a.m. . . . and yeeeow, we careen into Kensington Park Road . . .

11.01.35 a.m. . . . and into Colville Terrace . . .

11.01.36 a.m. . . . and the wrong way down Portobello Road, scattering American Hugh Grant fans like pigeons . . .

11.02 a.m. . . . and I can't believe it. I come shooting in triumph out on to Ladbroke Grove again, having done a kind of cat's cradle of the neighbourhood.

And the *News Of The World* Land Rover is just waiting for me, and we can almost see his grin through the shaded window. What has he got? Transponders? Homing devices?

12.30 p.m. But when we get to the motorway the contest with the Land Rover ends decisively in my favour. So it damn well ought to, what with my being at the wheel of a 155 mph sports car, and him driving a machine designed for towing cows out of bogs. He manages to keep me in view through the Hammersmith traffic, but when we are on the M4 . . . good night, baby and amen . . .

1 p.m. In fact, I am so enjoying the speed and prowess of the Nissan that I stop really looking in the rear-view mirror. It is only when we reach the turning for*****that I vaguely notice that there is an Audi Quattro behind us, and that he seems to be going to much the same place.

'Oh boy,' I think. I slow down. The Audi slows down. Yup – I should have realised that the paparazzi wouldn't rely on a Land Rover, and go up to the Quattro, who parks up on the kerb. He rolls down the window, I know what he is going to say. 'I am only doing my job, Boris,' he whimpers.

3 p.m. to 6 p.m. And so it goes on, all afternoon. At one stage, while I try to shake off the beastly Quattro down some muddy lane (another dead end, more embarrassed reversing), the posse swells. Another paparazzo turns up, in a clapped-out Toyota Corolla. I am afraid at this stage I give up, and we go back to London in a kind of OJ Simpson convoy down the motorway, the fugitive Nissan pursued by a fleet of photographers.

And in the course of those few hours it would be fair to say that matters evolve, in the phrase of Emperor Hirohito, not necessarily to my political advantage.

But at least I have driven a fabulous 350Z, and shaken off at least one of my pursuers, and if the boys at Nissan are disappointed by my evasive capabilities, let me point out that I had much on my mind, and it took three of them to pin me down.

FOREIGN AFFAIRS

Soon after arriving in Brussels, in 1989 I went down to watch the Euro-parliament in Strasbourg. The highlight of the week was a demented attack on America, and especially Coca-Cola, by a virtually mummified French film director called Claude Autant-Lara. It is in a way reassuring to find that fourteen years later, the language of French abuse of America is unaltered. In the meantime, Europe has lamentably failed to get its act together on the first Gulf War, the Yugoslav crisis, and the second Gulf War. Everyone admits that the Common Foreign and Security Policy is a joke. By contrast, the 'special relationship' between Britain and America would seem to be in robust good health. But whatever you think of the French, they deserve admiration for one huge geo-political coup. They have created a European currency which is at least potentially a rival to the dollar.

I include this story because the Daily Telegraph was the first UK paper to record the shooting of Gerald Bull, almost certainly bumped off by the Israelis for attempting to supply a supergun to Saddam (March 24, 1990).

Weapons dealer found murdered

A leading international arms dealer has been found shot dead outside his flat in a Brussels suburb. Mr Gerald Bull, 62, an American, was president of the Space Research Corporation, a multinational which sells rockets and other military hardware.

Belgian police have ruled out robbery as the motive because $20,000 (£12,500) in cash was found on the body.

Sounds familiar? Faced with the challenge of Saddam, a British foreign secretary desperately tries to get some action from the Europeans.

Hurd warns EC of US anger at Gulf response

Mr Hurd, Foreign Secretary, gave warning last night (December 4, 1990) of an anti-European backlash in the United States over the EC's disunited and patchy response to the military challenge of the Gulf crisis. He said: 'There's a feeling in the US, as they look at the Gulf, of the disparity of effort between the US and its European allies.'

Speaking after a meeting of foreign ministers in Brussels, he said there were now compelling arguments for much closer EC co-operation over defence and security.

The subjects will be high on the agenda at the inter-governmental conference on EC political union next week.

Mr James Baker, US Secretary of State, has already protested to the EC Commission at the slow pace of aid to the front-line states of Egypt, Jordan and Turkey.

Senior British sources made clear that Washington was even more concerned about the number of soldiers Europe was prepared to commit.

Mr Hurd will be drawing up plans in the next 10 days, for presentation at the Rome summit, outlining new British ideas for closer EC co-operation on security.

The Government insists that any moves in this area must not diminish Nato's role. Mr Hurd has also rejected French proposals that detailed matters of foreign policy co-ordination, such as sanctions, could be taken by majority vote.

He envisages a 'triangle' of the EC, Nato, and the Western European Union, a nine-strong defence co-ordination body, although last night he gave few details about the exact relationship between them.

Foreign ministers agreed yesterday that Italy, current holder of the EC's rotating presidency, could hold talks with Iraq if meetings proposed by President Bush between the US and Iraq take place.

Mr Hurd told a news conference that the question of Western hostages in Iraq and occupied Kuwait would top the agenda in any such talks.

The eternal verities of French European policy.

After Mitterrand nothing much will change

We stood in the Salle des Fêtes of Napoleon's Elysée Palace as the old man gave out the Légion d'Honneur. Above us hung chandeliers the size of small cars, from a gilded ceiling writhing with putti and mermaids. The honorands stepped forward: a man who had consecrated his life to the study of the circumflex accent; Sylvie Guillem, the ballerina; a stout old man who once escaped the Nazis. Each received the thanks of the President of the Republic, with a perfectly turned speech; and each then kissed François Mitterrand on either cheek, somewhere in the region of the ear, with the mixture of devotion and egalitarianism that marks the French presidency.

The ceremony was made all the more moving – and it *was* moving – for the small audience of family, loyal Mitterrandist politicians, and the odd interloping journalist from London, by the fact that we all knew, looking at his waxy skin and hair thinned by chemotherapy, that it might be the last. By May, at the latest, Mitterrand must leave this palace, his allotted span of two seven-year terms fulfilled.

One wondered what eulogy Mitterrand would himself deserve. He would like to go down, no doubt, as one of the progenitors of a more united Europe. But the Mitterrand legacy is under threat. He has failed even to nominate his successor. The Socialist Party he created is in ruins. The blood of Michel Rocard, his one-time prime minister, is on his hands, and Delors has bowed out. With four months to the presidential election, French politics is in a kind of frenzy, the bright young men in a delirium of doubt about which Right-wing horse to back.

Will it be Jacques Chirac, the snarling, brilliantined leader of the Gaullists? Or will it be Edouard Balladur, the Jeevesian wearer of cardinal's mauve socks whom Chirac mistakenly allowed to be prime minister? The betting is heavily on Balladur, though Chirac has the advantage of the party machine. Whoever wins, something has changed with the passing of Mitterrand. In the Elysée, the feeling is elegiac. Europe, they say, will founder without his florentine skills. 'It is a question of élan,' said an aide, 'the difference between a static and a dynamic vision.'

The inevitable triumph of the Gaullists has been hailed in London. If we are to believe the Foreign Office, we shall see a return of the Gaullism which places the sovereign state foremost and deprecates Brussels. If it is true that we are about to witness the obliteration of all M Mitterrand's efforts to construct a Franco-centric Euro-polity, that would be of momentous importance, for Britain and Europe. Such an assumption would, however, be premature.

Let us state, as powerfully as we can, reasons why Downing Street might be cheerful about a Gaullist French president. Agreed, the fall of the Berlin Wall fundamentally shifted the European balance of power. The old equilibrium between France and Germany has gone. Britain, so long despised and rejected of nations, is also to be clasped to the gallic bosom. 'It is simple good sense that France, Britain and Germany should be the directing countries of the EU,' M Maurice Couve de Murville told me. Yes: the self-same Couve de Murville who, as prime minister, blocked Britain's entry to the EC in 1963.

France and Britain have been brought closer by the experience of Bosnia. More effective than 100 Francophile speeches by Douglas Hurd has been the sight on French television of General Sir Michael Rose commanding French troops and speaking a kind of French. France's politicians have finally followed Britain's too, in spotting that there are votes in bashing Brussels. M Pasqua, the Corsican who aspires to be prime minister under President Balladur, has more or less scrapped the Schengen plan to abolish frontier checks, which once threatened embarrassment for Britain.

If anything, the French view of the Euro-parliament is more caustic than Britain's. London's excitement at the imminent Gaullist administration will be intensified, more-over, by signs that it will mean further Thatcherian privatisation, of Radio Monte Carlo, and who knows, even Air France, as well as an attack on the enormous employer contributions to the welfare state.

There is a difference, though, between a Gaullist modulation of rhetoric and a political earthquake. One should not exaggerate, first, the desire of the French Right to follow Britain's economic lead. In France, where growth is poised to overtake Britain's, and where the Bank of France last week predicted that the criteria for monetary union would be achieved by 1996, the attitude towards Britain's economy remains irritatingly compassionate. A Chirac victory is assumed by Tory Right-wingers to be the best outcome; yet in some ways he is more Left-wing than Mitterrand. His Gaullist concept of the nation would mean a France even more bloody in defence of its farmers; even more prone to flout EU competition law; even more protectionist of its workers.

Granted, federalism is now as bad a word in the French political lexicon as it is in Britain's. M Balladur's officials say they want to chastise the Brussels Commission, which appalled the French establishment by using its prerogatives to negotiate for freer world markets. And yet the solution of the Gaullists is a million miles from what might be acceptable in London. I heard a group of Gaullist senators outline their plans for the 1996 Inter Governmental Conference. They want to squash the Commission with a permanent Council of Ministers in Brussels, and a second chamber for the European Parliament: in other words, two more centralised EU institutions.

Whether the next president is Chirac or Balladur, the French remain committed to creating a European *pouvoir politique*', said one political scientist. One politician fanatically opposed to the single currency warned: 'I would say to Mr Major, do not think the French are going to abandon their strategic goals'. Too much, perhaps, has been made of Delors's decision not to run. The reality is that it might not have made much difference. When Delors was finance minister in Paris, he was hardly Monsieur Europe. He restored exchange controls and devalued four times against the Deutschmark. It was Jacques Chirac who signed the single European Act and who last week wrote a dizzy article in *Le Monde* lauding the Franco-German axis.

Mitterrand is now an old man in a hurry, desperate to plot a future he will not see. If you ask, has France's European programme lost its quasi-religious urgency with his departure, the answer must be yes. But if British politicians believe that the French have abandoned their policy, that European institutions, based in Brussels, offer the best means of protecting the French language and culture, projecting French influence, and controlling the Germans, then they are guilty of fantastic self-deception.

The triumph of Delors, Kohl and Mitterrand.

The birth of the euro

Snow had fallen in Madrid yesterday (December 1995), snow on snow. In the bleak midwinter, wise men came, mainly from the East, to behold a wondrous thing.

They came to bear witness to the nativity of the single European currency, and they came to give it a name.

From this day forward, the apostles of Euro-money will be able to spread the glad tidings in a vast Brussels propaganda campaign.

'Euro, Euro, Euro' the bumf will chorus, as it drops through the letterbox of a yet unknowing continent.

'As Peter was the rock on which the church was built, so the Euro is the rock on which the European Union will be built,' raved Antonio Guterres, the Portuguese prime minister. Babes unborn will lisp the name.

If the commission plan succeeds, Euro will litter the daily conversations of millions; and our grandchildren will ask themselves how on earth Britain could agree to this neologism, in half-an-hour before lunch on a freezing December day in Madrid's equivalent of Canary Wharf.

Did the Government not have a view? Did the sentiment of the ordinary people of these islands count for nothing? If ever a coin was the lowest common denomination, this is it.

This is a name which can be pronounced no less than four ways in Denmark – Ayooro, Aeaeooro, Yuro and Oiro – and all of them translate roughly as 'Yuck'.

And when the little ones turn to us and ask with big round eyes, 'Grandma, Grandpa, why is our money called the Euro?', we will blush and say: 'Well, darling, nice Mr Major didn't have much of a choice.

'He had these people called the Tory Euro-sceptics waiting for him to come back from Madrid.

'They were cruel, blinkered men who often plotted to get rid of Mr Major. If he had really pushed for a better name, like Florin or Crown, they would have been very cross. They would have said he was preparing to give up the pound.'

And the little ones will pause and look thoughtful, and then say: 'So John Major sort of said nothing?'

'That's right, darling.'

'And so he agreed to Euro because he didn't dare say anything much on the subject at all.'

'That's right, darling.'

It will be especially difficult to explain events if, as seems likely, the Germans cheat. It was Herr Waigel, the German finance minister, who yesterday proposed 'Euro', and who pronounced himself thrilled with the result.

That is because it remains Germany's intention to win round their public to monetary union by calling the currency the 'Euro-mark' abroad, and, slyly, the mark at home. Britain, true to form, will stick to the rules it apathetically agreed. If Britain ever joins the single currency, Euro it will be.

Ah well, you may say, there's the rub: surely the Government believes that monetary union will never happen?

Far from it. Yesterday's most astonishing development was Mr Clarke's admission that he believed there was a 60–40 per cent chance that European monetary union would actually take place. Hitherto, no doubt to reassure those Westminster sceptics, the Government has taken a different view.

Mr Major has famously compared the foreigners' deliberations about a single currency to a 'raindance'. And his Chancellor has said that EMU had 'less chance than a snowball in Hades'.

Well, it would seem the Government has good news for the primitive tribes of America: your average raindance has a 60–40 per cent chance of generating rain.

And Mr Clarke evidently believes – as indeed did the ancient Greeks – that Hades could be rather chilly, a place where a snowball could easily have a 60–40 per cent chance of survival.

As they looked out at Madrid's wintry landscape yesterday, plenty of officials could be found who put the odds on the Euro even higher. As for the survival chances of a snowball, they were better still.

Clinton puts his finger on a major intellectual difficulty facing the Euro-federalists.

Bill Clinton is right

Bravo, Clinton. Well said. After eight embarrassing years, in which we have had to endure his ego-sexo-psycho-drama, the President of the United States has made a major foreign policy pronouncement, which is at once exciting, profound and far-sighted. What bliss it would have been to have sat among the corpulent Euro-worthies last week and watched with them as Bill received the Charlemagne Prize for 'contribution to European unity', which is, these days, the highest honour the Continent can confer. The day before, the *Financial Times* had published an oleaginous leader, congratulating Mr Clinton for supporting EU integration. Yet, when he spoke after accepting the gong, he made a suggestion so stunning, so alarming to the tender federastic sensibilities of the *FT* that the newspaper hissed that he was 'not entitled to make such an offer'.

He spoke with the simplicity of the child who spied that the emperor was naked. He recommended that Russia should be admitted not just to Nato, but to the EU as well; and one can only imagine the girning he evoked among the Continent's elite. Mr Clinton's point is unanswerable, which is why they fear it. If you say that Mr Clinton is wrong and that Russia is not a European country, and is therefore not admissible under the terms of the Treaty of Rome, then you have to say what Europe is. So what is it?

In their efforts to exclude the Turks it has been customary for German Christian Democrats, and the likes of Jacques Delors, to hint that the EU is the successor to Charlemagne's empire, in that it is coterminous with Christendom. This will obviously not do. If 'Europe' means

Christendom, then you might as well include America, North and South, where there are far more Christians per head than in most European countries, and you certainly couldn't exclude the Russians. More furtively, some in Brussels will hint to you that Europe really means chaps like us: you know, white men on the end of the Eurasian landmass.

Let us leave aside the racism this implies towards the Turks, the Israelis and other inhabitants of the Mediterranean littoral, though it is worth noting, in passing, that all those who accuse Eurosceptics of being 'xenophobes' are in reality defending a political construction whose avowed intent is to keep out the Muslims. Even if this, deep down, is the rationale of the builders of Little Europe, they still have no answer to the question posed by Bill Clinton. Let us suppose that Ken Clarke, Michael Heseltine and Tony Blair are really so ugly in their prejudices that they want to build a Europe to keep out the 'towelheads'; they still have no reply to the claims of the Slavs and the Balts and the endless vista of Christian white folk stretching to Vladivostok.

What Mr Clinton, or whoever wrote his speech, has realised is that in the last ten years Little Europe has lost its geo-political logic. European integration was a noble idea, born of the desire that France and Germany should not go to war again. As the 1950s and 1960s wore on, the Americans strongly supported an integrated EU as a valuable bulwark against the Soviet threat. In 2000, more than ten years after the fall of the Berlin Wall, both those considerations look absurd. There will be no war between France and Germany, and the Soviet threat is a busted flush. That leaves no urgent necessity to create a tightly unified Little Europe, except in the hearts of those who are so anti-American that they would abandon national independence in the chimerical hope of creating a rival superstate. To that end, they continue to pour out federalising legislation (this week, abandoning its pretence of defiance, Labour accepted a new EU law to change the burden of proof in race discrimination cases) and militate for Britain to join the euro.

Everything is intended not just to complicate the lives of businessmen, but to frustrate would-be applicant countries. What is the point of this preposterous new Charter of Fundamental Rights, which is to be bestowed upon us by the EU? Why do we need Brussels to give us 'the right to reconcile family and professional life'? What the hell has this to do with the free movement of goods, people, services and capital? The objective is to pull up the drawbridge against those nations, especially, perhaps, the Turks, who cannot subject their national traditions to such a detailed and intimate destruction. Tony Blair has indicated that he will veto the Charter when it comes before the Nice summit at the end of the year. Let us hope he does so, though his record of resistance is not convincing.

Before then, the Prime Minister might tell us whether he agrees with Bill Clinton, his political mentor. Is Russia part of Europe? Is there any reason why Russia should not ultimately be admitted to membership? If not, why not? If the Prime Minister or one of his gnomes in Downing Street would like to write us an article, our columns are open. Come on, Mr Blair: is Chekhov a European author? Is St Petersburg a European city? Yes or no?

And here is the man who was to prove Saddam's nemesis, interviewed in February, 1999.

George Dubya Bush

'Good to see ya,' said George Walker Bush, and without any preliminaries, even as we shook hands and his blue eyes zeroed in with seasoned intensity, I blurted the obvious question. The question that *le tout* Washington wants to answer as they prepare to wash that man Clinton right out of their hair.

'Are you going to run?' I asked; and you didn't have to be Sherlock Holmes to work out what he was thinking. The polls say the 52-year-old should run. His daddy, to whom he bears an eerie resemblance, says he should run; not to mention the 30,000 remaining financial backers from his father's machine.

More and more pundits believe this is the man who will defeat Al Gore in 2000 and recapture the White House for the Republicans after the Babylonian follies of the last seven years. He cantered through the formulae of indecision.

'It's a big sacrifice,' he said, adding swiftly that 'it would be for you, too; it would be for anyone. If I do this I will never be a private person again.' And he knew of what he spoke, having seen at close quarters what it meant to be the most powerful man in the world. 'It's a decision of the head and the heart.'

The head was getting near to deciding, he intimated, but the heart was lagging behind. 'I've got two children going through college right now. That's a pretty interesting time. It's a time you want to spread your wings,' he said – and not have secret agents follow you around the 'frat' parties.

And he has only just been re-elected as Governor of Texas which, by convention, he must extol as the 'best job any Texan could have', especially since G W Bush Jnr is really an 'uberpreppy' from Kennebunkport, Maine, who, like his father and grandfather, went to Yale before making a fortune in property and buying a Texan basketball team.

Look at the magnificent pink granite capitol building in which we were standing in Austin. Why should he swap that for the White House?

He was wearing some black ostrich skin cowboy boots marked Governor and emblazoned with the Lone Star. What need of the President's seal, the bands playing *Hail to the Chief*, when his wife Laura is already called 'The First Lady' and has her own recipe for hot chocolate on the Internet?

He has huge powers under the federal system, powers of life and death. Indeed, he cannot leave Texas before June, so heavy is the legislative programme, and under a far-sighted restriction the Texan legislature cannot meet for more than 132 days per year.

As for his lead in the polls, he said: 'The polls said George H W Bush was ahead of Clinton 11 months before the '92 election. I don't take polls.'

But for all the Hamlet stuff, it was pretty clear which way his mind was moving. His father's Cabinet colleagues, former Secretary of State George Shultz and former Defence Secretary Dick Cheney, have been coaching him in world affairs.

Do they want him to go for it? 'They do. They all do,' he said. That very evening he was off to Louisiana to confer with the Governor. Aha. What about?

'We're gon' talk about crawfish ay-touff-ay [étouffé], haw haw,' said Mr Bush, and everyone guffawed with him, since he is as popular with the media here as he is with the voters. 'We're gonna talk some politics,' he conceded.

Whatever it was old Ma Bush used to feed her sons – Jeb, the younger brother, is Governor of Florida – they have the Right Stuff coming out of their ears. Like 'Poppie' Bush, George Jnr was a navy flier, and he exudes a sense of clean-cut, square-jawed, straight-backed, hot-dang all-American values.

If we see a second Bush presidency, it will be marked by his patented 'Compassionate Conservatism' which entails, among other things, long recitation of literacy statistics among minorities.

And no, said Bush Jnr, Compassionate Conservatism was more than Blairism or Clintonism.

'Our philosophy heralds the individual, and trusts the individual,' he said, while Democrats and New Labour still prefer to trust to the ministry of the state. 'There's tremendous scope to go with the grain of human nature.'

Not that there's anything soggy about this compassionate business, or even libertarian. He's in favour of parental notification for abortion, tighter drink-driving laws, and has authorised the judicial bumping-off of 40 murderers.

His eye alighted on my garish watch. 'I'm not sure about the wristband,' he said. On learning that the face bore the picture of Che Guevara (I blush), he said: 'Now that's an interesting statement. We're kind of tough on people like that down here, so be careful.'

I tried pathetically to explain that it was my wife's, just a joke watch, the other one having bust under six Gs in an F15E; but he was off to Louisiana and stuffed crawfish.

'What you bo's gon' do now? You should head down to 6th Street to the bars,' he said, flinging out an arm.

Should we mention his name? 'If you do and you go to jail, you ain't never gon' get out.'

These are just some of the machines that make America the most powerful nation on earth.

Flying a Scudbuster

The dratted toggle for the oxygen mask still won't fit when Matt Moeller, my US Air Force pilot, makes a pumping motion with his hands and the men on the runway go 'yessir' in lollipop language; and help, we start to move.

The helmet is still not sorted as we taxi past the other Strike Eagles, 92 of them arrayed on either side like a guard of honour on their high, spindly legs, £4 billion worth of testosterone wrapped in steel and titanium.

It is a January day of abnormal beauty here in North Carolina. Prowling behind us in plane number two are the British exchange pilots, and in a few minutes I'll have the answers to several key questions. Can these things really do what the military claims: post a bomb through Saddam's letter-box and hit the Serb's bottle of slivovitz just as he is raising it to his lips?

And how on earth do you fit the oxygen mask? And will I be very ill, or just slightly ill? You've no idea of the strings that were pulled to get us this 'facility' at Seymour Johnson Air Force base, home of the F15E Strike Eagle – Scudbuster to you and me. A four-star general in the Pentagon had to give final clearance, and even then I wasn't allowed to fly with one of the British pilots in case we kidnapped the plane and headed for Bermuda.

On the Tarmac, almost weeping with envy, is MoD press man, Squadron Leader Tom Rounds, who says he would 'bite his arm off' to be in my G-suit now; and as we come to the end of the two-mile runway, we turn. Matt Moeller, 34, aka Moleman, call-sign 'Sludge', says, 'OK Boris?' Air traffic control come over the headset saying Sludge 31 has clearance for vertical take-off . . .

And thank heavens, the oxygen mask doodah slips home. The two engines make a kind of yip-yip noise as the jet nozzles tighten like sphincters to maximise the thrust, and we are on our way. After about three seconds Matt sings out '100 knots' and the nose is starting to rise. As the after-burners kick in you can feel the pressure on your back, and at 200 knots we are airborne, the base, the cars, the trees flashing by like a past life. Then it dawns that we are essentially strapped on top of two rockets in the process of sucking in 23,000 lb of fuel and in a couple of ticks, when we hit 450 knots, Matt has promised to 'pull the stick back'.

Then we will ascend vertically into the blue heavens in a $60 million taxpayer-funded firework. As everyone has been saying for the past two days, there is a small risk of death, and a rather great risk of being sick.

At the egress – ejector training – session Captain Erin Pickel jovially recounted the fate of the Australian photographer who was forced to bale out at 20,000ft. Then there was the guy who forgot to unclick his parachute when he landed and was dragged to the bottom of a lake; and the guy who, ahem, unclicked his parachute 200ft up. There was the pilot who took a 6ft turkey vulture in an air intake and listened while it destroyed the engine. They lost a plane last year and two years ago they lost a pilot, too, though the ground staff suggest they 'don't want to say a whole lot about it'.

But, hey, everyone has been saying, you'll be fine. If Matt makes the triple arm-pump, which means let's get out of here, I have strapped to my rump the following items: a five-inch hunting knife; a mosquito net, diarrhoea tablets, emergency drinking water, a 16-in saw for fire-wood, aspirin, Band-aids, soap, razor blades, antiseptic gauze pads, a tourniquet, malaria tablets, a silver combat casualty blanket, green dye to mark the sea as in the Apollo splash-downs, a six-foot inflatable life-raft with a CO_2

canister and two olive drab sponges for bailing out water.

More useful, perhaps, are three sickbags stowed in the knee pocket of the flying suit; and I should explain that some machismo is attached to the vomiting issue. The only other British journalist to be allowed in one of these machines, Jeremy Clarkson, tossed his cookies 11 times. They have not forgotten it.

'These screens are very expensive,' said Lt Col Del Grego, the squadron's second-in-command, in the mess-room beforehand. 'We'll have to charge the UK Government.' He guffawed, and so did everyone else. So I'm braced for the challenge now as the joystick is pulled right back, and you suddenly feel the pressure on the chest.

You stare straight up at the sky; and the thing ascends with a shivering roar and if you hold your breath and swivel your encumbered neck in the canopy, you can see the ground shrinking beneath you and then, at least if you are me, you let out a groan because the ground now appears to be where the sky used to be, and you are turning backwards upside down . . .

And aaaargh: my abiding impression of the first 30 seconds in the F15E Strike Eagle is not of its technical capacities, astounding though these doubtless are. In the view of Rich Walton, one of the British exchange officers now taking off behind us, 'It is the best fighter aircraft in the world', while Graeme Davis, his fellow British pilot, advises me to think of this outing as 'the Grand Prix of flying'. And although each of its engines is now developing 32,000 lb of thrust, and though its pods and missile emplacements are almost infinitely adaptable to new software, what strikes me is how close this machine is, spiritually and mechanically, to – well – a Sopwith Camel.

It has the same stick, the same pedals for the flaps. It's the same war between a pilot's audacity and caution, except that it's not made of wood and glue and goes at two-and-a-half times the speed of sound; though now, since we've swooped down until we're sliding only 500ft above farms, Matt is going easy on the big throttle lever.

The yowling pain in the ears is fading. The G-forces which everyone warns about have been, so far, barely noticeable; and the exhilaration begins. Oh, you can say, it is just a PR stunt. But as Graeme Davis and Rich Walton come wing-tip to wing-tip, two British fliers in an American machine, you could argue that our little sortie is a symbol of something important.

In a neat piece of historical symmetry it turns out that these very American squadrons, the 334th, 335th and 336th, originated in the bosom of the RAF. It was in 1940 that a gang of American preppies went to plucky little Britain and formed 71 Eagle Squadron. For the two years until America entered the Second World War, they flew Spitfires, and still these clean-cut Kevin Costner characters wear RAF wings at the squadron's Friday night pizza and chicken beer busts.

It is a relationship still proved weekly in the attacks by America and Britain – and no one else – on Iraq. And it is a tribute to the intimacy of this relationship that two foreign pilots are allowed not just to fly this machine, but to teach Americans to fly it. Graeme, 31, a clench-jawed Biggles who 11 years ago transformed himself from bank clerk to Top Gun, has been here for two-and-a-half years and is clearly a star. He and his wife give Battle of Britain theme parties. He has 16 USAF personnel under him.

'He is the first exchange officer I know of to become an instructors' instructor,' says Don Seiler, his squadron leader. 'I've taken one of my billets and given it to an exchange officer.' Rich, also 31 with a young child, is a graduate of City University. He hasn't been here so long, but he loves everything except the American habit of spitting chewing tobacco into Coke cans; and I don't think the base commander, General Randy Bigum, is being mawkish when he says he'd like to have both of them under his full-time command.

So in formation the Anglo-American strike force heads east, picking up speed and height. Somewhere 80 miles away on the marshy coast in a deserted bombed-out waste-land is a big white container propped on its end – let us call it Saddam's bunker – and our mission is, as they say, to 'shack that baby'!

As we turn at high speed, we start pulling serious Gs, and it is time to prepare your mental state. The point of the G-suit, which consists of all kinds of embarrassing bondage in the groin area, is to stop the blood from your brain draining into your feet; and as the turn begins, your internal organs are squeezed, and your feet feel as if you have been queuing for Monet but far, far worse, and your lips are going blib blib blib.

You grunt as you have been told to grunt, and then suddenly it stops again. That was – phew – six Gs. They say it gets really tough at more than six, but I'm feeling perky enough. Now Rich and Graeme are circling over and over us, our metal skins only feet apart, and you have a sense of the planes shaping the air like a pair of hands. You can see why they call it an Eagle, with its massive hunched shoulders around the air intake and the soaring arrogant nose. You never saw a machine more expressive of speed and aggression. We pass a flock of swans far below on a sunlit lake. This thin Perspex canopy can take a 4lb bird full on at 480 knots. We haven't discussed what happens to the canopy at 490 knots except that if you pull this toggle with yellow and black stripes, two rockets will go off – one to push your seat slightly forward and the other to send it smashing out through the canopy, and all in four-tenths of a second.

At least I think it's that toggle. Or what about this button that says 'Select Nuclear Option'? There's one button I'm not meant to discuss because it might give the Iraqis ideas. I'm toying with the little red blip that releases the precision-guided munitions, the AIM-9 mike sidewinders and the AIM-20 alpha slammer, and I'm reflecting on the words of Graeme: 'I wake up. It's a nice day. I fill up the car for virtually no bucks and then I go and fly F15Es.'

What a life, if you have the Right Stuff . . . but do I? Matt reminds me of the little button that stops the noise from my Wizzo (Weapons System Operator) seat coming through to his part of the cockpit. 'Just a courtesy thing,' he says because the next bit 'will be a little more violent'; he doesn't want to hear any distressing noises as, oooof, we pull another six Gs, and the earth and the sky swap round again.

Now is the test. General Bigum has told me, 'The more our leadership wants a bomb to put through a window 100 per cent of the time, the more they are going to call on this plane.' Do these machines have the accuracy that democracy demands?

As I feebly try to keep my fluttering eyes on the instruments we begin the bombing run, just as they do them in Iraq: a series of hideous lunges and jack-knife turns and then, ceeee-ripes, we're pulling up again to avoid the triple A. 'That was the most perfect pass I ever made,' says Matt afterwards. Saddam's bunker was truly shacked, he says, though whether the bomb went through the letter-box I cannot testify. Because although I was the weapons systems operator, they wisely decided not to prime the weapons.

Frankly, my mind is by now on other things, like the cold sweat of nausea. Which Matt astutely alleviates by taking us through the sound barrier as we cross out over the Atlantic and then – I feel a sort of melancholy to recall, because there may never be another thrill like it – he gives me the plane to fly.

'Push it hard to the left,' he says, and we turn over and

over like a tumble-dryer in an aileron roll, and then I push it to the right; and I will never forget the sea rushing up not far from Kitty Hawk, where the first plane ever flew, and the beauty of that mad corkscrew downwards, so fast that we leave the noise of the engine behind.

'Uh, I'll take the plane back now, Boris,' says Matt and then it is home into the sunset, feeling very lucky indeed, very proud not to have been sick, and that Jeremy Clarkson is a big girl's blouse.

Why are the liberal London media so beastly to Bush, when they just lurved Clinton? They are both Bible-bashing death-penalty fiends from southern states, and seem to pursue the same global agenda. Is it cos Bush is Republican?

Good on you, Bush baby: you go ahead and tell 'em

You know, whenever George Dubya Bush appears on television, with his buzzard squint and his Ronald Reagan side-nod, I find a cheer rising irresistibly in my throat.

Yo, Bush baby, I find myself saying, squashing my beer can like some crazed redneck; you tell 'em boy. Just you tell all those pointy-headed liberals where to get off. Even if you felt that he was jammy to attain the White House; even if you are troubled by his syntax and his habit of turning the lights out at 9pm, you will surely agree that there is something magnificent in the way he has taken on the great transatlantic Left-liberal consensus-loving Third Way-ers and turned them into a state of stark, staring, bug-eyed, heaving-bosomed apoplexy.

He's a monster, shrieks Polly Toynbee in the *Guardian*,

214

adding that America has become a 'rogue state' in the two months since Clinton left office. In the *New York Times* and the *Washington Post*, the old Lefties are beside themselves with rage and grief, accusing Bush of cynically pretending to be a compassionate conservative in order to win the White House – not that he won it, they snarl; stole it, more like.

He's a nutter, they say; he's a reformed alcoholic basketball freak who got the job only because of daddy, and he doesn't understand that, if he carries on like this, it's going to be early lights out for everyone. And the more they scream, of course, the more I find myself secretly admiring the guy's style.

He sticks it to North Korea, which is still, after all, a barbaric Stalinist regime. He refuses to apologise to the Chinese for the downing of the EP-3 spy plane; and why should he? It was their fat fault that one of their fighters bumped into the American plane, in international air space, and consequently crashed into the sea. He's going ahead with his promised tax cuts of $1.6 trillion over the next 10 years; and that seems wholly reasonable, given that he said he would do so before the election, and that the American economy is badly in need of a stimulus.

He's decided to scrap the 1972 Anti-Ballistic Missile Treaty, which also seems sensible, since that document is now about as meaningful as the Treaty of Versailles. You may doubt that it is possible to build an umbrella against nuclear attack, whether by Russia or anyone else. But I have never quite understood why, on those defeatist grounds, we should stop the Americans from even trying to defend themselves, not to mention the rest of humanity.

But of all the tough-guy acts that Bush has performed in his first few months, of all the pieces of exuberant Reaganism, nothing has so intoxicated the world with hate as his decision to scrumple up the Kyoto protocol and use it for putting practice in the Oval Office.

Malcolm Bruce, a Liberal Democrat MP, has already accused Mr Bush of being a mass murderer; not for his record in executing felons in Texas, but for consigning future generations to a dust-bowl planet. Yesterday in the Commons, a Labour MP with a beard asked Tony Blair how America could be so incredibly selfish, given that the earth belonged not to Bush, but to every soul who walks it.

Polly Toynbee, my old friend, tells her readers that America is 'morphing into an evil empire of its own'. A special EU delegation went to Washington on Tuesday, consisting of Kjell Larsson, the Swedish environment minister, and Margot Wallstrom, the EU environment commissioner. It is not clear whether Bush had time to see these great ones personally, what with his heavily charged agenda of jogging, golf and watching movies, but, according to the *Financial Times*, they received 'short shrift'.

You can see where all this is leading. It will not be long before we are told that America is so selfish, so isolationist, so obsessed with its sovereign right to put its broad-bottomed people in gas-guzzling Chevy Suburbans, that she can no longer be trusted with global leadership.

We will be told – we are already being told – that Britain must make a choice, between America and Europe. We can either go for the rampant commercialism, the casino capitalism of George Bush's America, where petrol costs a dollar a barrel, and where Dubya has just scrapped some Democrat laws against arsenic in the water supply; or we can go for Europe, a softer, gentler, landscape of earnest Swedish commissioners and worker participation, and higher taxes, and tighter regulation.

If Bush is going to be so frighteningly tough on China and Korea, people will say in their fat-headed way, then perhaps we had better build up this Euro-army. And they will be guilty of a stupendous error.

Because we still need a rich, confident America; not just

to provide the cash for the global military leadership that the United States has given from the Gulf to Kosovo, but also to keep the world economy moving. The hypocrisy of the Europeans over Kyoto is staggering. They attack America in hysterical terms, and yet the 15 EU countries have never come close to meeting their own eight per cent target for cuts in carbon dioxide emissions. They have not even agreed which countries should cut the most. If America were to meet its Kyoto targets now, it would require a cut of 30 per cent in emissions, and how, exactly, is that supposed to work in the current economic downturn?

There will come a time when the market, and, inevitably, US technology, will deliver a greener planet, when cars run on water, or photo-voltaic cells. But it is plain ridiculous to ask America to make such cuts in emissions now, as Clinton recognised when Congress voted against Kyoto by 95 to one.

It would exacerbate the recession, and when Bush says no, he is doing what is right not just for America but for the world. And by the way, we Europeans already allow 50 microlitres of arsenic per litre in our water.

Without any UN backing at all, Bill and Tony decide to bomb Milosevic.

Blair and Clinton – will Bill let Tony down?

It was so beautiful. They were Achilles and Patroclus. They were the two young leaders of a new generation, fighting the first 'progressive' war.

'President Clinton is someone I am proud to call not just a colleague but a friend,' said Tony Blair huskily at the White House in February last year, at the height of Bill's difficulties over Monica Lewinsky; and Bill has reciprocated wherever the pair have met.

Now Blair must be wondering whether he is about to join the long line of people who have been disappointed in President Clinton, from Monica to Mike McCurry, the spokesman, George Stephanopoulos, the aide, and countless others who have worked with the brilliant and manipulative President.

As soon as the war began, there was a division of labour between the two leaders. The United States has supplied well over 80 per cent of the military effort. Those B2 bombers which have been attacking, among other things, the Chinese embassy, have not even been touching down in Europe in their round trips from Missouri.

And yet Clinton scarcely bothered to prepare the American people for what was coming, save for a weird and rambling press conference on the night of the bombing, in which he urged his listeners to consult their atlases. Ever since, it has appeared that the rhetoric of the war has been contracted out to Blair and Labour, as though it was the kind of theatrical service industry at which New Britain excels.

It was Alastair Campbell, not an American, who went to Brussels to sort out the Nato PR machine. Young thrusters like Julian Braithwaite from the Foreign Office have been sent to allied headquarters at Mons to help Gen Wes Clarke sharpen his act. All the while Tony Blair has supplied a crescendo of bellicose rhetoric, which yesterday showed no sign of diminishing.

'No compromise, no fudge, no half-baked deals,' he warned the tyrant of Belgrade, though Britain's military contribution, in terms of sorties flown and bombs dropped, is estimated at 5.6 per cent of the Nato effort.

At what is being seen as the turning-point of the crisis, the Nato summit on April 23–25, it was Blair who was the hawk. The air war was not going well. Civilians were being killed. Milosevic was acquiring an almost Churchillian persona in the eyes of the Serbs. Blair was said to be urging the consideration of ground forces; and if he was, he was not successful.

We are now seven weeks into the war and plans for a ground invasion – the only means of speedily restoring the Kosovars to their ruined homes – appear to be dead. And who suffers, politically, if Nato fails? In a way it ought to be President Clinton who takes the rap. He made the mistake of believing Madeleine Albright and thinking Milosevic would soon buckle under a spot of bombing. Blair was merely the number one cheerleader for what was an American-inspired policy.

And yet the paradox is that because he was so zealous in his propaganda, so unbending in his Gladstonian wrath against the Serbs, it is Blair, somehow, who seems the more politically exposed. When Bill Clinton speaks to the American people these days, he speaks as much of gun control and classroom morality as of the war in Kosovo. When Blair speaks, he seems engaged in a way that Clinton is not. 'We are not talking here of some faraway place of which we know little. We are talking about the doorstep of the European Union, our own backyard,' he said yesterday in Aachen. The trouble is that for the American electorate, that is just what Kosovo is; a faraway place of which they know little. No American lives are being lost: that is the whole objective.

Somehow it is Blair, not Clinton, who has contrived to intertwine his fortunes with those of Slobodan Milosevic. Several times the Prime Minister has said there can be no future for Serbia or Kosovo with Milosevic at the helm. Clinton has been careful to say no such thing, and seems to envisage a settlement in which Milosevic retains sovereignty not just of Serbia, but of Kosovo, too.

The United States started the Kosovo operation. Only America can bring it to a successful end.

Without the determination and resolve of his friend in the White House, Blair's warlike words will amount to nothing more than a forlorn and embarrassing parp of the trumpet.

Needing someone to fill my interview slot, I chance on the famous thug and mass killer. In retrospect, I feel embarrassed about the tone. He was a monster, and he doesn't deserve to be treated as if he were some buffoonish back-bench rebel.

Arkan

You instantly recognise the baby face across the Hyatt tea room, the face that is in a sealed war crimes indictment in The Hague. He's the owner of Yugoslavia's No 1 football team, proprietor of the 'Serb Crown' bakery chain, husband of Serbia's No 1 folk singer and the man singled out by the Defence Secretary as the incarnation of Serb mayhem.

He's called Zeljko Raznatovic, aka Arkan, and he has a message for us. No, he wasn't in Kosovo when George Robertson said that he was at the outset of the conflict. But his 'tiger' paramilitaries are in training all over Yugoslavia and Arkan is waiting . . .

'If you are coming with ground troops, I will be going to Kosovo. I was brought up in Pristina, the capital,' says Arkan, so that we know how personally he takes it. The paramilitary-cum-entrepreneur is surrounded by some very smart women, including his wife in a blue satin trouser suit, and some very tough-looking eggs.

One of these is called 'Colonel Igor Igorov', a flat-eyed Russian in a dark suit. Igor sits in on our conversation while another pair of Arkan helpmeets sits behind me. So tell us, Arkan, what about your Bosnian war crimes?

'I kill many people in a fair fight because I go first and my army is going behind me. All the time I can't live without danger. There were no atrocities in Bijeljina [a town in eastern Bosnia where his men drove the bulk of its Muslim residents from their homes]. There were 40,000 Muslims and 20,000 Serbs. Those Muslims started shooting and, after that, we came in the town and we killed those bastards. Muslim people and Serb people they welcomed me and I made a speech and I address the people and they start screaming "Thank you Arkan, thank you Arkan" because I saved them from the Muslims.

'I respect Muslims. I don't eat, for instance, pork meat but I'm not a Muslim. I simply don't like pork,' says the 47-year-old father of nine.

That's a jolly fine ring there, not a knuckleduster is it, I say, pointing to a diamond the size of a Smartie. No, he says. 'My wife gave me that present. She made a seventh record and she gave me that for my birthday,' says Arkan, who used to live in London and speaks French fluently.

And what about current Serb atrocities in Kosovo? 'It's possible that some Serbs got angry and they acted as they shouldn't,' he says. 'In this country, we have law and order. In this country, we don't have a president who is a war criminal.' And the rapes? 'It never happened. I will be the first to shoot a Serbian soldier who does this immediately. He will never live two seconds. We are not savages. We are not Nazis. We don't kill people.'

Do you think there will be a ground war? 'Of course. Why do you think I've cut my hair? Not to look tough but, when I put my cap on, it helps if the hair is short.'

Are you sure you will win? 'I don't doubt for any second

that we are the winners. After that, we will be singing *We are the champions*.'

On a more peaceable sort of note, has he any business wheezes up his sleeves? 'I will sell the plastic bags, because you will need a lot of plastic bags for your soldiers. That will be good business.'

Expressively, Colonel Igor goes to turn the hotel tea room music off. Er, nice suit, I say. It is white with a thin black pinstripe. 'An Italian friend of mine brought it from Italy. I would like to be like Martin Bell. I consider him a friend of mine.'

Won't it be a shame if he can't travel around Europe now, what with this indictment for war crimes in The Hague? 'I don't give a damn. I really don't recognise that court.

'We are warriors in our blood. My grandfather fought the Austro-Hungarians and the Germans. My father was a partisan. I will tell you the truth: we don't care. We are defending our country. We are defending our children. Anyone who is outside, we will kill. You have to understand that we are better fighters than the Vietnamese and we will make you a new Vietnam in the heart of Europe. The moral is on our side and we are ready to die. We will raise an army of two million. My wife will shoot you. My boys of 15 will shoot you.'

Aha, Colonel Igor and the others, are they, you know, armed? Igor shifts. 'Er, well of course they carry something,' says Arkan. 'But not in the hotel.

'Personally, I will be after the Brit troops because they killed a friend of mine and they said he was a war criminal.'

'From the back,' says Igor tonelessly.

'He was not even armed and they killed him: the SAS,' says Arkan. 'You could see from Blair, from Robin Cook, the British are mostly raising this war up and anger against the Serbs.'

He touches his ear and mutters to Igor. 'They are bombing right now,' he says to me. 'I hear it. You do not have a good ear.

'That rugby captain. They destroy him for nothing, for fun. And that topless thing; you want to kill her as you killed Diana. You British have something cruel in your mentality and that is why you conquer.'

Four angry despatches from Belgrade.

Incompetent swatting from above the clouds

It may not be today. It may not be this week. But I have a hunch that some time in the near future this demented war will end. Amid a crashing Beethovian finale of bombs from the American air force, Chernomyrdin will fly in for one last time to Belgrade.

Slobodan Milosevic will sign something involving Nato principles, G8 principles and UN declarations, and everyone will leap to the rostrum to proclaim a triumph. 'Slobba caves in', the *Sun* will say under instruction from Alastair Campbell.

A proud Prime Minister will address a grateful but secretly apathetic nation, while much the same happens in Washington, though with more accent on the apathy; and in most of Serbia, where the population relies mainly on RTS Serbian television for their news, since newspapers are expensive, there will be jubilation.

For the first time since the bombing began, Milosevic will address his people directly, instead of being endlessly filmed at a green baize table, surrounded by his nodding ministers, or greeting delegations from Moscow or Athens. He will claim victory for the Serbs, in the sense that they have survived a 70-day rain of death from the most advanced and terrifying military power in the world, fending off an alliance whose collective GDP is several thousand times greater than their own.

Who will be right, in this coming cacophony of propaganda? Let us look at what they call the facts on the ground. According to its own boasts, Nato has given Yugoslavia – which was already a poor country before March 24 – a thorough pasting indeed. I've seen the bridges, the electricity plants, the government buildings, the 'fuel reservoirs', aka petrol stations, which have been turned into blackened enigmatic lumps; not forgetting the schools, hospitals, old people's homes and homes in general which have been blasted to kingdom come.

Almost every day journalists leave Belgrade in a kind of corpse convoy to see the latest enormity; and I wish I could say our eyes were deceiving us. In the past 48 hours, the bombs have been feeling especially dumb, hitting a bridge packed with shoppers and a sanatorium full of old people. While Jamie Shea at Nato pretends that he will rootle around and investigate this or that alleged blunder, adroitly delaying confirmation in order to take the heat out of the story, the tally mounts up, to around 1,200 civilian deaths so far.

And as for poor Kosovo, the mountainous Yugoslav province of Kosovo for whose sake we are waging war, what do we see there? We don't really know, since one of the consequences of the unsupported air strikes was to make it very difficult for aid agencies and media to work in the war zone. Nato says that 340 Albanians have been executed by Serb forces, which seems a low estimate. We have no idea what kind of carnage will be exposed when the fog lifts.

We do know that there are around 1.3 million Albanian refugees waiting to go home, and we also know, from the experience of Bosnia and Croatia, that a great many of them will refuse to go. Who can blame them? Many of their homes will have been destroyed.

Under any forthcoming deal, Milosevic will be allowed to keep at least some Serb forces in the province. Remember those slippery conditions the Prime Minister keeps setting out: 'His troops out, our troops in, and the refugees back home.' We lack the crucial quantifier 'all'. Above all, as President Clinton has accepted, neither the G8 principles nor the Nato principles impugn Yugoslav sovereignty over Kosovo.

The Belgrade rumour mill is now humming with the notion that Slobba will shortly accept Nato soldiers as part of the peacekeeping force, including some kind of American and British presence in Kosovo, or in enough of Kosovo for Tony and Bill to claim that their conditions for victory have been satisfied.

If he does, Milosevic can expect something in return. Perhaps the Western powers will go easy on that war crimes indictment, as they have gone easy on Ratko Mladic and Radovan Karadjic. Perhaps they will lift the trade embargo. Whatever happens, poor Yugoslavia will stagger on, groaning under its crony-infested socialist system, and Slobodan Milosevic will remain in power.

War is stupid. War is hell. But never has there been a war so stupendously incompetent in matching methods to aims. There are plenty of theories here about why civilians have been killed in such numbers, and you can see why the Serbian population thinks the aim is to terrorise them. Nato succeeded in decapitating a priest as he crossed a bridge in broad daylight on the feast of the Holy Trinity. They killed a toddler as she sat on her potty.

Of course this was not intentional, in the sense that some brasshat at Mons did not target this priest or that toddler. But you could say it was intentional in that Nato dropped bombs from 15,000 feet in the sure-fire knowledge that civilians would be killed. One of the truly amazing things about reporting from Belgrade, where the bombs go off night and day, is that you never see the planes.

Nato is flying nigh on 1,000 sorties a day, and they are so high that you can't see them. No wonder they hit hospitals by mistake. The reason they fly so high, of course, is that this war is being conducted on the basis of a moral calculus which says that the lives of Yugoslav or Albanian civilians are worth very little next to the lives of allied soldiers and airmen. That moral calculus explains why the planes have not gone low enough either to risk the flak or to be sure of their targets, and why Mr Clinton and Mr Blair are reluctant to launch a ground war.

You might defend the air war if it was somehow stopping Serb forces from launching brutal purges in Kosovo. But that is just what it is not doing. Quite the reverse.

Yes, there was a case for intervention to protect the Kosovo Albanians. Yes, I and many others might have supported an immediate, massive ground operation. But there was no case for starting a war, if the reality of American domestic politics meant it was fought in this cowardly way, incompetently swatting from above the clouds and then trotting out these phrases borrowed from the IRA about regretting civilian casualties.

If and when there is a Nato 'victory', and Blair and Clinton are paraded in triumph, then I hope there is a man behind them on the chariot to whisper in their ears, not only of their own mortality, but also of the mortality of the people they claimed to be protecting.

The Serbs will blame us and they will have a point

So we won. We blitzed the Serbs so thoroughly and with such abandon that today I walk the streets of Belgrade the bashful citizen of a victor nation.

While the talks were going on at the Macedonian border, we gave the Pancevo oil plant another going-over, killing a father and his two-year-old son. Last night, I was watching an awesomely violent film starring John Travolta on the hotel television, while the ack-ack was erupting in orange flashes outside and the petroleum was going up like white sheet lightning, and, after going to the window a few times, I just gave up and watched John Travolta blowing up planes, and boats, on the ground that it was somehow more plausible.

Yes, as this column has predicted from the very outset, Tony Blair ends up covered with glory, the laurels on his brow, his feet dripping with the slobber of his media admirers. It cannot be long before we have some carefully choreographed visit by the Prime Minister to Kosovo to escort a weeping Albanian family back to their homestead – and the Serbs will fight and lose their last great battle of the media war.

Appalling things will be found to have taken place in Kosovo. And the Serbs will have no defence. If their troops and police carried out a fraction of the killings, burnings and rapes of which they are accused, then Nato's war, even its barmy conduct of the war, will seem to be justified a hundredfold.

The crackpot raids on sanatoriums and old folks' homes, the bombing of trains and bridges, all will be eclipsed, forgotten. The public will be queasily grateful to have ended up so crushingly in the right, and will turn their thoughts to the excitement of the Royal wedding.

Some of us might say that the pogroms would not have taken place if Nato (and, in particular, Madeleine Albright) had not been so foolish as to launch unsupported air strikes, which meant first clearing Kosovo of media and monitors. But we who enter such protests will be accused of casuistry, and, in any case, it won't get the Serbs off the hook.

It will be no use them saying that they individually had no part in it, or that it was all the fault of Vojislav Seselj, the glass-chewing ultranationalist who urged Serbs to kick out the Kosovars as soon as the bombing started; and no doubt plenty of Albanians will be produced in the next few weeks, who will testify that it was Nato bombing that drove them from their homes.

That won't wash, either. Belgrade will ask us to lament the fate of the 190,000 Serbs in Kosovo, who will shortly be purged in reciprocal violence from the Kosovo Liberation Army, the extremely nasty terrorists supported by Nato.

If there was any justice, we *should* care about these Serbs in Kosovo, as passionately as we have cared about the ethnic Albanians. Many of them will be utterly innocent of crimes against their Albanian neighbours. But in so far as we give them a thought, we in the West will stretch, yawn and say they had it coming.

The very word Serb has become a kind of synonym for violence or racist intolerance. You say Serb, close your eyes, and you see a tattooed, close-cropped figure in combat fatigues and dark glasses, swigging slivovitz and waving his AK47. We all know that the stereotype is unfair, that the Serbs can be gentle, peace-loving, donnish types of the kind you see in Belgrade's squares, tugging their beards over chess. Having been here for two weeks, and having endlessly consulted Vokspopovic, the Serb in the street, I can testify to his great natural politeness. Only one man has shouted about the bombing, and that was immediately after his roof was blown off. Call me a dupe, but I seem to like most of the Serbs I have met, and feel sorry for them.

To explain how things have gone so badly for this people, so that they are not only losers, but also villains, you have to look at a toxic confluence of factors. There is a natural tendency to racism all over the Balkans, where people are instantly categorised according to their grouping. In Serbia, that hidden poison has been potentiated by the manipulation of Slobodan Milosevic.

As soon as Yugoslavia began to break up – an event he had himself precipitated – he began to whip up fear that they would lose out. They did. They lost in Slovenia, in Croatia and in Bosnia, they lost Sarajevo to the Muslims and, as they indefatigably point out, more than a quarter of a million of them were 'ethnically cleansed'.

They also did terrible things. They massacred Muslims and Croats. But the beauty of Milosevic's state-controlled media was that these atrocities could be minimised along with the sense of guilt, and Serb paranoia could be fed by the rich sequence of defeats.

The more they lose, the more nationalist they become. The Democratic party, no doubt one of those Serbian opposition parties that Robin Cook fondly hopes will one day force Slobba from power, has described its policy towards Muslims as 'castration' and even Vuk Draskovic, on his day, can spout the rhetoric of nationalism.

Now Milosevic has completed the programme of defeat. He has almost certainly lost Kosovo, in the sense that there seems little he can now do to protect the Kosovo Serbs; and instead of blaming Milosevic, the Serbs will blame Nato.

Instead of blaming their leader for their country's ruin, they will blame the West; and since Nato blundered into the air war, without thinking it through – how long it would take and the suffering it would involve – they have a point.

It would be nice to think that Nato will be rewarded by pushing Milosevic from power. In reality, we may all have played a part in his elaborate game of bolstering resentment, paranoia and nationalism. In five, 10 years, Kosovo and its holy places could be the sundered homeland, the instant claptrap of anyone seeking to arouse irredentist fervour.

The Nato bombing may have been in some instances a disguised blessing, in the cruel sense that antiquated factories such as Zastava can now be rebuilt from scratch. But what will your average Serb see in that? Nothing but a Western plot to seize the best of their economy. And who will profit from the forthcoming deals to rebuild the place? Milosevic, of course, and his Socialist cronies.

Nato's problem in Yugoslavia has been fighting not just nationalism, but a manipulative brand of socialist quasi-tyranny; and you can't get rid of the one without first getting rid of the other.

If anyone should hang their heads, it is those in the West who, for the past 10 years, have connived at keeping Slobba in power.

How the Serbs were turned into a nation of victims

You see, if you were a Serb, you might observe nothing here except a charming rural cemetery in the south of Kosovo. The blue sky, the tumbling hills, the babbling birds. You would point triumphantly at the hollyhocks that have been put by the mounds of earth.

230

And you would shut your mind to the fly-buzzing evil of the place. Okay, so a lot of people would seem to have died at once, you might say. Perhaps there was a nasty dose of Spanish flu in the village, heh, heh. Fair enough, it seems odd that no one has bothered to write the names of the deceased on the little wooden stakes. Odd that they should use only numbers.

You would shrug, knowingly, and perhaps make a little joke about literacy rates. But if some hysterical Westerner tried to tell you that this was a mass grave, a war crime, and that beneath this earth were in all probability the mangled bodies of 89 Albanians who had been put in a road tunnel, grenaded and then shot, your mind would immediately go into autolock.

You would freeze, and whatever the evidence before you, no matter how overwhelming, the facts would immediately become part of the great anti-Serb conspiracy. They would be relegated to that tainted corner reserved for things you just don't want to know. If you are a Serb and you see a blazing block of flats on the outskirts of Pristina, you will turn logic on its head. You will defy probability, to prove to yourself and to others that this was the work of the KLA.

Yes, you will say furiously, it was the Albanian terrorists who did it. This was a Serb flat, you will say, brazenly: and when it is later revealed that it was an unoccupied Albanian property, unquestionably put on fire by Serb militiamen who had moved in to use it as a command post, you dismiss the suggestion as the propaganda of those who would make Serbs the new Jews of Europe. Even as you drive out of Kosovo, as I did last night, and you see the Albanian bars burning with freshly laid fires, and you see the very hayricks alight in the farms, so that the returning Muslims have nothing for the winter, you will perform stunning mental gymnastics.

231

Somehow you will want to convince any Westerner in your company that it is perfectly probable that the fleeing Serbs have done this themselves. They have burnt their farms rather than see them taken by the KLA murderers, you will insist. The mere fact that this might be true in a couple of cases begins to mean, to you, that it is true in every case; and in your topsy-turvy Balkan mind you will start to blot out the hideous destruction of innumerable Albanian homes in the past two months.

The reason you think like this, of course, is largely, though not entirely, the work of one man. You think like a victim, because every day you are told you are a victim. Unable to slough off communism, with its cosy comfort blanket of oppression, you and your media conspire with Slobodan Milosevic in his terrible game. Why does he pick these stupid wars, which he invariably loses? Because, in a way, he wants the Serbs to lose.

The more wounded, and fearful, and wronged they feel, the more they turn to the racist and nationalist politics that sustain him. Like all racism, the Serb variant comes from fear: fear of being belittled, of losing old privileges, of losing in the race to populate; and the fear produces the nationalist anger on which Milosevic depends. You could see both on the faces of my Serb friends as we pulled out through KLA country.

Their knuckles were white on the steering wheel as we drove at about 80 mph round winding defiles, and they later revealed that they had been wearing bulletproof vests (though not, of course, seat-belts; that would be sissy). Looking at their obvious terror, I suddenly understood what drives an otherwise companionable man to say, gesturing at a group of Albanians returning to their village after two months in hiding: 'They are some kind of stinky monkeys.'

He feels that about the Albanians partly because he feels

worsted by them; and for that he has to thank Milosevic. He picked the fight with Nato. He lost it. And as usual when the Serbs lose, state television shows the same awful images: the Serbs being turfed out of their houses, in their thousands, like the slow, flapping columns of Serbs who were yesterday leaving Suva Reka in the patent Balkan method of flight: red TS 133 tractor, plus family arranged in attitudes of despair on the trailer, like the Raft of the Medusa. And if we in the West cough politely, and remind them that terrible massacres of Muslims are alleged to have taken place in Suva Reka, and will probably be proved in the coming grisly disinterments, we are accused of bias. See how the West is against us, Milosevic will say.

The Serbs have fallen for it in Slovenia, in Croatia, and in Bosnia. Can Slobbo pull it off again, and dupe them into victimhood? It is possible.

At the end of the conflict, Milosevic is still in power in Belgrade, and the Tanjug news agency can talk of nothing but the injustice done to the Serb refugees. The British Army is doing a magnificent job in Pristina, bringing life back to the streets and generally displaying the kind of fairness that fills one with bursting, Soamesian pride. If, however, they begin to fall foul of the KLA, then that is all grist to Slobbo's mill. See, he will say: stupid British, poking their noses into our business. We told them they were terrorists.

As for the poor Albanians, Serb propaganda holds, in a fine piece of post hoc ergo propter hoc-ery, that the Nato bombing caused them to flee. That is certainly right in the sense that Nato's inept strategy allowed the butchery and expulsion to happen. Those mass graves were filled by Serb killers while Nato was bombing from 15,000ft. But can the Serbs conceivably exculpate themselves this time? Can they shut their eyes again?

This time, surely, Milosevic has pushed his luck too far.

As one Serb woman put it to me yesterday: 'You know, with 19 nations against us, it is time to accept that something is wrong.' This has been in many ways a miserable war. But something tells me that it will not be long before the Serbs finally rise up and chuck out the man who has for so long perverted their patriotism, allowing their country to be destroyed to prolong his rule.

And what about other evil tyrants?

Zimbabwe – we won't do anything for them

Get me the atlas, darling, before I have a seizure. Let's send a gunboat to Matabeleland, via the Limpopo. No: here we are. Let's canoe the marines through Lake Kariba and simultaneously deploy the SAS to guard the homesteads in Mashonaland. How long can we sit idly by while our kith and kin – our flesh and blood – are brutally turfed out of their farms by Mugabe and his bunch of panga-wielding thugs?

I don't want to sound hysterical, or frivolous, but does anyone agree that it is about time we did something to help these people? Every day we see fresh pictures of innocent white settlers, farmers who have toiled to make a living out of the African earth, with blood pouring down their faces. More than 1,000 farms have so far been invaded by armed 'squatters', egged on by Robert Gabriel Mugabe, the country's Marxist leader. Mobs are storming houses, firing automatic weapons and kicking out the occupants.

A race war seems to be afoot in southern Africa, and for once everyone in this country – from Right to Left – is against the Zimbabwean leader. In the higher reaches of the Government, and in the *Guardian* editorial conference, he has fatally lost sympathy ever since he said that New Labour was composed of 'gay gangsters' (though, ahem, you could say there was a grit of truth in that observation). Peter Hain, the Foreign Office minister, a man whose formative years were spent campaigning for the end of white rule and the installation of Mugabe, has denounced him. Robin Cook has denounced him. In the Commons, Francis Maude, the Tory spokesman, has accused the Government, not without some justice, of vacillation and drift and dither. The Right-wing columnists bellow for their sundered kinsmen on the veld, like the bellow of a stricken wildebeest as she sees her young being seized by the jackals.

It is time, we are told, to avenge the betrayal of Lancaster House, when slippery Carrington sold the British settlers down the Zambezi. It is time to get out the solar topees and blanco the spats and take up the white man's burden ... Except, of course, that we won't do any such thing. If we were going to do anything about Zimbabwe, we might have done it long ago; but instead we acquiesced in the handover, 20 years ago, to a Marxist who had already warned that 'none of the white exploiters will be allowed to keep an acre of land'.

Of course, some were intellectually soggier than others, as they saw the new man arrive with his curious hairy-caterpillar moustache. As Tony Benn recorded in his diary on March 4, 1980: 'Robert Mugabe has won the Rhodesian elections outright. It is a fantastic victory, and I can't think of anything that has given me such pleasure for a long time. When I think of the systematic distortion of the British press, it's an absolute disgrace. The Tories must be furious.' But, as Stephen Glover points out in this week's *Spectator*, Benn was not alone: the Thatcher government (though not Thatcher herself) emitted its own squeaks of optimism about Mugabe, if not in such lunatic terms.

The Tories didn't do anything in 1982, when Mugabe launched his war in Matabeleland and the North Korean-trained Fifth Brigade of the National Army killed between 20,000 and 30,000 black civilians; and we won't do anything now, when the country has been brought to its knees by the corruption of one-party rule, and when Mugabe is finally turning the mob on the white farmers who remain, and who have so far been sensible enough to keep out of politics. What can we do? The terrible truth – or so the Labour Government will whisper – is that Mugabe's actions have a weird sort of logic. Yes, these expropriations are hideous and indefensible; but in his imagination, they are historically symmetrical with the actions of the white settlers, who were driving blacks off the land until the 1950s.

Under the Lancaster House accords, it was agreed that Britain would pay to help resettle thousands of poor black farmers; and though Britain has contributed a few million, the operation would cost billions if it were done properly. Will we pay for that? Of course not, and neither should we, since all the evidence is that the exodus of white farmers leads to agricultural disaster: the eating of the dairy cows for beef and the smashing up of the irrigation system to make pots and pans. If there was ever a case for British help, that case has been destroyed by Mugabe's actions in dishing out the land to his cronies. And even if we had done as he wanted and coughed up for the resettlement programme, is there any guarantee that he would not now be fomenting the same kind of unrest against the remaining whites?

Some will say that Hain and Cook were always Mugabe-backers in their hearts; that they are overgrown student union politicians, remnants from anti-apartheid rallies, and that, when they look at dispossessed white settlers, they see a colonial order getting its comeuppance. Perhaps there is a trace of that instinct in their performance, which may explain their curious oscillation, from softly-softly tactics to pseudo-hardball. But that is not the determining factor in Britain's relations with Zimbabwe. That is not why we are doing nothing.

The reason we are doing nothing is that we *can* do nothing. We have neither the will nor the means to protect our kith and kin. The Americans are not in the least interested in the fate of a few British farmers in a landlocked part of Africa. The Pentagon will not be sending over the stealth bombers. This is not Kosovo, fulcrum of the Balkans. There will be no ethical foreign policy here, because it is not convenient for Washington to impose one.

We have precious little to console us, in fact, except this: that Zimbabwe has not yet collapsed; that, as I write, no settler has yet been killed (though a black policeman has, an event not widely reported in the British press); and that there is still a chance that Mugabe will not only hold but also lose the elections next month. It is not trivial that he is holding elections, or that there is an independent judiciary, or that there is still a free press, which is continually interviewing Ian Smith. Indeed, the whole set-up is a tribute to the British empire.

If Mugabe goes, it may be that sense will return to Zimbabwe, and that the white farmers will be allowed to carry on; and if he carries on with the pogroms . . . well, we will do such things, what they are yet I know not, but they shall be the terrors of the earth. Like seeking Zimbabwe's expulsion from the Commonwealth, perhaps.

*There probably is, alas, a clash of civilisations, and it is
very largely about feminism. I am proud to say that Polly
Toynbee copied this piece almost exactly.*

What Islamic terrorists are really afraid of is women

So we're going in. In the next few days, our boys will be
taking on the Taliban, and we must all pray they succeed.
Let them winkle him out of his cave. Let them blast Osama
bin Laden's arms dumps and blitz his followers, and car-
pet-bomb the Khyber with pineapple chunks, to appease
the civilians, and then, and then . . . er: nobody seems sure
what happens then, because this is a war against terrorism
unlike any other.

We have had our own such war for the past 30 years,
and we know that it is accompanied by a stately hypocrisy.
On the one hand, we do our best to catch them, or sometimes just shoot them. On the other hand, we secretly talk
to them and give them what they want. We invite them
first to Cheyne Walk, in 1973, and eventually to Downing
Street. My dear Gerry, my dear Martin, what would it
take to get your lads to stop blowing us up? A ministerial
Rover? Done. The end of the RUC? Say no more.

The trouble with the war against Islamic fundamentalist
terror is that the terrorists themselves have no interest in
talking. Bin Laden calls on his followers to kill all infidels.
Then, he says, the killers will go to heaven. There is not
much room for negotiation there, not even over tea at
Number 10. We are not only horrified by the actions of
the 19 suicide killers; we are still baffled, two weeks on.

What is it really all about? What is the true well-spring
of this rage? We have all read that these crazed young men
resent America for supporting Israel; that they believe the
sufferings of the Iraqi people are excessive; that they hate

their own corrupt regimes, especially in Saudi Arabia, and blame America for backing them. None of these geopolitical reasons, I am afraid, quite does the trick, for me. There must be some deeper offence to their pride.

I think it is to do with their sense that they are representatives of a culture under siege. They fear that American morals and values will take them over, just as Coca-Cola and McDonald's have conquered the Earth. And what is the biggest single difference between their culture and Western culture? That's easy: it's the treatment of women.

Not all Islamic societies are equally sexist. You may not believe it, but the Turks gave women the vote before the British did. But listen to the casual bias of bin Laden's address to 'brother Muslims'. Look at the wacko women's gear that the BBC's John Simpson wore when he smuggled himself into Afghanistan, a sort of blue tent with a letter-box hole for the nose.

This is a world where women are lashed for adultery; where little girls are denied education; where female teachers are sacked; and where women are kept from elementary health care. Mohammed Omar, the Taliban leader, says that mingling men and women is Western and decadent, and leads to licentiousness. To call these views medieval is an insult to the Middle Ages. And yet they are held, with varying intensity, across the Muslim world.

In Kuwait, the country for which we fought, they recently decided against giving women the vote. As one enlightened Kuwaiti MP, Ahmad al-Baqer, put it: 'God said in the holy Koran that men are better than women. Why can't we settle for that?' The Kuwaiti tribunes later had a debate on the Sydney Olympics, in which a fruitcake called Waleed al-Tabtabaie called for the banning of women's beach volleyball, on the ground that it was 'too sexy and indecent'.

In Kano, Nigeria, the Muslims banned female soccer. In Dhaka, Bangladesh, women have been banned from working for NGOs. A Malaysian minister recently announced that any kind of skirt is an invitation to rape. Iranian magazines may not show unveiled pictures of Monica Lewinsky, or any other woman who has had sexual relations with President Clinton. The imam of a mosque in Fuengirola, Spain, one Mohamed Kamal Mostafa, has just published a handy guide to when you may beat your wife. Only hit the hands and feet, he says, using a rod that is thin and light. Of course, it's all grotesque. It's nutty. But these prejudices are so deeply held by Islamic fundamentalists that they will die to preserve them.

They look at America, and they see a world full of spookily powerful women, such as Hillary Clinton. So terrifying have been the advances of Western feminism that her ludicrous husband can almost be expelled from office for having a sexual liaison with an intern. The Muslim fanatics see denatured men, and abortion, and family breakdown, and jezebels who order men around. It tempts them and appals them and, finally, enrages them. Mohammed Omar says that 'only ugly and filthy Western cultures allow women to be insulted and dishonoured as a toy'. What he means is that only the West allows women to be treated as equals.

Now, there will be plenty of British conservatives who think these Taliban chappies run a tight ship, women's lib is not an unalloyed blessing, look at all these poofters these days, and so on. There are even ex-feminists, such as Germaine Greer, who will take a perverse pleasure in announcing that women can look very beautiful in a veil.

These points may or may not be valid, but they are essentially irrelevant. Female emancipation has been the biggest social revolution since print. In trying to resist it, the Muslim fanatics are establishing themselves as doomed cultural Luddites. Let me say what the Left cannot say, since it chokes on the contradictions of its position, at once feminist, and yet relativist.

It is time for concerted cultural imperialism. They are wrong about women. We are right. We can't have them blowing us up. The deluded fanatics must be helped to a more generous understanding of the world. Female education is the answer to the global population problem. It is the ultimate answer to the problem of Islamic fundamentalist terrorism.

The hunt for Osama.

We should try bin Laden first

Suppose you are one of the lads from Bravo Two Zero. You're up there in the frigid wastes of Tora Bora, and all around you is the devastation wreaked on the al-Qa'eda positions by the daisycutter bombs. It is a terrifying lunar landscape of rock splintered by TNT, littered with blood-spattered clothing, kettles, tins of food, and the mortal remains of the Arab terrorists.

And then, like the soldier in the Wilfred Owen poem, you find yourself stumbling into some dark tunnel full of corpses; and suddenly one of those bodies rises before you, and, as the poet puts it, lifts distressful hands as if to bless. You look into those dark eyes, and at once you know the man.

His turban may be askew and his cheeks grimy; but this is he, the face that launched a thousand air strikes, the ultimate objective of the war on terror. It is Osama bin Laden, badly injured, and against all predictions, he is trying to surrender. The man who encouraged demented young men to take their own lives is making a pitiful attempt to save his own.

What do you do? Do you blow him away? You could sort of accidentally squeeze the trigger and pow, no more bin Laden; and if you did, there is hardly a person in the West who would condemn you. To be sure, there would be long editorials in the *Guardian*, denouncing the shoot to kill policy of Her Majesty's Armed Forces, and John Pilger would accuse you of being a war criminal.

But almost every other well-adjusted member of the human race, on hearing that bin Laden had been whacked accidentally-on-purpose by the SAS in a mountain cave would conclude that it could not have happened to a nicer guy. Amid the general jubilation, there would be profound relief, in Washington and Whitehall, that a major diplomatic and military problem had been snuffed out with a single bullet. But it might be that you could not bring yourself to take a life in this way.

No matter how angry you might feel, and how vividly you recalled the events of September 11, you might think, as you raised your rifle to point at his chest, that British soldiers are not taught to murder unarmed people in the act of surrendering. You might suddenly be overcome with feelings of compunction, and dim memories of the Geneva Convention.

And if you were afflicted by such scruples, you would have my sympathy. Of course, it would be the neatest solution if the terrorist maniac were to be dispatched in the coming days, whether by an M16 carbine or a 10-rupee jezail. But it would not be the best or most satisfying outcome. Bin Laden should be put on trial; not in Britain, but in the place where he organised the biggest and most terrible of his massacres, New York.

He should be put on trial, because a trial would be the

profoundest and most eloquent statement of the difference between our values and his. He wanted to kill as many innocent people as he could. We want justice. It was a trial that concluded the tragic cycle of the *Oresteia*, and asserted the triumph of reason over madness and revenge.

There are those who worry that a trial would give him the chance to grandstand. They say that putting bin Laden in the dock, week in, week out, would merely boost his status as a martyr, and that the Arab 'street' would rise up in revolt at his treatment by the West. Well, there are already plenty who see him as a martyr and hero. It seems just as likely that a trial would expose the cruelty and emptiness of the man, the muddle of his beliefs, the mushy-minded chippiness of his politics.

Osama bin Laden is not a modern Socrates, a sage whose self-defence can be expected to shame his accusers and echo down the ages. He is both sinister and ludicrous at once, and a trial would expose that. If it is really true that a trial would provoke a revolt in the souks, then that is a small price for showing the souks how we in the West obey the rule of law.

Fair enough, say the opponents of a trial; but how can you be sure that we will get a conviction? What if it becomes the OJ bin Laden trial, a grotesque pantomime of top-dollar human rights lawyers, trying to pull wool over the jurors' eyes? To which one can only respond that the evidence was pretty good on September 11 that bin Laden was responsible for the massacres. It is now, thanks not least to the bragging of the man himself, over-whelming.

It seems inconceivable, if bin Laden were produced in a New York court, that he would not be convicted of mur-der. Yes, say the opponents of a trial: but what of those jurors? Would not they and the judge be potential victims of bin Laden's suicide squads? To which the retort is that if the safety of judges was the paramount consideration of the judicial system, there would never be any trials of Mafia goons. The whole point of the exercise, the whole point of the war against terror, is that we believe in due process and the upholding of civilisation against barbarism.

All right, say the opponents of a trial: but how can you possibly send him to America, where they have the death penalty? It is true that there is currently an absurd ruling, which seems to mean that we could not send him from Britain to America without securing an undertaking that he would not be killed. That does not apply, however, in the event of our capturing him in Afghanistan, where British forces are expected to turn him over to the Americans without any such agreement. Yes, they probably would fry him, if we hand him to US troops. But I wouldn't be prostrate with grief; and at least they would try him first.

As an embattled President bombs Baghdad in 1998, a Gulf War veteran reflects on our earlier failure.

We blew the chance to finish Saddam

So, that's it. Mission accomplished. Saddam has been 'degraded' to the satisfaction of Washington and London. He's been 'attrited', in the magnificent word of Colin Powell.

Hundreds of cruise missiles costing $1.3 million (£812,000) each have blown up bits of Baghdad real estate. The Iraqis are burying their dead, tending their injured and generally going around with the dustpan and brush.

And who comes on the radio to tell his people they have been heroes? Not him again? Not Old Walrus Moustache?

Hasn't he had the decency to implode with shame at the destruction he has brought on his country?

The West sent half a million men to wage war on this fellow eight years ago. Here we are again, at the end of another campaign, and he's still vowing the mother-in-law of all revenges.

Why do we always seem to let him off the hook? We can trace the error, perhaps, to Feb 28 1991, the day the Gulf War effectively ended. Col Mike Vickery remembers it well, and with frustration.

For three days of intense fighting he had led his 53 Challenger tanks of the 14/20th King's Hussars north from Saudi Arabia into Iraq, and then east into Kuwait, crushing bunkers beneath the treads, killing and taking prisoner thousands of troops in what he calls the 'application of a serious amount of violence'.

Then, 35 miles west of Kuwait City, they were stopped. 'It was "End Ex", as we say – the end of the exercise. There was a great deal of shock among my soldiers that we hadn't defeated Saddam at all, and then we found out he was turning around and beating up his own people. There was shock and disgust.'

What checked his advance was the furore following the bombing of Highway 6, or the 'Turkey Shoot', as it became known. As the Iraqis fled north on the road to Basra, they were shot up.

In reality, it now looks as though many of the vehicles had already been abandoned. But to the media – deprived of Western casualties about whom to wax indignant – it was an atrocity. Gen Norman Schwarzkopf came under immediate pressure from Washington to cease fire.

'That precipitated the end of the war,' says Vickery. 'That sort of thing is bad PR and PR counts for a lot.'

The trouble was that Saddam was by no means a spent force. 'He's a lunatic, but he's a splendid chess player. He fed us all his pawns while he deployed all his smarter pieces round the back, and very few of them were taken. They were to become his power base after the war.'

The Allies could have destroyed those forces without breaking their United Nations mandate, he believes. 'The UK division could have gone straight on. We could have got ourselves poised and barricaded him in the Basra pocket. That is something we could have done and we didn't do it. We didn't want to carry on and slaughter innocent Iraqis. We wanted to finish the job.

'I would have very much liked to have stopped him killing the Marsh Arabs and the Kurds. It was a scandalous mistake to allow him to keep his helicopters. He said he needed them for peaceful operations and he used them as gunships.'

He also believes Saddam should have been made to surrender in person at Safwan airfield.

Vickery does *not* believe that the Allies should have gone on to invade Baghdad. 'In good old-fashioned imperial terms, you have to take it over and run it, and none of us was prepared to do that.'

He believes simply that far more could have been done, legitimately, to demolish Saddam's hardware and to foster opposition. 'I regretted the lack of support for the dissident elements who may well have been told – I am walking on eggshells here – that we would be supportive.'

Vickery is now a defence consultant, and has spent his Saturday shooting, with greater accuracy than Iraqi anti-aircraft guns, he says, though less than a cruise missile. He supports the latest operation, and no, he doesn't believe Clinton started a foreign adventure in the hope of getting out of trouble at home. 'It hasn't, and he knew it wouldn't,' he says.

For a cavalry man, Vickery has surprising faith in the bombing. 'These Cruise missiles are one-window-in-a-building accurate. The Iraqi casualties are staggeringly few, considering what has been dumped on them.

'What is very much the coming thing is the bloodless war.' He even defends the term 'degrade', and takes it to mean reducing an enemy's threat by a certain percentage.

'But what you can't do is win a war and take ground and hold it with planes.' The bombing has not been valueless, but it has been 'a limited war', he says. 'There was a question in the Sandhurst exam about whether there can be a limited war. This is it.

'I don't think it'll lead to his downfall. It'll prevent him from reassembling this sort of weapon for a while. They can rebuild, and it'll take them a long time and cost them a large amount of hard-earned money, but I don't believe that will defeat Saddam or destroy his wish to do whatever he wants.'

We had a chance to do that eight years ago, and we blew it.

The fear, the squalor . . . and the hope

We could tell something was up as soon as we approached the petrol station. There was an American tank parked amid a big crowd of jerrycan-toting Iraqis. Unusually, the soldiers were down and walking around, guns at the ready. Then I heard shouting and saw the Americans using their carbines like staves to push back some of the customers, who were evidently trying their luck. Just then a black sergeant near me started shouting at an Iraqi. 'You, I've told you to get away from there,' he said, swinging his gun round.

The Iraqi appeared to be a phone technician, with pliers and a handset. He was standing before an open relay box, up to his ears in wire, and trying to repair some of the damage that has left Baghdad for three weeks without telephones, electricity, and in some places without running water and sanitation. The American repeated his command; and again. Still the Iraqi did not move, while others vehemently and incomprehensibly tried to explain what he was doing. Then the American seemed to lose his temper.

'Let me put it this way, buddy,' he shouted, lifting the gun to his shoulder and aiming at the Iraqi's head from a distance of a couple of feet. 'If you don't move, I'm going to shoot you!' At this point, since it did not appear out of the question that there would indeed be a tragedy, I am afraid that I intervened. 'I say, cool it,' I said – or rather, croaked. Three pairs of US army shades turned on me, and a couple of American guns waggled discouragingly in my direction.

There is gunfire the whole time in Baghdad. It barks around every street corner. Every night is enlivened by the rippling and popping, as if someone were tearing a sheet a few feet away. Within the space of the last half-hour, I had slunk past a ten-year-old with an AK47 over his shoulder, chewing the fat with his dad in the door of the shop. Just five minutes ago I had flinched when another shop-keeper cocked his automatic in my face to show how he dealt with the plague of thieves. But in my three days in Baghdad, this was easily the scariest moment, and the one time I really wished I had bothered with the flak jacket kindly loaned to me by Fergal Keane of the BBC. 'You!' screamed an American, whose stitched helmet name-tape proclaimed him to be Kuchma, blood-type A neg. 'Who are you? Go away! No, wait, give me that,' he said, shaking with anger when he saw my camera. 'Give me that or I will detain you.'

I refused; but it was only a couple of minutes before Kuchma and I had calmed each other down. He explained to me the huge pressures his men were under, trying to keep order in a city with no recognised authority, a gun under every Iraqi pillow, and with only a fraction of the troops necessary. I apologised, as we shook hands, for accidentally interfering with his work. I gabbled some congratulations on the amazing achievement of his men and the rest of the American forces.

It wasn't just that he had the gun and I didn't. I meant my congratulations, and I still do. Like everyone in Baghdad, Kuchma asked what the hell I was doing there. I went partly to satisfy my curiosity, but mainly to clear my conscience. I wrote, spoke and voted for the war, and was hugely relieved when we won. But owing, no doubt, to some defect in my character, I found it very hard to be gung-ho. My belligerence never burned with the magnesium brightness of, say, Mark Steyn.

It was troubling that we were preparing war against a sovereign country that had, so far, done us no direct harm. And the longer Blix and co. fossicked around in search of weapons of mass destruction, the more cynical I became about the pretext. If you took it that the WMD business was just a rigmarole, an abortive attempt to rope in the French and others, there was only one good argument for violently removing Saddam Hussein from power; and that was not just that it would be in the interests of world peace and security, but that it would be pre-eminently in the interests of the Iraqi people.

It was, therefore, a piece of utilitarian arithmetic. You had to weigh the disasters of war against the nightmare of life under Saddam. You had to set the misery of old Iraq against the uncertainties of a free country. That is the calculation; and it would be quite easy to construct a powerful case for believing that the exercise has been a disaster. You don't need to be Robert Fisk. You just shut one eye in Iraq, and look around you.

As we drove into Baghdad from Jordan, I saw some sights familiar from Kosovo, like the way a smart bomb deals with a motorway bridge: the writhing steel reinforcements twisted like spaghetti; the concrete shaken free as if it were plaster. But about 50 miles away from the city, in the neighbourhood of Ramadi, it became obvious that this was a much, much bigger deal than Kosovo. The tanks were not just neutralised; they were frazzled and oxidised, and in some cases they had flipped their lids – with the gun turret blown right out – like a biscuit tin. Cars had been crushed like balls of paper, and chucked over the side of the bridges. In every cock-eyed anti-aircraft gun, in every useless and deserted gun emplacement, you could read the humiliation of the Iraqi army.

We drove past the Baghdad Museum, which has still not recovered the Warqa vase and the 300-kilo bronze Akkadian king, and which every Iraqi believes was looted with the collusion of the Americans, or the Kuwaitis, or both. We went by a shopping centre flattened by bombs, as the vast buttocks of an American security guard might accidentally squash a cardboard box of cornflakes on the front seat of his Stingray. My interpreter pointed out the Ministry of Irrigation. Irrigation is the word. The thing was fuller of holes than a watering can.

But it is not the Americans who have done the worst damage to Baghdad. Weeks after the invasion, buildings are still burning, not from missiles but from the looting. Most of the shops are shut. There is glass everywhere, and rubbish all over the streets, because there are no municipal services; and there are no municipal services because civic order has broken down. Little Japanese pick-ups scoot by, laden with copper wires uprooted from the streets; and the very same looters shake their fists and complain that there is no electricity. Like every other reporter in Baghdad, I have done dozens of vox pops, shoving my notebook under the noses of passers-by, virgins to this procedure, and canvassing their opinion on the traumatic change we have made to their cityscape and their political arrangements. With my interpreter, Thomas, I went down to Sadr City, formerly Saddam City, where two million Shiites live in scenes of unremitting squalor, with markets petering out and starting up again on the wide, tank-friendly streets.

'Hello there,' I asked Hamad Qasim. 'How is it for you? Are you happy that Saddam has gone?' The djellaba'd shepherd chopped the air with his hands, as if brushing a fly off each ear, and said, 'We lived for 35 years under oppression and we are very happy that the Americans are here.' He then tried to sell me one of his malodorous brown ewes for $50. Others thought his words needed amplification. 'The Americans have come and purified us [Thomas's translation] from Saddam, but until now we have seen nothing from the Americans,' shouted another man, and the mood of the crowd became more assertive as, finding my Arabic inadequate, they engaged in choleric altercation with Thomas.

'Where is our gas, our electricity? They just make promises!' And as they grew more emphatic in their views I buttoned up my jacket and we found ourselves retreating to the car. A skinny man in a waistcoat stuck his nose through the window. 'I have no job. I have no money. There are gangsters everywhere shooting people. If this goes on,' he cried, flapping his waistcoat in ominous demonstration, 'I will make myself a suicide bomber!'

Those are the kind of words that terrify men like Kuchma, the harassed marine at the petrol pump, and which tempt them to blow away someone who might be a phone-repair man, but who also might be about to set something off. Two and a half weeks after toppling Saddam, the American forces are pitifully ill-prepared for the task of rebuilding the country they conquered with such brilliant elan. Behind the scenes, under their breath, Iraqis are starting to make comparisons with the former regime. 'When the last Gulf war ended,' said Thomas, whom I suspect of being a bit of a Baathist, 'it took only a week before Saddam restored everything.'

Yes, agreed Mohamed, his colleague, you needed two Saddams to run this country. 'Your William Shakespeare has written in his novel *Julius Caesar*,' said Thomas, rolling his eyes and waving his finger, 'a country with a tyrant is better than a country with no leader at all.' Indeed, said someone else, Saddam may have been a thug and a killer, but at least he had a policy on law and order. Somehow, perhaps because we have so far failed either to capture him or to produce his moustachioed corpse, the shadow of the dictator still hangs over this town like a djinn. Where is he? What happened to him?

Some say he was seen at the Adamiya mosque on the day that American column sliced through Baghdad's pathetic Maginot Line. Some say he is holed up in Ramadi, the badlands to the west of town which fought on for six days; others that he is being ferried between the many households prepared to give him hospitality. I'll tell you where he is not. He is not at the bottom of that enormous hole made by the US air force in the posh district of Al-Mansour, when they had a tip-off that he was having a working dinner with his henchmen. He may indeed have been at the Al-Saab restaurant, a fine establishment that gave me a topflight Shoarma and chips, but the bomb landed about 100 metres away from the joint, doing it no damage whatever. There were twisted bedsteads, snatches of curtain and other remnants of four civilian houses. But there was no Saddam.

It was theoretically his birthday on Monday (actually, no one knows when he was born, in the miserable village of Ouja near Tikrit; like everything else in his life, Saddam swiped his birthday from someone else), and everyone was gripped by a delicious paranoia that he would pop up, like some awful Saddamogram, with a special birthday commemoration. Almost all his images have been shot up, or defaced, and Mohamed, my driver, was very happy to join in, jumping up and down on a fallen statue. But the image is still there, on every corner, the grin still visible beneath the bazooka holes.

It is obvious why the name Saddam is still potent, and can still, incredibly, be spoken of in terms of grudging respect; and that is because no one else has taken power, at least not in the way that Iraqis appreciate. A charming Foreign Office man briefed the international press on Monday night, flying in and out on a lightning visit with his minister, Mike O'Brien. He sat on a desk in his salmon-pink tie, blue shirt, chinos, and twirled the toes of his brown brogues. Asked about law and order, and the creation of a new government, he said we were on a 'process' or a 'journey' in which he hoped the Iraqi police would shortly start to do the job themselves.

So far the Iraqi police are finding themselves unavailable for work, no doubt owing to heavy looting commitments. The Americans roll by in their Humvees, or sit behind their shades and their razor wire. They do not have the numbers to mount foot patrols; they have abandoned any attempt to confiscate the guns of the population, since it is a bit like trying to confiscate all the cannabis in Brixton. The result is that they do not control the streets. No one does. Iraq in 2003 will be studied for generations by anyone interested in power, and the emergence of authority in human society. Into the vacuum have flooded competing hierarchies – religious, military, secular – and a hilarious range of political parties, already exhibiting Monty Pythonesque mutual loathing.

Saddam's palaces are now controlled by the Americans, and I was repeatedly frustrated in my attempts to gain admission. But there are plenty of other looted palazzos, formerly belonging to Baathist kingpins, and all sorts of people seem to be in charge. A sign outside the home of Saddam's half-brother, Watban Al-Tikriti, proclaimed that it was now the headquarters of the Democratic and Liberation party. What were their political aims, I asked the shuffling men who allowed me in. They grinned. The charter of the Democratic and Liberation party is to liberate, in the most democratic fashion possible, the possessions of Watban Al-Tikriti.

Then I went to the villa of Tariq Aziz, in a hopeless attempt to emulate David Blair and find some documents incriminating Western politicians. My fingers clutched greedily at some papers scrumpled outside; and – yes! – they were indeed communications between Iraq and a foreign power. They were letters from the Swedish ambassador, dated 1982, complaining about the mugging of his au pair, and registering the import, to Baghdad, of a Ford Capri. I decided not to trouble the *Telegraph* copytakers. Apathetically overseeing me was a group called 'The Military Liberation Force of Officers'. Their aim, they said, was to purge the army of corruption.

They might as well have had 'looter' tattooed on their foreheads. I went to the next looted palace, formerly owned by a Baathist vice-president. Yet another gang was in charge. 'We are a new party but we do not want to give you the name,' said a raffish, amply constructed fellow. Oh, all right, I said, what is the name of your leader? 'He is a religious man. I do not want to give his name.' I see, and what does he want? 'He wants a government.' What sort of government? 'He wants a patriotic government. He wants freedom.' These are some of the Shias who make up 60 per cent of the population, who were repressed by

Saddam, and the people Thomas, the Christian Baathist, fears most.

Everyone has seen the pictures of the nutty head-cutters of Karbala. But what makes the Shia clerics dangerous is their appetite for power, and their shrewd understanding of how to get it. The leading mullah in Baghdad is the evocatively named Mohamed Al-Fartusi, who has already been arrested once by the Americans. On Monday night the coalition convened an extraordinary meeting of all those who might have a political role in rebuilding Iraq. There were perhaps 250 in all, including 50 sheikhs, tribal leaders in full headdress; there were Iraqi intellectuals who had suffered under Saddam, and there were émigrés who had come back to help.

But there was no Fartusi. Not only had he not been invited; he would have boycotted the proceedings anyway. Nor was he available for interview when I turned up at his mosque. But as you studied the crowd at his gates, begging for arbitration from the holy men on questions of usury, theft or divorce, you could see why Thomas the Christian feels so threatened. They want to close down the booze shops, he said. They are mediaeval, he said, and he is exactly right. Sharia law means that there is no separation between church and state. The clerics are doing the job of the civil courts, and in the absence of any other authority their influence will surely grow. And who is there to rival them?

No one thinks much of Dr Ahmed Chalabi, whose Free Iraqi Fighters are in the pay of the Americans. For a couple of days Baghdad had a Chalabi-backed mayor called Zubeidi. Unfortunately, his first act as mayor was to loot $3 million-worth of TV production equipment, and the red-faced Americans put him under arrest on the charge of 'exercising power that wasn't his'. So who does have power? Not Jay Garner. 'Who's Jay Garner?' asked one marine, guarding the building in which I was told the proconsul resided.

Power is being contested on every corner, between Shia moderates and extremists. It is being fought for by umpteen Kurdish parties, Assyrian parties, secular parties. Of course there was something absurd about the conference organised by the Americans, the endless jabbering of groupuscules under a mural of a semi-naked Saddam repelling American jet bombers. There was a priceless moment when Mr Feisal Ishtarabi could not remember whether his party was called the Iraqi Independent Democratic party or the Iraqi Democratic Independent party. But does it matter?

There was also something magnificent about the process. It was a bazaar, a souk, in something the Iraqis have not been able to trade for 30 years. It was a free market in politicians. In a word, it was democracy. Sooner or later there will be elections in Iraq; and no, funnily enough, most people do not think that the Shiite extremists will sweep the country, or that government will be handed over to Tehran. There will be no more torture victims, like the man who showed me the ivory-white sliced cartilage of his ear, cut off by Saddam to punish him for deserting from the army, or the stumbling old man who claimed his three sons had all been killed by the Baathists.

If there are any weapons of mass destruction, the good news is that they will not be wielded by Saddam or any group of terrorists. And since it is time to put the good news into our utilitarian scales, here is a statistic that you should be aware of, all you Fisks and Pilgers and Robin Cooks, who prophesied thousands and thousands of deaths. I went to see Qusay Ali Al-Mafraji, the head of the International Red Crescent in Baghdad. Though some nametags have been lost, and though some districts have yet to deliver their final tally, guess how many confirmed Iraqi dead he has listed, both civilian and military, for the

Baghdad area? He told me that it was 150, and he has no reason to lie.

Of course it is an appalling sacrifice of life. But if you ask me whether it was a price worth paying to remove Saddam, and a regime that killed and tortured hundreds of thousands, then I would say yes. What do you see now when you walk past Iraqi electrical stores, which are opening with more confidence every day? You see satellite dishes, objects forbidden under Saddam. One man told me he had sold ten in the last four days, at between $200 and $300 a go.

Snooty liberals, and indeed many Tories, will say that this is vulgar and tawdry, and make silly, snooty jokes about the poor Iraqis now being subjected to *Topless Darts* and Rupert Murdoch. What such anti-war people don't understand is that the Iraqis are not only being given their first chance to learn about other countries. They can now learn about their own. They can now watch channels not wholly consecrated to the doings of Saddam.

There have been terrible mistakes in this campaign, though those who followed the cataclysm at the Baghdad Museum may be interested to know that, when I went there, three big boxes of artefacts were being handed over, having been recovered from the looters. I suppose that, with 170,000 objects stolen, there was a slight glut in the market for cuneiform seals, no matter how old.

As George Bush gave his speech on Tuesday night, I happened to be watching it with three Iraqis. When he said that 'the windows are open in Iraq now', meaning that people could talk without fear for their lives, they laughed and banged the table. I can imagine the anti-war lot in Britain, with their low opinion of Bush, also laughing at his folksy rhetoric. But when I asked the Iraqis what they thought of the speech, I found I had completely misunderstood their laughter.

'We agree with Bush 100 per cent,' said one, and they all passionately agreed. Really? I said. 'Yes,' he said. 'We are free now.' Iraq has huge problems, including colossal debts. It is barely governable. It would be unthinkable for America and Britain to pull out. But he says that his country is now free, and that, to me, is something that was worth fighting for. Saddam may be a ghost, but that is all.

Way to go, Dubya

New York

Come off it, I am thinking to myself. The last time I saw Tuesday night's Republican keynote speaker was only a week ago. I was lying comatose on a motel bed in North Carolina, flipping from channel to channel, and he arrived, starkers, in a Plexiglass bubble from space. As I recall, he then changed his batteries by carving a hole in his thorax, destroyed much of downtown Los Angeles with a runaway crane and narrowly failed to avert the annihilation of the earth.

It is hard to take a politician seriously when his undraped form has been likened to a condom stuffed with walnuts, and when most of his roles involve him telling rival robots that they are 'Terminaded'. But the Americans take him seriously, increasingly so.

By some fluke I am in the 'friends and family' section of the amphitheatre, only a few feet away from Dick Cheney, and can monitor the star's reception closely. Every time Arnie mentions some key state such as Ohio or Pennsylvania the crowd seethes around that state's name-standard and Mexican-waves its approval, and there is one man behind me literally screaming 'Arnold!', as if the former bodybuilder were treading on his corns. Indeed, the more Arnold talks, the more fervent become my own nods of assent.

In a simple and direct way the reformed android is explaining the greatness of America, and what it means to him. 'There is no country more generous, more compassionate and more welcoming than the USA,' he says. This is a man who couldn't even speak English until his twenties, whose Austrian accent is so thick that audiences laugh at it around the world; and yet he is governor of California, for pete's sake. It *is* astonishing. It *is* marvellous, and it deserves to be greeted with ululations of rapture.

Now Arnie is explaining not only why he is a patriot but why he is a Republican. He had lately arrived in the US when he saw a 1968 presidential debate between Richard Nixon and Hubert Humphrey. Arnie was appalled, he tells us, by the socialist poltroonery of Humphrey, so he got a friend to translate Nixon.

'He vos talking about free ennerprise and it sounded like a breath of fresh ear.' (Cheers.)

'It vos about cutting taxes and getting ze state off your back.' (Yeehah, etc.)

'I said, vot pardy is he from and zey said he is a Republikan and I said zen I am a Republikan!!' (Yeehah Granmaw, cheers, screams, etc.)

Yo, I am thinking. Way to go, Arnold.

'If you believe zat your family knows better how to spend your money zan ze government does, zen you are a Republikan!'

Fair enough, mein freund, I think. Then Arnie goes for the killer pay-off, the message that is blapped between the eyes of this audience with all the monotony of a special-effects explosion. There is only one man who can deliver those values for the nation and that is GEORGE W.

BUSH (ovation, ovulation, etc.), says Arnold, and a chant begins:

Four more years!

Four more years!

He starts to bellow like a branded bullock, the great square ruminant jaw working with the effort, and across the hills and dales of Madison Square Garden the countless Republican herd lows its answer: Four more years!

In the cacophony two unsettled questions buzz in my head. Will Bush win these years? And then there is the prior question. Does he deserve to win? It may seem unwise to forecast the outcome of an election when there are 60 days to go and even pollsters, such as my old friend Frank I. Luntz, say that the result will be a matter of 1 per cent either way; and it may seem especially perverse for me both to think that he will win, and – on the whole – to want him to win, when the charge sheet against Bush is so long and so devastating.

First there are the little pinpricks of unease. There is something unsettling about a man who never touches alcohol, goes to bed at 9 p.m., holds Bible-study meetings every morning and who is unable to eat a pretzel without nearly dying. Then there is his command of English. At one point Bush was on the giant screen before us, explaining that his wife Laura believed children should be encouraged to read. 'She wants America to be the most literate nation for every child,' he said, the gears of his brain audibly crunching.

One can see what he means, but it's just maddening that when asked to form a simple declarative sentence on child literacy the leader of the free world is less articulate than my seven-year-old. Then there are the things that are really worrying. There were the steel tariffs, which destroyed his free-trade credentials, and the agricultural subsidies grosser even than those applied in Europe. There is the Cecil B.

De Mille expansion of the state, exemplified by the prescription drug benefit that – whatever its merits – is going to cost $534 billion over the next 10 years.

There is Iraq. It is disgusting that no one in the US government has resigned over Abu Ghraib. Only this week it was reported that Lt Gen. Sanchez, the senior military commander in Iraq, sent a memo which included an enjoiner to his interrogators to exploit the Arab fear of dogs. Now we know why those rednecks used Alsatians to terrify naked and hooded Iraqis, thereby undermining the case so many of us relied on: that this was a war to end torture in Iraqi jails.

They did it because they were told to. Shouldn't someone pay the price for that? It is an eternal reproach to Bush, as Commander-in-Chief, that he invaded Iraq with such inchoate plans for governing the country and such a muttonheadedly inaccurate anticipation of the popular reaction. Why the hell can't the US government – why can't our government – give us any idea of how many Iraqi civilians have died in this enterprise?

And yet as British Conservatives have found, it is hard both to support the war and to quibble about the execution. For instance, one may support the broad aims of the war and call – as this magazine did last week – for the impeachment of Blair on the grounds that he was wilfully misleading about the weapons of mass destruction. That position is intellectually coherent; but it must be confessed that it lacks political simplicity. And if Bush has an over-riding virtue as a politician, it is that he at least appears to keep things taxi-driver simple.

You either suck or blow. You're for the war, or you're against it. That is where he has the edge over Kerry; and there are other tricks that might be instructive for us British Conservatives and which, if he wins, will explain his victory.

261

Bush is good at uplift, and optimism. He talks about inclusion and hope in a way that seems genuinely persuasive to minorities, especially Hispanics. Several times on Tuesday night his team treated us to a good compassionate conservative phrase that sums up black educational failures: 'the soft bigotry of low expectation', they said, and the Bushites applauded knowingly and compassionately.

Most telling and thought-provoking of all, he eschews altogether any claim to be a 'small government' conservative. He may cut taxes, but he certainly doesn't cut government, in the way that British Tories feel they must pledge to cut government. On the contrary, he has presided over a Gordon Brown-style explosion in the public sector. This is government of the people, by the people, for the people – of, by, for, with lots and lots of the people.

In so far as he is at all right-wing, it is that this spending may be said to be accompanied by reforms that lay stress on individual responsibility and initiative, such as choice in schools. Here he is bolder than British Tories, still nervous that the punters don't really want choice.

And then there are the socially conservative moves he has made that are probably not open to British Tories, and yet which are increasingly popular in America. The audience just lurved it when one speaker said, 'An embryo is biologically human. It deserves moral respect.' That received one of the most heartfelt whoops of the night, as did any mention of marriage, whose joys and pains Bush is determined to confine to heterosexuals.

All this seems very tough to some of us British, with our mushy, secular approach. Many of us probably think that if the gays want to get married – indeed if they want to have babies by some horrible form of monotreme parturition – then that is a matter for them. How, we ask, can you have a nation conceived in liberty and dedicated to the proposition that all men are created equal when the President institutes a constitutional amendment to ban gay marriage? Is that really what America wants?

It's what the Christians want. Just drive through rural Virginia, as we did the other day. Darn it, I said, we're lost: just 20 minutes ago we had passed those three crosses, arranged in Gethsemane formation on the hillside. Then we realised that this was a different set of crosses, and that in fact the crosses were everywhere.

Now you or I might think a cross was a pretty odd thing to erect in your paddock, but that's what they do here. They have rows of churches, not dilapidated or in the process of being converted into yuppie flats, but full of God-fearing folk bawling their hearts out. Bush knows that five million Christians failed to turn out in 2000: so he uses abortion and stem-cell research and gay marriage to ginger them up and get them to the polls – rather as Blair continually offers his disillusioned Left the prospect of a ban on hunting.

The last reason why Bush is likely to win is of course that this is a country at war, and Kerry has made a cretinous error of judgment in evoking his record on Vietnam. Every hour there are Swift boat veterans on CNN, reminding us of what Kerry said about the Indochinese disaster and those who fought in it. The effect is to elide Kerry's opposition to Vietnam with his opposition to Iraq, and to turn him into the once and future whinger, the guy who doesn't support our boys. With 144,000 Americans risking their lives in Iraq, that is not ideal political positioning.

As Frank Luntz points out, it is the flip-flopping over the war, the supporting it and yet not supporting it, that is damaging to the challenger. 'Credibility is more important than ideology. It's more important than principles. He keeps changing his views too often, and we respect people who stick to their principles.'

That is why the war is now the number one issue for Bush's tactician, Karl Rove. That is why Arnie closed his remarks with an anecdote about a wounded soldier he met in Iraq. According to Schwarzenegger, this chap was in a very bad way, full of holes, leg gone, etc.

'He said he vos going to ket a new leg and zen he vos going to ket some therapy, and zen he vos going to go out again and fight with his buddies ... And you know what he said to me ... he said, "Arnie, I'LL BE BACK!"' (Widespread epilepsy, Holy Trinity Brompton-style convulsions, followed by rhythmic chanting of USA, USA, USA.)

There are – who knows – perhaps five or ten years in which America's supremacy will be unchallenged, and in which she can try in one way or another to promulgate her values; and that will not always be a bad thing. 'If you work hard and you play by the rules, then this country is truly open to you. You can achieve anything,' said Arnold. That is true of America in a way that it isn't quite true of Britain. Colin Powell, the Secretary of State, might have been British – he was born in the West Indies – but he once said that he could never have risen as far in the UK as he did in the US.

That is harsh, but maybe fair, and it reflects great credit on America. In the words of the statesman Schwarzenegger, 'America is still the lamp lighting the world ... It is a great idea that inspires the world.' (Cheers.)

In the words of America's first Republican president, it is the last, best hope on earth. Kerry's trouble is that he doesn't seem to see it that way. We don't have much of a choice in this election: between a man who inspires not much confidence and a man who inspires fractionally less. But at a time when so many people are full of an irrational dislike of America, I'd rather have a president who is not just optimistic about what America can accomplish but who also believes unashamedly in America's essential goodness.

Even the bombs couldn't spoil this day

Baghdad

Bombs? I said. What bombs? I heard no bombs. I don't mean to affect any false war correspondent-style nonchalance, but when they mortar-bombed our meeting yesterday, I simply did not notice. Had you told me that four shells had landed only 100 metres away, scattering shrapnel, I expect I would have hurled myself to the floor like any other self-respecting MP, a species widely credited with a cockroach-like instinct for survival. Had the crump not been drowned out by other noises in the room, I would certainly have been scared, and I would like to reassure the poor, incompetent, deluded terrorists on that point, because they must, today, be feeling very disappointed. However many mortar bombs they fired at the convention centre in Baghdad, they totally failed to disrupt the event. For days we had been told to expect fireworks; and in the end the terrorists fizzled.

There took place yesterday morning on the banks of the muddy Tigris a ceremony that was in many ways beautiful and moving, and deeply consoling for anguished souls like me who voted for a controversial war. Shias, Sunnis, Kurds, Assyrians, you name it: speaker after speaker stood up to hail the birth of a new democracy in the Middle East. Surrounded by vast sprays of plastic gladioli, reminiscent of a banqueting hall in Ceausescu's Romania, the party leaders celebrated a free Iraq.

There were smooth émigré businessmen, returned in the search of power, and ancient caramel-coloured Bedouin in traditional headgear. There were angry Kurds, who insisted that every syllable be translated in their language, with all the passion of a Plaid Cymru man on a speeding charge, and above all there were the men of God. One man, a key figure in the Supreme Council for the Islamic Revolution in Iraq, began with the words, 'We praise Allah and thank him that he has accomplished the ambitions of the people,' and ended with: 'You are the best lord and the creator of our destiny and we praise you lord of the world, peace be upon you.' In between, he attributed almost everything to the beneficence of Allah, foreign, domestic, monetary, fiscal.

And as the many Shias on his list gave tongue in response, and answered his Koranic invocations, we could see the difficulties ahead. First they have to form a government, which will be difficult enough, with the Kurds and the Shias jockeying for possession of the oilfields of Kirkuk, and then, before August 15, they must draw up a constitution. There is a risk that the Shi'ites will try to grab the steering wheel, and turn Iraq into an Iran-style theocracy, complete with restrictions on female education. Then there is the continuing risk to the security of every person in this room, the fury of the rejectionists and insurgents who make so much of Iraq a no-go area for foreigners and democratic politicians.

Yesterday the Italian government of Silvio Berlusconi – formerly a fervent supporter of the war – announced that it was pulling the 3,000 Italians out, in response to the killing of an Italian security operative at the hands of American troops. I think that is sad and regrettable. Something very remarkable is happening in Baghdad, and whatever the rights and wrongs of the war, those of us who were involved in it should stay until this nascent democracy is safe.

As I poked through one of Saddam's bunkers yesterday morning, I came across a reminder of how much has been achieved, and why it was right to do it. It was a fantastic bunker, built by the Germans, with three-ton steel doors supplied by the Swiss. There were map rooms and war rooms and huge untouched generators, machines built by Siemens of Germany and Bobinindus of Belgium, so colossal that they had defeated even the looters. There were emergency operating rooms, and places where corpses were allegedly stored.

But as we poked around with our torches, the spookiest detail we discovered concerned the security system. Saddam cared so much about his bunker, and so little about the loss of human life, that he had installed a system to combat fire. As soon as there was the risk of losing the premises, they were automatically programmed to fill with halon gas, suppressing oxygen – and killing any human being left in his creepy passages. That is the kind of man he was, and the kind of regime he ran: where people could not only be tortured and killed, but where the safety of his employees counted for nothing.

And why did they count for nothing? Because they could not vote to punish him for his madness. That is why we need to keep working to make this democracy thrive in Iraq, and that is why it is so wrong of the Italians to retire. As it happens, Mr Berlusconi was wrong in his whole handling of the rescue of Giuliana Sgrena. By allegedly paying a huge ransom to the kidnappers, he merely added incentive to the nutcases to kidnap others; he raised the risks for the hundreds of British, among others, who are struggling to help rebuild the country.

Efforts to provide water, sewers and electricity are already being hampered by the need for every Western worker to be accompanied by his or her own private security detail, composed of hugely competent Ulstermen with shades and pistols on their thighs. The security problems are not only frightening; they are frighteningly expensive.

We need Western troops to remain here until the Iraqis are capable of fighting the terrorists themselves. The day may not be far off, but in the meantime I did not meet a single person here who wanted us to leave – far from it – or who regretted the change we have brought about.

Having started this operation, whatever its faults, we have a moral duty to help see it through. If that means sending more British troops to make up for the Italian deficiency, we may have to do it – and there would be many brave Brits in Iraq who would agree.

It's simple: no democracy, no nukes

The Iranian ambassador is an immensely distinguished-looking fellow, tall, erudite, with a coiffure so perfect that he could be a barber shop model, and as we sat in his parlour in Prince's Gate – once famously redecorated by the SAS – it seemed rude to dissent from anything he said.

But the more he spoke of his country's nuclear non-ambitions, the more that famous old crack of Sir Henry Wootton's floated in to my mind: 'An ambassador is a good man sent abroad to lie for his country.'

Look here, Mr Ambo, said my friend and colleague, Stuart Reid, deputy editor of *The Spectator*, you say you need these civilian nuclear power plants; and yet Iran is the second biggest oil producer in the world. Come off it, my old mate, suggested Reid: why would you need to build a load of expensive atomic plants – of a kind we in Britain are in the process of abandoning – when the lands of Persia have fossil fuel energy bursting from every crevice?

My friend's implication was clear: that Iran is busy enriching uranium for one reason only, and that is that the country wants a nuclear bomb. Wasn't that right? we demanded; and the ambassador, of course, supple in argument as a Qom seminarian, was having none of it. A bomb! he said, in a Lady Bracknellish way. A nuclear bomb!? That was the last thing his country wished to obtain, since whatever firework the ayatollahs eventually produced would be no match for the American arsenal. Why pick a fight, he demanded, with a country that could boil the sands of the desert to molten glass?

So I tried a different tack, and what I believed to be a cunning line of argument. If I were sitting in Teheran, I said, I might think that my first and most urgent task was to equip my people at once with weapons of mass destruction, and in particular nuclear weapons.

What other possible conclusion could one draw from the history of Saddam Hussein? The only reason he was deposed, and Iraq subjected to a humiliating invasion, was that he didn't have such weapons. It was precisely because he had nothing more lethal than a few old Scuds – about as ballistically effective as a trebucheted cow – that the Americans felt able to go after him with such abandon. To the various despots around the world, lesson number one of the Iraq business is surely to equip yourself with nuclear weapons as soon as you can.

The ambassador was, as you might expect, far too fly to fall for my gambit. Did he not represent the land in which chess originated? He continued to chew his mutton and pilaf, a smile visible in his immaculate beard, and then repeated the Teheran line, that no, they have no nukes, and as far as they are concerned, no nukes is good news. All I can say is that I suspect that is not the whole story, and if experts such as Ali Ansari of Chatham House are right, then what is really happening is the slow build-up of a capability that we in the rest of the world will find alarming, but which there is precious little that we can do to stop.

So before we start to panic, we might as well ask the prior question: on what grounds, exactly, should one country – no matter how powerful – be able to prohibit another sovereign state from acquiring a weapon that the government of that country may desire?

Here we are in the United Kingdom, about to get seriously worked up about the limits to our self-government envisaged in the European Constitution. What gives us and the Americans the right to tell the Iranians what they may or may not spend their money on by way of defence? Do we have such a right, and, if we do, what is the principle at stake?

When I was a child, I used to stare with real horror at the pictograms in the paper of the rival nuclear arsenals of America and Russia. I had a feeling that, in spite of their record, the Americans were unlikely to launch a nuclear first strike; but the Russians . . . ?

It worried me that Russia was run by elderly men in the fervid grip of a bizarre ideology; people who might launch an irrational strike in the belief that they somehow represented the will of the people; and that, surely, is the trouble with Iran. The Russians now have a democracy, more or less, and they certainly have a secular, pluralistic and free-market society in which everyone is harmlessly engaged in getting and spending, not least on English Premiership football clubs.

But, in Iran, they do not have democracy as we understand it. They have imams who settle all manner of political questions, and their elections are rigged. This is a country that still actively pays for people to go and strap on a suicide bomber's jacket and blow up Pizza Huts in Tel Aviv. In deciding whether a country is suitable to wield nuclear weapons, you may think that its promotion of suicide bombers is not an encouraging sign.

So there, in conclusion, is my criterion. It is amazing

that Israel remains the only nuclear power in the Middle East, with 200 nukes at its disposal and more plutonium in stock than America, France, Russia and Britain put together. But that is a good thing, as long as Israel is the only democracy in the Middle East. And that is why it is so disastrous that the Americans have been so careless as to allow the Pakistani dictatorship also to acquire these weapons, and why India-Pakistan remains the world's most dangerous flashpoint.

Iran is making progress, and they want to be friends: why else invite us to lunch? But it is a theocracy. Rather than threatening them – which may only encourage them to get nukes as quickly as possible – they should be invited to consider that, as soon as they have a full and functioning democracy, they can have the bomb that goes with it.

Bush owes Blair – and must deliver

In a hotly contested field, the most dismal awakening of my life took place yesterday morning, alone, hungover, in a hotel bedroom in Tel Aviv, when I found that the television was still burbling from the night before and that Don King, the infamous boxing promoter with a conviction for first-degree manslaughter and the Van der Graaf Generator hair, was on screen announcing to an appalled planet that the American people had awarded a second term of office to the cross-eyed Texan warmonger George Dubya Bush.

If ever there was a moment for burying your head in the many superfluous hotel pillows, and issuing a groan of self-pity, this was it.

Not four more years of a man so serially incompetent that he only narrowly escaped self-assassination by pretzel, and also managed to introduce American torturers to Iraqi jails. Who on earth, I moaned, can conceivably have supported this maniac with his monochrome Manichaean rhetoric that has done so much to encourage the nasty strain of anti-Americanism that now afflicts so much of the world?

Who did it? Who were the idiots who backed him, I whimpered, in that weak pre-breakfast state.

And then I remembered. I backed him, come to think of it. In fact, not only did I want Bush to win, but we threw the entire weight of *The Spectator* behind him. We wrote a magnificent leading article in which we recounted these well-known weaknesses of Dubya, and then set them beside the weaknesses of John Kerry: his air of Herman Munster gloom, his flip-floppiness over Iraq, his greater hostility to free trade, his love of higher taxes. We then closed our eyes and, in a tumultuous final paragraph, we exhorted the people of America to vote for Bush, as marginally the less undistinguished of two undistinguished alternatives.

It is well known that *Spectator* editorials can have an explosive effect, even among populations not normally thought of as avid readers. It may even be that we tipped the scales in Ohio, and there will always be part of my heart that suspects it was the *Spec* wot won it for Dubya.

But not all readers will be satisfied by this account, and will be wondering what other factors saved the President. A certain amount of mild tosh will be written this morning about the 'lessons' for the Tories from the Republican victory, and the way British Conservatives need to become more like their hot-dang Bible-bashing church-going American cousins, and how we need to emulate the family values of the vast suburban flyover country that voted for Bush.

I am not certain that these qualities, however admirable, can be easily implanted into the brains of suburban Brits;

but in any case, the championing of such attitudes was not the most important cause of the Bush triumph.

As Karl Rove predicted, in a speech I heard him make at the Republican convention, Bush won because of the war. He won not because he'd handled it well (he hadn't), but because he was a president at war, and because in the end an anxious population – especially, I think, women – wanted his certainties rather than the ghastly nuances and tergiversations of Kerry.

And in presenting himself as a half-successful war leader, and a man in whom his country could place confidence, he had one invaluable testimonial. Perhaps even more important than the support of a British weekly, he had the support of Tony Blair. Time after time, on the stump, he invoked the name of our Prime Minister in token of his international approval.

He did not bother with the leaders of Spain, South Korea, Australia, Afghanistan and other such coalition members. Blair was the name that resonated with Americans; Blair is big in America, and now Bush owes Blair big, and for all our sakes Blair must now make sure that Bush delivers.

I have spent all day charging around Israel and the West Bank, the high stony landscape of Judaea and Samaria, where the feeling of injustice is the proximate or anteproximate cause of so much Muslim hatred of America. I can see the limitations of what any American president might accomplish. There is no way he can instantly stop the Israelis building their tragic and disastrous wall; there is no way he can stop Hamas from luring poor confused young men to blow themselves up in crowded markets.

But there is one thing Bush can do in his second term. He can use all his influence – the influence that comes with more than $3 billion of support for Israel – to speed Ariel Sharon in his plan for disengagement from Gaza and, we must hope, from almost all of the rest of the occupied territories. Too few people in Britain understand the immensity of what Sharon is planning to do next year.

He is planning to winkle 6,000 settlers out of Gaza, a territory they consider to be theirs by act of God. He faces the kind of psychotic reprisals the settlers visited on Rabin. Bush needs to help Sharon, to encourage him, and to insist that he stop the evil of building new settlements – an act that is cruel to the settlers themselves, since their houses will one day have to be abandoned. And if Bush won't act, then Blair must insist, publicly, that he does.

One other thing. Some of us voted for the Iraq war. We gave Bush and Blair a vote of confidence, and do not feel, to put it mildly, that it has been repaid. Britain went along with an operation without being consulted on the practicalities, and it might, in retrospect, have been better to have had a closer discussion of the Pentagon's plans. If Bush is about to unleash violence against Fallujah, then we deserve, as coalition members, to be consulted.

Bush has a chance to be a great second-term president. If Arafat vanishes, there is a fantastic chance to push for peace in Palestine. If Bush fails to push, it will be Blair's failure, too.

Getting our knickers in a twist over China

Quite often on a Wednesday lunchtime I find myself conferring with my friend Rudi the sandwich man about the madness of Ken Livingstone, and his latest monstrous scheme for London. Rudi blames the congestion charge for pushing up his costs. I can't stand the evil frankfurter buses that crush cyclists to the kerb.

This week, however, the newt-fancier has exceeded our

wildest fantasies. Do you know how he has chosen to spend £1 million of our cash? That crazy old Trot has bought in 100,000 doses of anti-chicken flu medication, to be distributed, presumably, so that his key workers can continue to clamp cars and impose their poxy charges while the rest of us are expiring during the approaching epidemic.

It is a ludicrous waste of taxpayers' money, and before you dismiss it as another case of Red Ken-ery, you should know that the madness has infected the Department of Health. They have drawn up a list of 'elite' figures, mainly government ministers and BBC high-ups, who would be required to keep the country going in the event of the chicken plague, and who must therefore receive free doses of the wonderdrug.

What drives me mad is not that I am excluded from this list (opposition politicians, you will not be surprised to learn, are thought to be dispensable to the running of Britain), but that we are getting in a flap about a chicken disease which has killed a grand total of 57 human beings since it was detected in 2003, most of them Asian owners of fighting-cocks who chose to give mouth-to-mouth resuscitation to their spifflicated birds.

To get these figures in proportion, as Ross Clark does in the current *Spectator*, you should know that nine million people are suffering from tuberculosis, of which two million will die in the next year, and half a billion people are suffering from malaria. So why are we scaring ourselves witless about this Asian fowl pest? Because it is all part of our new phobia about the Far East, and China in particular.

China is becoming in our imaginations the fashionable new dread, the incubator of strange diseases, a vast polluted landscape of Victorian factories where coolies sit in expectorating rows, nourished on nothing but rice and the spleens of pangolins, producing whirling typhoons of cheap bras and lingerie that race across the seas and reduce the native industries of the West to matchwood.

It has become a cliché of geopolitical analysis to say that China is the next world superpower, that the 21st century will belong to Beijing, and that we had better get in tutors to teach our nippers Mandarin if they are to make it in the new world order.

It is all stark staring nonsense, and founded on the same misapprehension as Peter Mandelson's demented decision to slap quotas on Chinese textiles, so that the mouths of the Scheldt and the Rhine are apparently silting up with 50 million pairs of cut-price Chinese trousers. It is idiocy, and not just because it is unlike Mandy to come between a British woman and her knickers.

Let me assert this as powerfully as I can: we do not need to fear the Chinese. China will not dominate the globe. We do not need to teach babies Mandarin. Our Sinophobia is misplaced. Even with 1.3 billion people, and fast export-led growth, the Chinese have an economy smaller than Italy's, but that is not really the point. World domination – superpowerdom – is all about hard power and soft power, military might and cultural impact.

Well, compared with the old British Empire, and the new American imperium, Chinese cultural influence is virtually nil, and unlikely to increase. Far from spreading overseas, as the English language has spread, and Hollywood has spread, Chinese culture seems to stay firmly in China.

Indeed, high Chinese culture and art are almost all imitative of western forms: Chinese concert pianists are technically brilliant, but brilliant at Schubert and Rachmaninov. Chinese ballerinas dance to the scores of Diaghilev. The number of Chinese Nobel prizes won on home turf is zero, though there are of course legions of bright Chinese trying to escape to Stanford and Caltech.

There are Chinatowns and takeaways all over the world, but in Britain the culinary impact of China is dwarfed by the subcontinent. The turnover for Chinese restaurants is about £282 million, compared with £2 billion for Indian restaurants. It is hard to think of a single Chinese sport at the Olympics, compared with the umpteen invented by Britain, including ping-pong, I'll have you know, which originated at upper-class dinner tables and was first called whiff-whaff.

The Chinese have a script so fiendishly complicated that they cannot produce a proper keyboard for it. And how many people do you know who can speak even a sentence of Chinese? If global domination means anything, it must mean the spread of culture, language and mores, in the way of the Romans, the British, and the Americans. The Chinese aren't even out of the paddock.

As for military might – hard power – our fears are again overdone. The Chinese may have 2.5 million men in uniform, but of the long-range missiles you need to be a global power Beijing can wield only 20, which would make for a pretty brief fireworks display if they came up against the Americans.

None of this, of course, is in any way intended to be disrespectful to the glories of Chinese culture: only that they are not in any way global or – and this is the point – intended to be global. The Chinese have neither the ability nor the inclination to dominate the world. They merely want to trade freely, and they should be encouraged. The emergence of China and its integration into the world economy has been a major spur to growth and a deterrent to inflation. It is an unalloyed good, and it is sad to see our politicians responding with such chicken-hearted paranoia.

The beginning of hope in the Middle East

But why did he do it? I asked the dark and bony young man in the yarmulka, still clearing up the scene of the murders. We were standing at the blackened steel counter of Shimmi's cheese and olive shop, where three people had yesterday been killed by a suicide bomber and 13 seriously injured. It is a testimony to the vibrancy of the Carmel market, Tel Aviv, that business had resumed at the neighbouring stalls within minutes of the detonation, as though an act of self-destruction and murder by a 16-year-old was as banal as a traffic accident. Shimmi's cheese shop still had ripped awnings and bust fluorescent lights, but fewer than 24 hours later the shop boy was getting ready to open again, and he didn't seem disposed to ponder on my question. 'I cannot imagine why anyone would do that,' he said. So I turned to Ran, my affable minder from the Israeli foreign office. Why did he do it? I repeated, looking at the sinister fatty globules still adhering to the counter.

A Jewish religious organisation called Zaka had been fossicking away for hours, in obedience to the code that says all body parts must be interred; but it was impossible not to speculate about the stains. Amar al-Far was just a kid, one of the youngest suicide bombers ever. What made him leave the Askar refugee camp near Nablus, pass through the Hawara checkpoint, and kill himself and three blameless Israelis, including Leah Levine, 67, a holocaust survivor? How could anyone persuade a child to do something like that?

'He was expecting the 72 Virgins,' said Ran, 'like you have written in your novel.' Flattering though this answer was, it didn't quite work, for me. Maybe it was true that Amar al-Far dimly expected to be cosseted in paradise by the 72 black-eyed ones of scripture, which some authorities say should be correctly identified with raisins rather than virgins. But was that hope really enough to encourage a sentient adolescent to come to a shop and blow himself into a compote of cheese, persimmons and human remains? No one seemed to have the answers in the Carmel market, least of all an old man who – so said that morning's *Jerusalem Post* – had stared at the mayhem and announced, 'It was the pork. It was the pork that brought on our doom.' He meant that the market was being punished for tolerating an outlet as exuberantly non-kosher as the Baboy butchers, two stalls down, which had a picture of a round, pink, beaming, curly-tailed porker, and the advertisement, 'Here we sell fresh pork.' A million Russian Jews have arrived in recent years, and their fondness for 'white steak' causes great offence.

So I left Carmel market with two barmy opinions from the rival theologies: the killings were either inspired by the heavenly promise of 72 peach-bottomed girls, or else by heavenly anger at the consumption of pork; and, since neither seemed adequate, I wanted to go to Nablus, where the kid's parents were saying the most extraordinary things.

The mother was sad, she said, that her child was dead, but the real pity of it was that he had died so young. They should have waited until he was older, she said, before turning him into a suicide bomber. And that was his mother! What kind of sick society is it, in these refugee camps, that a mother could condone the suicide, at any age, of her son?

The trouble with going to Nablus was that it meant giving my nice Israeli handlers the slip, and when I reached the checkpoint I found that I couldn't get in. No way, said an Israeli soldier, unimpressed by all the credentials I could muster, including a new Israeli press pass. The town was closed for an 'operation'; by which it turned out he meant the search for the associates of the suicide bomber, and the customary destruction of his family home – intended to be a deterrent to other families. But as I looked at the Palestinians queuing to get into their own town, waiting to be passed by Israeli troops through the urine-soaked turnstiles, I had an inkling of the frustrations that might produce a cult of suicidal martyrdom. It wasn't the promise of 72 Virgins that drove a young, talented female lawyer to escape from the Occupied Territories to Haifa, a mixed Arab-Israeli town. I don't believe it was the notion of carnal bliss in heaven that made her order lunch in a crowded restaurant, pay for the meal, then stand by a baby's trolley (the suicide bomber manuals always recommend standing up, in buses or restaurants, for the decapitating effect) and blow herself up. It is all about a sense of powerlessness, and rage, and hatred, and a sense of injustice.

And if you want to see the physical embodiment of that injustice, then you must go to the wall, or fence, as the Israelis prefer to call it. The wall/fence now runs for only 200 km of its projected 700 km, and as a security measure it must be rated a triumphant success. In its wall incarnation it is huge, much higher than the Berlin wall, grey and forbidding and covered with wire and watch-towers. But it is a wall only for very short stretches, and just as effective when it appears as an electronic fence, equipped with no anti-personnel devices whatever.

We were shown inside a monitoring station, where young female Israeli soldiers sit staring at the screens and other imaging devices of great complexity (provided, oddly enough, by the French company Alcatel). As soon as the fence is touched the monitoring station is filled with the opening bars of a pop song by Queen. 'Dum dum dum dum,' it goes, 'Another one bites the dust!' Immediately the site flashes on the screen, wherever it is on the 55 km stretch, and within five or six minutes an Israeli army jeep can be on the scene. As a direct result of the wall, say the Israelis, suicide bomb attacks have declined by between 75 and 90 per cent. Even car thefts have declined considerably. The station commander described how one potential bomber had been trying to get round it, and became lost. 'We heard him asking directions,' said the Israeli soldier. That's right: they intercepted his mobile phone call, and pounced. And who can deny that the Israeli government has a perfect right, a duty, to use such means to protect its citizens from the insanity of the suicide bombers? The figures speak for themselves: 126 people died from suicide bombs in March 2002; there was a time when they were happening every week. Yesterday's was only the second in this calendar year. And yet the wall is itself, of course, responsible for inflaming the insanity it attempts to seclude.

Jacob, our gun-toting guide from the Israeli Defence Force, kept explaining what a piece of cake it is if you are an Arab olive farmer, and you want to bring in your olives, half of which are on one side of the fence and half on the other. You just go to the nearest agricultural gate, press the buzzer, and, hey presto, a detachment of friendly Israeli troops shows up to let you through. Jacob's voice dropped confidentially as he informed us that in one case a family of Arabs had proved so trustworthy that the IDF gave the head of the household the key! Could he tell us the name of this family? Alas, no: security reasons.

This sunny analysis was not shared by the Palestinians I later spoke to in the village of Turmus Aiya. There the discussion turned on Israeli shootings, stolen olives and stolen land. As any candid Israeli politician will tell you, there is not the slightest intention to redraw this wall/fence, and remove all its anemone-tentacle protrusions into the West Bank. Those salients enclose large numbers of Israeli settlers, and under any peace map those red-roofed villas close to the 1967 Green Line will remain Israeli. 'The truth is you don't build a fence within your own country; you build a fence between your two countries,' an Israeli MP said, and he was a moderate. Successive Israeli governments – even Barak's – have connived in or encouraged the settlement of territory that the world ascribes to the Palestinians.

Take that injustice, add the fetid conditions in the refugee camps and the brain-washing by Hamas, and you have the conditions for madness and martyrdom. But there is a final reason why the Palestinians are driven to kill themselves, and why the Israelis have created the dreadful expedient of the wall; and that is the abominable leadership of Yasser Arafat, now dying in Paris, who for more than 35 years has taken his people from one disaster to the next.

For a final verdict on the motives of Amar al-Far, the teenage suicide from Nablus, I went to Arafat's compound in Nablus. 'I think he must do that,' said a guard who showed me round. 'They killed his father, they destroy his home. What else can he do? The Israelis destroy everything. They kill old men, women, children. What can we do? We can only stay and wait. Look at this,' he kept saying, pointing to a kind of sculpture park of vehicles, flattened by Israeli tanks in 2002, 'look at this. What would you do? What can a man do?' he said, smacking his brow with his palm; and after a while I'm afraid I grew impatient, and wanted to suggest to him that since the damage had been done more than two years ago, it was time to clear it up.

But that would be to miss the essence of Arafat's approach, which is always to be a martyr. It is meant to be a sad but necessary fact of life that terrorists graduate to the role of statesman: Kenyatta, Begin, McGuinness, and so on – all have made the transition. The most glaring and pathetic global exception has been Yasser Arafat.

To judge by the deals he was offered in 2000, at Camp David and later, he wasn't interested in statesmanship or statehood. He was offered 93 per cent of the West Bank, and a deal on the holy sites of Jerusalem by which Israel would have effectively delegated sovereignty over the Dome of the Rock, rather as an embassy is deemed to be foreign soil. Arafat was offered east Jerusalem, a concession that amounted to political poison for Barak. He had several Palestinian negotiators ready to do a deal, who thought he should. The Israelis were ready, since all sensible Israelis – even Sharon – know that there must be a two-state solution.

There are now 3.5 million Arabs living in the West Bank. Add to those the 1.2 million Israeli Arabs, and you have 4.7 million Arabs living in the whole area. In spite of the huge Russian influx, there are only 5.5 million Jews, and, given the faster Arab rate of reproduction, the Jews face the appalling prospect of shortly being in the position of the white South Africans – a minority race depriving the majority of full civic rights, and ruling that majority by force. It cannot last, and that is why Ariel Sharon is unilaterally pledged to pull out of Gaza. So why did Arafat say no, four years ago, to a much better deal? Why did he launch the second intifada, which has claimed the lives of so many thousands, including the teenage suicide bomber and his victims in Tel Aviv?

He said no, because any such accommodation would have robbed Arafat of his martyr status, and therefore of his power. Throughout his career he was the physical expression of victimhood. With his runty physique, his pendulous lips like a pair of rotting apricots, he has invited sympathy; he has been the epitome of underdoggery and chronic injustice, and it did not suit him to have that role taken away. He has been an egotist and a narcissist who has required his people to adopt the endlessly defeated tones of that guard in Ramallah, so that he could maintain his chosen role as their martyr and leader. He is also a killer, the founder not just of Fatah but of Black September. It was Yasser Arafat's organisation that killed the Israeli athletes at Munich in 1972; Arafat's voice can be heard on a tape, ordering the execution of the US ambassador to Sudan, and others. With one breath he tells English language reporters that he is calling a ceasefire and discouraging suicide bombings; with the next he orders the crazed young men of Palestine to continue their jihad.

It is bizarre, in retrospect, that everyone should have sucked up to him for so long, and that his impending death should move a BBC reporter to tears. Such sentimentality was forgivable in this sense: that behind the mask of a revolutionary eccentric, behind all the crazy demands, we assumed there was a man with a plan, a man who wanted to be at the apex of a set of new political institutions. But instead of being the father of his country, Arafat will die a political juvenile.

It was his tragedy that – as he revealed in 2000 – he had no ambition to make that transition from terrorist martyr to grown-up politician. It was the Palestinians' tragedy that he represented their aspirations for so long. His death comes too late for thousands who have died in the intifada, most of them Palestinians. But his imminent departure brings hope: that Israel will be demographically obliged to renew the Barak offer, and that the Palestinians will find a statesman with the wisdom and authority to accept it.

MANNERS AND MORALS

People tend to tie themselves in knots these days trying to explain what Conservatism is. Are we libertarian, authoritarian, vegetarian or rotarian? Should we be a little bit Rastafarian now and then? Here, in these articles, is how I think we should be: free-market, tolerant, broadly libertarian (though not, perhaps, ultra-libertarian), inclined to see the merit of traditions, anti-regulation, pro-immigrant, pro-standing on your own two feet, pro-alcohol, pro-hunting, pro-motorist and ready to defend to the death the right of Glenn Hoddle to believe in reincarnation.

Alcohol is good for you

'Waiter, my cabernet sauvignon is being drunk by someone else,' said the dark-haired young woman opposite – whose card now reveals her to have been called Carolyn Panzer of the Portman Group of seven big British drinks companies – looking accusingly in my direction. Somehow, by the third course of the lunch given by a new and wonderful society called 'The Case for Moderate Drinking', things had indeed become muddled up.

It is a vintage Strasbourg scene. In an alcove of the members' dining room in the Euro-parliament, the windows have steamed up against the cold air outside. The *huissiers* in their black tail-coats and gold fobs glide about, settling Europe's representatives at table: here a Belgian Green, there a former SS Stormtrooper.

About 20 MEPs, and the half-familiar faces of assorted Euro-consultants and lobbyists, have gathered to celebrate the self-evident proposition that alcohol is good for you. Before us, for starters, is a scrummy *chiffonade de la laitue* with prawns and cooked oysters, garnished with a large indeterminate crustacean.

It had been a hard, dry morning of lectures on the medical evidence supporting 'moderation', here taken to mean consistent but not excessive spending of money on alcohol. Now was the time for the practical. One young blond man's face is so suffused with the '*Bienfaits de la Modération*' that he is the colour of a letterbox.

Now, the *chiffonade de la laitue* could mean anything as far as I am concerned – probably French chef for lettuce leaf. Actually, it turns out to be a delicious sort of patty stuffed with boiled greens. The roar of the company dies a little as the sea creature is broken up and sucked dry, and a toast is drunk to the 1988 chardonnay.

This is also terrific, and has apparently been made by my left-hand neighbour, an energetic, deep-voiced, turtle-faced Californian in his sixties. 'We only make very high quality wines,' he says. 'They have their own style and character, but they have helped to set the pace for wine-making worldwide.'

It suddenly becomes apparent that I am sitting next to a colossus of the wine world, and had better get with it. This is Mr Robert Mondavi, as in Robert Mondavi of the

Napa Valley, California. What, apart from the fame of the members' restaurant, brings him to the Strasbourg Euro-parliament, home of lost causes?

About two years ago, Mr Mondavi became concerned at the neo-puritanism that was sweeping the United States and the world. His father, an Italian American, made his money during prohibition by exporting grape stock all over the United States, so that ordinary householders could ferment their own wine. But those profits were nothing to the serious wine business that Mr Mondavi had conducted in the Napa Valley.

The pinot noir arrives, also made by Mr Mondavi, and we analyse the growing global tide of intolerance. In France, they have just passed the Loi Evin, which restricts advertising to mere representation of the bottle and how the wine was made; the 1990 Mammi law has imposed sponsorship restrictions in Italy, and tighter controls are planned in Spain, Luxembourg, Denmark and Belgium.

This lunch in Strasbourg is the culmination of a world tour to campaign for the right to drink – moderately. 'They are taking away our freedom of choice and expression. We want education, not control,' says Mr Mondavi.

Who are They? Our host intervenes with an amazing fact. This is Mr Peter J. Duff, chairman of the morning's symposium, Director of the Robert Mondavi Alcohol Initiative and European Consultant to the Wine Institute of California. He reveals that the huge financial resources of Saudi Arabia are being poured into the coffers of the growing world temperance lobby.

'The Koran states that the drinking of alcohol is a sin, though you can drink in the next life. They want to destroy alcohol,' he explains. It seems there is evidence of heavy Arab influence in the World Health Organisation, the UN body which last year decreed that world alcohol consumption must fall by 25 per cent. More hatefully yet, the WHO concordat mentions alcohol in the same breath as drugs.

Some Westerners seem to be involved. There is a man called Dr Craplet in Paris, whose name is savoured richly around the table: 'ha ha ha . . . only a little one!' And there is a man called Dr Derek Rutherford, who has drawn up the obnoxious 'Alcohol Charter for Europe'. But Mr Duff points out that they are in a minority. 'Where do they get their money from? If you read the names, these are not European or US names,' he says. They are Arabs . . .

The only way to fight their reverse crusade is with science, and that is why this morning's key speaker has been Dr Agnes Heinz, now sitting two away from me. She is a Director of Nutrition and Biochemistry at the American Council of Science and Health. (Why is it that this sort of job is always done by very good-looking women in their thirties, anthropologists, palaeographers, gorilla experts, etc? Is it some concession to Hollywood?)

Dr Heinz's talk was a piece of scrupulous scientific balance. There was a downside to alcohol, no doubt about it. But the message of hope stood out like a beacon for us all: 'The liver is an enormous recuperative organ . . . moderate drinkers live as long or longer than abstainers . . . alcohol can prevent coronary heart disease.'

What! Alcohol staves off heart attacks? It seemed worth pursuing this with Dr Heinz at lunch, as the Napa Valley Cabernet Sauvignon arrived. Yes, it is true. Researches at Harvard have concluded that those who drink wine have a 25–40 per cent less chance of sustaining a heart attack. In addition to relieving stress, alcohol helps build the vital, life-giving HDL, the High Density Lypoprotein. This is useful in some way, though Dr Heinz smiled bashfully, indicating that I was unlikely to understand exactly how.

Anyone who has seen journalistic colleagues return to their desks after three pints of beer and seven whiskies, and produce perfect copy in 20 minutes, or fellow students taking finals so drunk that they cannot push their spectacles up their noses, will have an instinctive understanding of the benefits of HDL. As she says herself, it is 'multifactorial'. Myself, HDL works the other way. After this particular lunch it produces a contemplativeness so deep that not even the dramas of the Euro-parliament debate can break it.

Riches have become the bad dreams of avarice

Seldom in the history of the British middle classes has there been such unanimous fury. Rarely has this nation known the same degree of moral outrage on the part of the many against the few. In certain quarters, you merely have to breathe the words 'top people's pay', 'share options', 'bonuses', 'executive pension rights', or 'Cedric Brown' to watch your friends' eyes pop in reflexive disgust.

Those who would normally consider themselves enthusiastic supporters of enterprise show the irrational righteousness, on this subject, that one imagines marked the witch-doctors smelling out corruption on behalf of Chaka the Zulu. Wrinkling their noses, they point at the boardrooms of Britain. See, they say, a coterie of mutual backscratchers determined to treat each other right, irrespective of the fate of junior ranks, voting each other stupendous handshakes and pay-offs, even if – sometimes, it seems, *especially* if – the firm is on the verge of ruin.

Almost every day bears new statistics stoking public wrath. Like announcements of wills, the newspapers publish details of what has become known as Boardroom Greed, the noughts streaming across the page: we learn that Lord Alexander of Weedon is to receive a £100,000 bonus from the NatWest Bank, that the executives of the privatised utilities stand to make £100 million, one way or another, among whom one might cite Mr John Baker, chief executive of National Power, who luxuriates in a £675,000 profit on his options.

His voice quivering with Calvinist contempt, Gordon Brown, Shadow Chancellor, bangs on the same point, day in, day out. City editors fulminate against the practices. Committees are set up to wring their hands over the question. Former Tory MPs such as Sir Anthony Beaumont-Dark warn the Government that the level of anger now eclipses that felt against the unions in the 1970s. If any issue has cooked the Tory goose at the next election, we are told by pollsters, this is it.

So against this tide of collective hysteria, is it not urgent that someone should take a stand? My friends, I appeal for calm. I appeal for logic.

Perhaps there is a legitimate case for discontent with the actions of the privatised utilities. It is hard to deny the general perception that men like Cedric Brown, the chairman of British Gas, have been able to swell their pay packets by becoming monopoly purveyors of life's essentials, while reducing costs by sacking thousands of employees. But this self-enrichment by a handful of utility barons has, in the view of the public, contaminated the motives and reputations of everyone earning more than £100,000. Or shall we say £50,000? Where does it end?

At the risk of an excessively colourful comparison, one is reminded of the rage whipped up by Stalin against the kulaks. Hardly anyone, not even Left-wing charities, escapes in this great smelling-out of perks and privileges. Yesterday, we learnt that Mr Pierre Sane, the rather underpaid francophone boss of Amnesty International, was in trouble with his subordinates for receiving an extra £3,000 per year for keeping his children in French-speaking education in London.

What has come over us? Are we experiencing some kind of communist backlash? Are the Levellers abroad again? If I asked you: 'Is there anything wrong with making money?' you would say: 'No, of course not, don't be so silly: it all depends *how much* money, and how you make it.'

But no matter how many Greenbury Committees the City sets up to study the question, there remains only one way of settling how much executives are worth and that is to leave it to the market. These people are, by definition, worth what they are paid, no more and no less. Even in the case of the privatised utilities, gas, water and electricity, where the market is rigged, you cannot entirely blame Cedric and his kind for their remuneration. They are there to make money for the shareholders. Provided they achieve that, it will be in their genetic make-up, as businessmen, to take their chance to squirrel something away in advance of what now appears the inevitable victory of Tony Blair and Labour at the next election. If anyone is to blame for high salaries in the utilities companies, it is the regulators, men like Professor Stephen Littlechild, and the Government, who, deliberately or not, underestimated their profitability.

Blaming Cedric is like getting angry with a dog for wanting to chase rabbits. And think it possible, gentle reader, that Cedric and his kind may be doing some good. When they rise before dawn to spend their long day thinking about making biscuits or selling gas, we cannot exclude the fact that these chief executives are adding value to their companies. It is understandable, in a way, this middle-class urge to scratch your neighbour's Rolls-Royce. It has spread with the recession, among those in the negative equity trap, who have been forced to take their children out of prep school, who have felt the pinch at Lloyd's. What goads them most is the disparity between, for instance, the pay rise of 173.7 per cent for Mr Keith Orrell-Jones of Blue Circle, and the 21.5 per cent for the company's staff. As Incomes Data Services testifies, the gap between the incomes of chief executives and middle management has widened fast in 1979 to 1995. Managers' pay went up 409 per cent, chief executives' 645 per cent.

In its spleen, middle-income Britain has fallen for an absurd redistributive fallacy, as if lopping a few noughts off Lord Alexander's bonus could make a difference to NatWest's customers. We seem to have forgotten that societies need rich people, even sickeningly rich people, and not just to provide jobs for those who clean swimming pools and resurface tennis courts.

If British history had not allowed outrageous financial rewards for a few top people, there would be no Chatsworth, no Longleat. The stately homes of England would never have been built, nor much great art commissioned. There would be no Nuffield Trust. Yes! Had a certain Quaker family not profited enormously from making chocolate there would be no Rowntree Foundation ... The point, surely, needs no labouring.

In the same way, and to make the face of his particular brand of capitalism acceptable, Cedric might in time sponsor a poetry prize, or endow a professorship in physics. Perhaps he will. Let us keep our fingers crossed. In the meantime, though, we should avoid confusing a genuine moral affront with the politics of envy.

Rights and Duties

One sometimes wonders whether the fire has died in the belly of the Parliamentary Labour Party. One wonders how they can contain themselves, those ex-miners, those shop stewards, those thin-lipped lawyers, as they watch Tony Blair drift off to the Right in search of Tory raiment. He has sent his son to a grant-maintained school. He has rewritten the sacred text of the Labour Party. He has given a lecture sponsored by the *Spectator* in which he banged on about Responsibility with a capital R. Yet from the Labour Left we hear not a squeak of protest. They appear to have lost the power of speech.

Perhaps it is just that they are content to watch the media chew again the supermasticated question of whether or not a change of leader might increase Tory chances of winning the next election. Perhaps they feel they need only wait for power to drop into their laps. Or perhaps there is a further reason why Labour's rank and file bite their tongue: that they can't quite believe their luck. The Left, I would guess, is secretly astounded at how the middle class, and especially the Right-wing media, have allowed themselves to be gulled by the new Labour leader.

Just listen to the credulous yippees of these last few days. Blair is applauded on all sides for apparently resuscitating Duty. He is said to be dragging Labour away from the idea of what we think society owes us, and back to the Victorian concept of what we jolly well ought to do by way of mucking in. All hail 'Responsibilitarianism'! Someone the other day suggested that Blair's moralising approach evoked Lady Thatcher. Well, we may all be forgiven for hungering for a change of government. And we hacks are professionally obliged to come up with paradoxical headlines, such as Blair is the New Thatcher or Freddie

Starr Ate My Hamster. But it breaks my heart that we should acquiesce so happily in our own deception.

Consider more closely Blair's new Clause Four formulation, that 'the rights we enjoy reflect the duties we owe'. This is suggestively phrased. Blair appears to imagine a sequence of nice equations, beginning with 'Your right to life: your duty not to kill' and continuing through 'Your right to chew gum: your duty not to stick it under the seat', and so forth. In fact, the balance between rights and duties is rather different. These days a 'right' is usually a legal entitlement, often costing taxpayers' money. Duties, on the other hand, are thought of as moral obligations, but with no compulsion attached other than the prickings of conscience. Rights and duties may sprout together, as Blair seemingly believes, like dock leaves and nettles. But it is not too obvious to point out that modern Britons are much keener to avail themselves of their rights than they are to perform their supposedly corresponding duties, just as they are keener, broadly speaking, to handle a dock leaf than a nettle. Smokers frequently prefer their right to light up to their duty to the health of others. Sufferers from ingrown toenails, as we discussed recently on this page, are sometimes quicker to exercise their right to call an ambulance than to think about their duty to those in genuine emergency. Some of the unemployed would put their right to benefit ahead of their duty to look for work.

The paradox and shame is that this rights-first culture has been greatly encouraged under the Tories. Contrary to its rhetoric, this government has presided over an explosion of rights and entitlements of all kinds; not just more spending on old entitlements, but on new entitlements as well. One might cite the Children Act of 1989, which gave children rights against their parents. One might mention the Disability Discrimination Bill, which the Tories brought forward in January, with its destructive costs for industry. One might mention, as a specimen charge, Mr Major's decision to update Child Benefit even for the richest families. Overall, the budget of the welfare state has risen by an astonishing 75 per cent *in real terms* since 1979. No wonder the Tory Right is furious and disappointed with Tory rule, and wishes it would end. The wretched truth, though, is that Labour, at least in this respect, would be far worse.

Tony Blair may have reintroduced Labour to 'duty', but he cannot ignore Labour's constituent interests, who remain dedicated to expanding 'rights' of all kinds. Not even Mr Blair has been able to erode the unions' conviction that we all have a 'right' to a minimum wage. Mr Blair is also fully committed, the instant he reaches Downing Street, to accepting the detailed entitlements of the European Social Charter: minimum holidays, minimum weekly rests, paternity leave.

Both the minimum wage and the Social Charter would palpably destroy jobs. And what is Labour's answer to unemployment? Everyone with an interest in the pressures impending on Prime Minister Blair should read *Tribune*, the organ of the Labour Left. In this week's issue Mr Roger Berry, Labour MP for Bristol Kingswood, has a wheeze for promoting the 'right' to work. He has worked out that to devise employment for each of the one million long-term unemployed, perhaps in fretwork or making macramé placemats, would cost a mere £20,000 per head. That is 'only' £20 billion on the budget, says Mr Berry, who is *Tribune*'s economics correspondent.

Labour will scrap the few improvements that the Tories have made to the welfare state, such as the Jobseeker's Allowance, which is intended to prevent people remaining in the dole queue without trying to get a job. Labour will abandon Tory efforts to build up private pensions, exposing future taxpayers to the crippling cost of paying for our old age.

Worst of all, Mr Blair's concept of 'duty' is, on careful analysis, perverse. Far from leaving responsibility to individual volition, he appears to want local authorities to have more powers to interfere, over noisy radios, dangerous dogs or truant children. That is not duty; it is legislative coercion, and a familiar Labour nostrum. Sitting in their ranks behind Blair, Labour MPs know that this new talk of duties is merely covering fire for the extension of rights, and, consequently, spending. Hence their ominous complacency.

The rest of us, meanwhile, should realise that sand is being thrown in our eyes. The way to improve British society is not to attempt to enforce 'duty' through new and interfering legislation. It is to take the billhook to the great accreted thicket of expensive and often universal rights and entitlements.

Thoughts on the ruin of Aitken

In ancient Greece they liked to curse the 'origin of evil', that seemingly innocuous event that started the ineluctable chain of causation that led to the downfall of some great man, the beginning of some war. Woe, woe, the chorus cries in Greek tragedy. If only Argo had never been built, Medea would never have killed her children. If only Paris had never stolen Helen, Achilles and Hector would still be alive, and thousands of doughty heroes with them.

Woe, cries the chorus of Tory elders, as they behold the awful comeuppance of Jonathan Aitken and the Tory party; if only Michael Howard – or, more accurately, his junior, Charles Wardle – had not shown such scruples; if only Mohamed Fayed and his brother Ali had been given British passports!

For then the owner of Harrods would never have gone to the *Guardian* with his tawdry tales, the Tories would never have been cursed with 'sleaze', Tim Smith would still be MP for Beaconsfield, poor Sir Robin Butler, the man who 'cleared' Aitken, would not have so much egg on his face, Neil Hamilton would not have been exposed as an alleged handler of brown envelopes, Christine Hamilton would not be a housewife superstar, Cash for Questions would have been a pilot quiz game, Ian Greer the lobbyist would still be plying his merry trade at Westminster, the children of Britain would not be having nightmares about Peter Mandelson coming to get them if they don't eat up their greens, and dear, dear John Major . . . John Major would still be in power!

The Tories would have won the election! Thrice woe. If only the Tories had not crossed Fayed, the wrathful merchant of Alexandria, groan the chorus, the Tories might have escaped the Pharaoh's revenge, the tragedy might have been averted. Such is the counterfactual history of the past few years. Yet one has only to put it that way to feel uneasy.

Suppose it were possible that the great Tory disaster was not determined in other ways. Even if we could go back in time, pacify Fayed, snuff out 'sleaze', would that have been any better? The trouble with counterfactual history – in spite of the fascinating new book by my erstwhile colleague Niall Ferguson – is that it so often seems to rob events of pattern, proportion and symmetry.

To abolish the wrath of Fayed would have been cheating, tampering with what in retrospect can be seen to be a perfect historical cycle. There is something in the story of Aitken, and, yes, of the Tories, that is both vastly suggestive and comforting. Take Aitken first.

It is a plot that has everything: brilliant, engaging Old Etonians, exotic Yugoslav heiresses, illegal arms exports; television stations; Cabinet red boxes – the sensation is scarcely dimmed by the fact that Mr Aitken lost Thanet South at the last election – all thrown away in a full-blooded, old-fashioned *ruin* of 19th-century proportions, and now a proper Lucanesque flight from the country aboard a private jet, it seems, to fool the tabloid papers, with Inspector Knacker of the Yard already puffing in pursuit. The last we heard of the tall, pin-striped former Chief Secretary to the Treasury, he was in 'the Americas'. One imagines that reporters are even now paddling up the Orinoco or quizzing the suspiciously well-spoken short-order chef in San Diego, California; and now news reaches us, perhaps brought in a cleft stick by some piccaninny from the steaming Mato Grosso, that he has resigned from the Privy Council. And we nod. It could not have been otherwise. It *should* not have been otherwise.

This was a man, as it will be pointed out ever after, who was willing to put his innocent teenage daughter in the dock, to ask her to perjure herself, and thereby to put her very liberty at risk. We may not think him quite as 'despicable' as the editor of the *Guardian* claims to do. But there is a touch of Darius Guppy about him, to take an example from my own generation, a Walter Mittyish refusal to face up to reality, and an inability to sort out right from wrong. Let us put the best possible construction on events in the Paris Ritz on Friday, September 17, 1993.

The most favourable explanation is that it was all On Her Majesty's Secret Service. It was all – wink, wink – in the national interest. The defence procurement minister needed to be alone with the chaps in tarbooshes because a certain Levantine touch was required, which might have shocked his Private Secretary at the MoD. Mr Aitken might try some such explanation if and when he returns. It won't wash. At the very least he was in breach of ministerial guidelines, to say nothing of the allegations that he attempted to procure prostitutes from among the good ladies of Kintbury, or the question of what he did or did not know about the arms exports of Bmarc to unsavoury places in the Middle East.

Like all tragic figures, Aitken was the author of his own downfall, and like most tragic figures, there was at least an initial dash of greatness, if not quite of heroism. Aitken may not have been a particularly brilliant Chief Secretary to the Treasury. But he was a man of considerable attainments, the author of a book on Nixon fat enough to mend a broken bedspring, possessor of some fancy houses in Lord North Street and in Kent. With his status went hubris.

Here was a man so sure of himself that he was prepared to stick his head in the lion's mouth of a libel action against the *Guardian*. It was the madness, the Ate, of those whom the gods wish to destroy. As Dr Robin Kirk, the principal of the Inglewood health hydro, said: 'I think he's slightly insane, he doesn't follow the normal behaviour of people like you and I would do.'

Then, inevitably, came peripeteia, or reversal, that shattering moment when he read the docket produced by the British Airways investigator, Wendy Harris, which proved that his wife was in the wrong city, like the moment when Oedipus discovers what he has known all along, that he married his mother. And then there was nemesis, flight, ruin, the national nodding over the cornflakes, the sense that the will of the gods has been fulfilled, the fear and pity excited in the populace by the spectacle of this great crash. Bent is the bough that might have grown full straight, we mutter to ourselves, and withered is Apollo's laurel bough, as we put down the newspaper and ask our wives to pass the marmalade.

And what is that feeling, that tiny smug satisfaction? It

is catharsis: the sense of cleansing, purging, of rightness, a smaller version of the same emotion that so many in this country seem to have felt at the end of the 18-year cycle of Tory rule. After the heroic achievements of the early years came the arrogance of too long in office, the slip-ups, the 'sleaze', until, even among those who accepted intellectually that the Tories had the best case to govern, there was such a yearning for them to leave the stage that on the night of May 1 the brutal forces of democracy smashed the Tories so violently that even Labour supporters may have felt some sympathy for John Major. In the morning came the feel-good factor, otherwise known as catharsis.

That is the basic drama of politics. Politics is a constant repetition, in cycles of varying length, of one of the oldest myths in human culture, of how we make kings for our societies, and how after a while we kill them to achieve a kind of rebirth – as Tony Blair would put it, new life for Britain. Some of the kings are innocent; indeed, some of them take away the sins of the world. Some of them are less innocent, like Mr Aitken. It doesn't really matter. They must die.

Moments of moral choice

You're in the car with your secretary after a party and trying to effect a ticklish exit from your parking place when, damn it, you bump the car ahead. Some bawling French brat has been squashed in his pram and his father's cutting up rough. You're a former Tory minister and you foresee all the embarrassment of being breathalysed, and suddenly, though you perhaps don't realise it, you're in one of those positions where you've got to do the right thing.

You must work out in a flash whether it is more sensible to stay and face the consequences, or whether it might not be quite as prudent, since you can see that the kid is perfectly all right, to drift off down the pavement. In that instant, the depths of your character stand to be exposed. Depending on how you behave, a lifetime's cultivation of respectability can be made to seem hollow.

Looking back afterwards in shame at these moments of moral apocalypse, we can all work out what we should have done. If we had our time again, we would not hesitate. The lucky ones are those who can spot the ball early, who can see at once that they are in a genuine left-or-right, yes-or-no moment of moral choice, without having the position pointed out to them afterwards by the press: 'You liar! You coward!' The lucky ones also divine instantly that a cover-up will be impossible.

It takes skill to recognise these moments, because the decisions, when they are required, are required with such urgency. It is difficult to keep a clear head when you've driven off the bridge at Chappaquiddick in the middle of the night, and the water is closing around your head and you have to order your priorities: save self; save pretty blonde co-passenger? And you then have to work out whether to deny all knowledge of Mary-Jo Kopechne in the hope of protecting your political career, or whether to do the right thing and come clean.

These decisions take skill, also, because most of us have so little practice. Contrary to the impression given by various theories of moral philosophy, modern urban life is not an endless series of bifurcations between right and wrong. We might waver for a second or two before chucking a pound coin to a man selling the *Big Issue*. But perhaps because of the giant apparatus of state control and welfare that cushion our society, most of us, thankfully, find it hard to remember the last serious moral dilemma we faced.

Indeed, the drama of Sir Nicholas Scott, the former Minister for the Disabled, is really the stuff of fiction. In essential respects the episode resembles the famous opening scene of Tom Wolfe's *The Bonfire of the Vanities* (which itself owes something to *The Great Gatsby*). For the embarrassment of the former Tory minister and his secretary, read the agonies of Sherman McCoy, the Master of the Universe (Tom Wolfe's hero), and his female companion, and the little accident in the Bronx that transforms their lives. In fact, these moments of revelatory moral choice are so rare that they sometimes have to be confected by those who wish to dig out the underlying character. One thinks of the cash-for-questions affair, in which MPs faced an artificial dilemma offered by the *Sunday Times*.

It is because these moments are so rare – or at least so rarely come to light – that they are so illuminating and important. What the inquiry by Lord Justice Scott tells us above all is that even the most experienced Cabinet minister can be prone to the same mad self-delusion as Teddy Kennedy or Sherman McCoy: that they can do the wrong thing and get away with it.

For any of the Cabinet ministers concerned, the moment of crisis, of decision, may have come like this: he is sitting up late doing his red boxes at home, his eyes pricking with fatigue and the whisky not helping, deciding whether or not to sign these curious papers, these Public Interest Immunity Certificates. He knows that both options are bad. If he allows certain documents to be produced in court, that will expose embarrassing modulations in the Government's embargo against Iraq.

On the other hand, if he signs the 'gagging order', he must know that he will be frustrating justice and that innocent men may go to jail. That is the choice at the heart of the Scott Inquiry. Never mind the sophistries of Mr William Waldegrave who, admittedly, seems to have produced an odd syllogism: 1) All change in policy on Iraq must be approved by Downing Street. 2) Downing Street did not approve the change of policy. 3) Therefore there was no change of policy.

At the end of all this, I would guess we are likely to forgive Waldegrave, who took a First in Greats and knows about Wittgenstein, for saying there can be a change which is not a change. Most reasonable people would accept that on sensitive matters of Middle East policy the entire diplomatic minuet need not be played out on the floor of the Commons. No, the moral dynamite is in the question whether Mr Henderson and his fellow directors of Matrix Churchill should have been faced with jail to spare the blushes of the British Government.

Unlike Sir Nicholas Scott on the pavement, these ministers had plenty of time to think. The amazing thing is that – and I should be surprised if this is contradicted by Lord Justice Scott's final report – they all, in varying degree, flunked the test, Clarke, Garel-Jones, Rifkind, Lilley, Baker. Heseltine may have shown the sharpest appreciation that this was a moral dilemma (or rather, that it would look terrible if it got out), an occasion for thinking ahead, and thinking straight. But even he signed the gagging orders.

What is even more amazing is what these ministers now say in mitigation: 'Lyell told me to sign it.' 'It was for the judge to make the decision to waive the certificates, not the minister.' There may be other excuses for the actions of these £65,000-per-year decision makers, with their vast powers of regulation, their armies of civil servants to do their bidding; these people whose entire profession and expertise is to select options not just for themselves but for millions of others. But they cannot say that they had no choice.

Who'd want to be a Tory MP these days?

You have to wonder why anyone should want to replace them, these great men now giving up their seats. Hurd, Baker, Renton, Biffen, Walden; yes, and more widely across the Tory benches, it is as if the old boys are waking up with a start, glancing at their watches and realising they have been there for about 25 years, and Good Lord! it is time to collect their K and make way for a younger person. As local Conservative associations begin casting around for candidates, one ponders the unceasing miracle of the party's regeneration.

For it is a miracle that anyone should want to embark on the struggle to power, with that rather expensive weekend at the Slough Marriott with a hundred other keenies wearing their names on their lapel badges, there to be catechised by the examining panel for the slightest sign of Euroscepticism, and thence, assuming you pass, to begin the humiliating crawl towards the Palace of Westminster. It is a common prejudice in that building that there has been no worse time in Parliament's history to try to become an MP, and not just because of the Conservatives' likely fate at the next election.

'There's no money,' says George Walden, who has just issued a fairly dyspeptic explanation for his reasons for standing down at the next election. By 'no money' he means that the salary stays at a measly £32,000 per year, and one sees his point. 'There's no sex,' he goes on; by which he means not just no illicit sex, but not even blameless difficulty with girls, not with impunity.

Listen to Walden, O ye generation of thrusters. Heed him well. Your private life will indeed be taken away from you and pushed back through your letterflap one morning in the italicised innuendo and non-sequiturs of journalism.

As a result of this drip-drip-drip denigration, the public now conceives there is something ribald in the very concept of a male Tory MP. 'People don't respect you as much as they used to,' says one member Eeyoreishly. 'It used to be something to be an MP. Oh! An MP! Best table in the restaurant, that kind of thing. Now they just snigger.'

You must resign yourself to inhuman patterns of work, small offices, sometimes overbearing secretaries, a phenomenal mortality rate, almost certainly assisted by beer and boredom. Under a rule devised in 1885, debates continue after dinner until ten o'clock, and, indeed, sometimes last all night. The job, in general, is increasingly like being an MEP without the travel, or the Strasbourg food.

And at the end of it all, my friend, you must prepare for failure. All political careers end in tears, said Enoch Powell. He might have added that a good many parliamentary careers hardly get going. It is a regular complaint that there is no such person in Britain as a successful non-ministerial parliamentarian. Apart from Bill Cash, Frank Field and one or two others, few backbenchers establish themselves as independent figures, respected for their mastery of a certain issue. Therefore, you must spend years oiling up to the whips, in the hope of securing a Red Box, or even attaining the bogus rank of PPS; and heaven help you, as Geo. Walden points out, if you show anything approaching independence of thought.

Consider Mr Iain Duncan-Smith, one of the brightest of the 1992 intake. Because Mr Major continues to punish this sage for his doubts about the Common Market, and has refused to promote him to ministerial office, Mr Duncan-Smith is likely to have to wait until the party gets back into office – in, what? five, ten years? – before he has a sniff of power.

Did someone mention power? Hah. Above all, at least according to the Walden analysis, the job has shrunk.

Britain is relatively poorer, and less important in the councils of nations. Power is seeping away from the House of Commons. The sovereignty of parliament is now disputed with the judiciary, and above all with Brussels; which may explain why so many Tory MPs have fastened on 'Europe', as an object of resentment.

When Patrick Cormack stands up to talk about Bosnia, he is heard respectfully, with only the most discreet rolling of the eyes. But no one believes that it matters much what he says. The continent of Europe does not hang on the words of a British MP, as it did when Gladstone took a dim view of human rights abuses in Naples or Athens. Far from twanging their braces and surveying the horizon, MPs complain that they are treated as glorified social workers. 'My constituents ask me about their marriages? What am I supposed to do about their marriages?' says Eeyore. To cap it all, Lord Nolan now hovers over everything like some puritanical bird of prey, ready to snatch the tiniest crumb of financial consolation from their lips.

Why, to repeat our original question, would anyone want to do it? There are many layers of gratification. There is vanity. In almost all of these MPs, I think, though, there is at least a tiny grit of an instinct to public service. Probably most of us should be gently dissuaded from becoming an MP, just as we should be dissuaded from writing a novel. But, as with writing a novel, there is a thousand to one chance that you will hit the jackpot. There is a chance that you will have a role, like Mrs Thatcher, or Norman Tebbit, or Nigel Lawson, in briefly shaping the destiny of the nation. The only place to do that is in the upper reaches of government.

That is why beneath them, as they prepare to depart, Cranley Onslow, John Biffen and the rest can already hear the drumming roar of Young Men in a Hurry, desperate to take their places. We are fortunate, in a way, that so many relatively good people are prepared to risk the tears and disillusion with which their careers will undoubtedly end.

The nation is lucky that so many relatively bright people will not be happy unless they are able to haul themselves to their feet at 3.15 on a Tuesday, with the square eyes of a select band of BBC2 viewers upon them, their pate burnished by Trumpers, waistcoat flatteringly tailored, and say, 'May I ask my Rt Hon. friend to what he attributes his great gifts of leadership?' That is still an honourable ambition. Without politicians, after all, there would be no political journalism.

Killing deer to save them

All the warning we had was a crackling of the alder branches that bend over the Exe, and then the stag was upon us. I can see it now, stepping high in the water, eyes rolling, tongue protruding, foaming, antlers streaming bracken and leaves like the hat of some demented old woman, and behind it the sexual, high-pitched yipping of the dogs. You never saw such a piteous or terrible sight.

In that instant we would have done anything to help the stag get away. I think we vaguely shouted and flapped our arms, but too late. In a trice, the stag had been brought to bay by the hounds, almost at our feet in the meadow. And then a man with an ancient-looking pistol, a bit like a starting gun, blammed it in the head and they cut it open in a kind of laparotomy.

I remember the guts steaming, and stag turds spilling out on to the grass from within the ventral cavity. Then they cut out the heart and gave it to my six-year-old brother, still beating, he claimed ever afterwards, or still twitching, and he went dancing home singing: 'We've got the heart! We've got the heart!' So we cooked it up with a bit of flour, and the German *au pair* girl left the next day.

No, you don't need to tell me that hunting with hounds is cruel. We don't need some report by scientists to show that the animals suffer 'stress'. No one looking at that deer could deny that this was a sentient being in the extremity of suffering. This wasn't the stopping of some Cartesian clock. This was savagery, and that is the case for banning hunting, stated as forcefully as I can – and it isn't enough.

When the 80,000 or so marchers for the preservation of country sports arrive in Hyde Park tomorrow, they will have my support, and I think Labour is mad, after its enormous success in winning over so many former Tories, to make an enemy of such a large slice of rural Britain by going ahead with a ban.

You may think it odd to take this line, having been exposed to the full horror of a kill and never having hunted myself; and, indeed, some of the pro-hunting points seem weak. There is the argument from inconsistency, which says that every day we kill thousands of cows in wretched circumstances, and moreover this fellow Mike Foster, the MP for Worcester tabling the Bill, is a competition angler, who yanks hooks out of the cheeks of fish, and the faster he yanks, the better he does. Why should he ban hunting? Such a ban, the argument runs, would lift but a pebble from the mountain of man's inhumanity to dumb brutes. As so often with arguments from inconsistency, this is not quite the knock-out point it seems. Just because we are unable to stop all cruelty to animals, this is no reason why we shouldn't be able to stop some. Medicine cannot end all human pain. That is no reason to abandon medicine.

Then there is the argument from tradition. Hunting has

been going on for a long time, part of the warp and woof, says this argument. You can be in some hellhole hotel, the Khyber Pass Marriott, and, like Stephen Glover's, your eye can alight on a hunting print in the breakfast room, and suddenly you're bathed in Rupert Brookeish emotion about a body of England breathing English air, washed by the rivers and warmed by the sun of home. Well, that is good as far as it goes. But then plenty of traditions have been dispensed with: slavery; male-only suffrage; absolute monarchy; and you'd have to be pretty reactionary to want them back.

And then there are some good arguments for keeping hunting. There is the simple argument from liberty. This is an ancient freedom. To take away people's freedom to do something they have always done is serious; and when it appears that hunting is to be banned by those who have no standing in the matter, the New Labour types who want to 'make a statement' about the kind of Britain they believe we should live in, without any thought for the effect on rural employment, or point-to-points, or gymkhanas, or tourism, then it is an odious interference.

And it is especially odious when, as so often, the antis do not really appear to be actuated by concern for the animals, but by disgust that people should enjoy hunting, mixed in with a healthy dash of class prejudice. If you want evidence that this is largely about class, look at the proposed Labour amendment to protect footpacks – which still rend the fox in pieces – but ban the toffs in pink.

The argument from liberty alone would probably be enough to make me want to keep hunting. But it is not the strongest argument for protecting the Devon and Somerset staghounds – and I pick the staghounds because those are the ones I have observed the closest and which are, in the popular imagination, even more brutal than the fox-hounds. The best argument in favour of keeping them is that hunting is best for the deer, as Dick Lloyd, the historian of Exmoor's deer, has shown. Ted Hughes set out the case beautifully last week.

The number of deer has fluctuated over the past 350 years in direct correlation to the success of the hunt. From early times, the deer were protected for baronial hunts, and the chief threat came from the resentful Saxon farmers. The deer population flourished until the Civil War, when the hunt's protection was removed, and by 1660 the red deer was almost extinct in the West Country.

After the Civil War, the hunt was revived under the auspices of the North Devon staghounds and recovered to about 200 deer. When the North Devon staghounds folded in 1825, the deer population again collapsed, falling to about 50 by 1850, most of them peppered with gunshot. And then the Devon and Somerset Staghounds was set up.

Farmers took part in the hunt, the staghunt became part of the farming way of life, and the deer were systematically protected. Since then, North Devon and Somerset have become a kind of free-range deer park, and the population of red deer has climbed to 2,500 according to the 1995 census, far more than ever before. When the huntsmen say that the population would fall dramatically if the hunt were abolished, that seems demonstrable on the evidence of history. Deer are already shot by farmers. If they were no longer valuable for a hunt, they would simply become pests which could be turned into meat. They would go.

Another time we were up on the moor and we came across the hunt, the cars parked up against the hedges. Standing on the roof we saw the deer, its coat more blond than red in the sun, going fast and well ahead of the hounds. We cheered as it jumped one hedge, and then another and then we saw it still going fast towards the sea, antlers disappearing over the brow of the hill. After-wards we found out that the stag had indeed escaped, and we were thrilled. But that did not mean we were against the hunt. Apart from anything else, without the hunt, there might be no deer.

Why Tony worships in the Temple of gammon

My hand hovered above the leg of lamb. In that instant, I had a sickening sense of what I was doing. Here I was, in Sainsbury's in Taunton, preparing to buy a leg of lamb from a supermarket. There, in the chilled meat section, round about aisle three, my conscience convulsed, and it hit me that only the previous evening I had been vowing, *vowing* to myself, never to buy meat from a supermarket again.

The night before, I had been on the roof of Exmoor, listening to a farmer who had been driven to the desperate extremity of shooting his sheep rather than lose money trying to sell them. He had been hammered by the madness of the BSE regulations. Pork and beef were in such super-abundance that the market for lamb was in free-fall.

And above all, he and his fellow hill farmers were being imperially screwed by the cartel of the big supermarkets: Sainsbury's, Tesco, Asda, Somerfield, Safeway. These five now sell some 70 per cent of meat in Britain. Their buyers call the shots in the livestock industry, inciting farmers to join their 'producers' clubs' and then using their domi-nance, as the only buyers, to drive down the price.

That haunch of cling-wrapped meat, which I had so glibly thought to slam in the trolley for Sunday lunch, and which J Sainsbury was offering to sell me for £7.45: how much had J Sainsbury paid the poor suicidal producer?

About an eighth of that amount. The supermarkets and their agents are now buying lamb for 76.5p per kilo, and selling it for £8.01 per kilo. In the 50th year of their existence, the supermarkets have become commercial and political bully-boys. They control agriculture. They dictate what we buy, and where we buy it. No politician dare stand in their way.

With their amazing distribution systems, the supermarkets are forcing British vegetable growers to go toe to toe with sub-Saharan Africa. When Cornish farmers came up with some perfectly delicious but yellowish cauliflower, the supermarket cauliflower chiefs said No, and 100 acres were ploughed back into the soil. Assisted by the *laissez faire* policies of successive governments, the supermarkets have built their great brick cathedrals outside town centres. Bustling butchers and grocers have been replaced by slot machine joints, frequented by forbidding youths. The market-place, the forum, the agora, the centre of every community since civilisation began, has been ripped out and transplanted to a car park in the middle of nowhere. Employment, inevitably, is reduced; and to cap it all, they are ripping us off.

Staple foods are 20 per cent more expensive in British supermarkets than in France; and a German professor yesterday revealed how a representative sample of 38 products from Tesco in Cambridge was 55 per cent more expensive than in a local grocer's in Kassel, Germany. All these thoughts, or at least some of them, flashed through my mind as the hand hovered above the chill cabinet.

And then I looked at my watch, and realised, Good Lord, that I had to pick my family up from the station in 10 minutes. In went that leg of lamb, and then, let me tell you, I gave that trolley some welly. In the space of about seven minutes I bought £83 worth of food and wine, took the tricky corner between household cleaners and babycare with all the ruthless daring of Schumacher on the Monaco hairpin, screeched through the chequered flag of the checkout, and had I not been in such a rush, I might have reflected that supermarkets, in a hotly contested field, excite the British to their highest pitch of humbug and hypocrisy.

Of course we hate them, in a way, for what they do to farmers and to town centres. But deep down, we love them, too. We love them for being so quick, so handy. We love the way we can shop on Sunday in these temples of gammon, marvelling at the 20,000 exciting lines that are now stocked in major stores. Maybe there really are some people who yearn for shopping as it was in the old days, when mothers and their children would spend Saturday fighting their way out of the old-fashioned, overcrowded butcher's and into the pullulating haberdasher's.

Maybe it would be lovely to go back to the age I dimly remember, when shopkeepers knew their clients, and gossip was exchanged, and there was a sense of community. The trouble is, there is just no evidence that this is what we really want. No sooner is a supermarket built, than people cynically desert their wheezing old grocer, and take to their cars. The supermarket question, in short, encapsulates the central dilemma of modern politics.

When Nicholas Ridley and John Gummer gave permission for the out-of-town shopping centres, they were following one of the two contradictory strands of Tory thought: the instinct to let the market rip, to let people decide how to run their lives, to give them choice. What they neglected was the classic Tory concern for the old way of doing things, for the little platoons, for communities. It is an unresolved tension.

We cannot disinvent the supermarket, and would not if we could. All we can say is that there are aspects of their current dominance which are legitimate political concerns.

They should *not* be allowed to crush small farmers by using their cartel strength to drive down the price at which they buy; and they should *not* be allowed to rip us off by inflating the price at which they sell. The Office of Fair Trading has shown what they are up to. Will the Government act?

Will it hell. It is a measure of Blair's opportunism that before the election, Labour policy was to be generally against new shopping centres. To the dismay of Frank Dobson and Michael Meacher, there was then a meeting in Blair's office, organised by John Mendelson, one of his advisers, and the supermarket barons. Labour policy on shopping centres 'matured' to a studied neutrality. Mr Mendelson has now left Mr Blair's office to set up the LLM lobbying company, briefly hitting the headlines during the Dolly Draper lobbygate affair, and numbers Tesco among his clients.

Tesco has given many millions to the Millennium Dome. Lord Sainsbury of Turville is a generous private donor to Labour, and is now a government minister. Somerfield sponsored the dog tags at the Labour Party conference. Labour has all but completed the selling of its soul to big business; and here, one would have thought, is a theme for William Hague and the Tories.

It is not simply a question of bashing the supermarkets, but of sticking up for the consumer, and for rural Britain. It is helping the underdog. It is the British way. Who better to lead the attack than the chairman of Asda and deputy chairman of the Tory party? Come on, Archie. Never mind the profits. Think of the people.

Call to raise the speed limit

Have you ever driven very fast on a motorway? I have. As the motoring correspondent of *GQ* magazine, I have sometimes attained velocities which are incompatible with my new status as a tribune of the people.

Not so long ago, I found myself at the wheel of a Ferrari Maranello Testadicazzo, or some such name, whose dashboard boasted it to be capable of 220mph, which, as my six-year-old worked out after much coddling of his intellect, is more than three times the national speed limit. Did you get that? Three times! Powee! If I'd really put the pedal to the metal, I'd have gone through this planet's event horizon and found myself in the middle of next week.

Who on earth needs a car that fast, you will ask. Who needs to bust out of the comfortable old corset of the 70mph restriction? Well, all I can say is get out on to a road near you, baby, and look around. It's you. It's me. It's everyone.

If you see anyone who is obeying the law, apart from the odd motorised rickshaw, please give me a ring. The national speed limit is, *de facto*, 99mph, because everyone knows that you lose your licence at 100mph. The law of the land is disregarded by good people, held in contempt by Middle England, and scorned by no less a person than Jack Straw, who saw fit to scream through the sound barrier when he was Home Secretary.

Oh, we'll sometimes make a passing stab at legality. If there's a police car on the road, we'll all slow down to a theatrical 70mph, and cluster round the cops like guilty sheep around a sheepdog; and for an interval we'll keep pace, dawdling politely along, until we feel the proprieties have been observed, and when we have nosed a couple of hundred yards ahead, we give it some welly and show the law a clean pair of heels. And what do they do? What can they do? Nothing. They haven't the time or money thoroughly to enforce a law that no longer reflects the power and safety of modern cars, and, above all, no longer reflects the custom of people who, broadly speaking, have a care for the interests of themselves and others.

The same point can be made, of course, about cannabis, which is now a subject of lively debate in the Tory party. Isn't that, by the way, just one sign that the Tory party is the coolest, chic-est and most happening place to be right now?

I appeal to all members of our nation's yoof who may be reading this article to get with it, join the Tory party, help lower the average age from 67¾, and come break dancing with Peter 'Tosh' Lilley and Charles 'Rastaman Vibrations' Moore, the apostles of liberty.

Forget about Tony Blair and his ghastly pretence at bourgeois values. Get with the Tories, who really understand about bourgeois values and how they may be changing. If you were to go to any great national festivity this summer – a regatta, for instance – you would see the flower of England's youth assembled. And if you were then to ask them all to turn out their sock drawers, and their handbags, and their pockets, you would find a fascinating harvest of objects looking faintly like desiccated hamster droppings which, on analysis, would prove to be Peruvian skunk or Colombian gunk, or whatever.

As the police have told me and anyone else who is interested, they cannot possibly enforce the letter of the law as it is currently framed. They can't bust all these people, and bring criminal proceedings against them, any more than they could arrest everyone who is speeding on the M40; and yet they naturally do intercept some abusers, which makes the application of the law seem uneven and therefore unfair.

Now there is an argument for living with such imperfection, and it is one that I have tended in the past to accept. There may be some laws, such as those on speeding and controlled substances, which are not there to delineate a precise boundary between what you may and may not do.

It may be that they are there to act as a kind of cultural drag-anchor, a tug of conscience. The 70mph speed limit may be regularly exceeded, but the mere fact of its existence survives as a whispered reproach to the motorist, and discourages him from being truly reckless. In the same way, cannabis may be smoked everywhere, but the fact that it is still technically illegal serves as an assertion of society's basic disapproval of drugs.

As bans, both laws are hopeless. But they are not meant to work as exact interdictions; they are attempts at mass psychological conditioning. The herd has crashed through the fence, and is busily grazing the forbidden pasture. But the animals do so a little bit nervously, and with a vague sense of restraint, because they know that some of them, sometimes, could still feel the cattle prod of retribution.

That argument, as I say, has tended to satisfy me in the past. I wonder, though, whether it really works. We pay the police to enforce the law, not to engage in a game of bluff with the motorist and the cannabis-user, in which the policeman's bluff is almost always called.

The speed limit is 10mph too low. It bears no relation to the speed motorists actually use, when, as Alan Judd points out in this week's issue of *The Spectator*, fewer people died on the roads in 2000 than in any year since records began in 1926. There were 3,409 deaths last year and 4,886 in 1926, when there were only 1·7 million cars on the roads.

Yes, cannabis is dangerous, but no more than other perfectly legal drugs. It's time for a rethink, and the Tory party – the funkiest, most jiving party on Earth – is where it's happening.

Thoughts on an Indian elephant

The elephant shuddered beneath me, and when I say shuddered I mean he positively heaved. He chugged, in out, in out, like an old Route-master bus about to expire, waved his dappled trunk, sprayed us with trunk snot, and gave an elephantine whinny. And if you could have seen the goad the mahout was using, you would have seen why.

This tool was about 6lb of forged steel, filed at one end to needle sharpness, and the blunt bit was now being thudded repeatedly into the top of the animal's warty, black-haired, double-domed pleistocene bonce, bonk, bonk, bonk, with the force of a navvy laying a rail.

Me, I didn't complain, because you don't try to back-seat drive an elephant. What is more, I was enjoying the ride, fantasising in my howdah about trampling mogul infantry. But the thought flashed across my mind, as the beast swayed on, and we undulated on top of his vast hips, that all this might soon be banned; not just the goadwork, but perhaps even the elephant routine itself. One day the global blender will complete its work, and western values will penetrate every aspect of Indian life. By New Year's Day 2013, I prophesy, there will be a campaign to stop the use of steel goads on elephants.

There may even be calls to end the custom of sawing their tusks, daubing their foreheads with paint, and allowing them to carry six heavy tourists up the hill to the Rajah's fort. There will be a parallel campaign to stop the clonking of poor deaf cobras with flutes by cross-legged men trying to persuade them to 'dance'; and all will be funded not just by the widow's mites of animal-lovers in Dorking, but by the Indians themselves. Borne by television, western values are seeding themselves everywhere. Many wonderful things will bloom, but some fine things will also be lost.

There could be no better education in the difference between Indian society and western society than to spend the past six days immersed in the preparations and rituals of a vast double wedding. The Indians take it very seriously, this business of being a family member. In India, families are big, not just because the Indians are enthusiastic reproducers of Indians. They stay in intimate contact with relatives who would be, in British terms, quite distant. They ring up. They pay calls. They endlessly confabulate. There is no word for a brother-in-law, or sister-in-law, or a cousin. Everyone is either a brother or a sister.

Looking at this intricate set-up, I found myself mentally contrasting the big American bestseller of last year, which described so well the atomised western family. Jonathan Franzen's *The Corrections* relates the wretched struggle of Ethel, an elderly woman, to convoke her small, scattered family for one last Christmas. Her husband, Albert, has incipient dementia. All three of her adult children know it would mean the world to her if they could be bothered to show up. Franzen paints a gloriously realistic picture, a kind of inverted Norman Rockwell, of their selfishness, their evasions, their instinct for self-gratification. There's one thing worse than the spoilt 11-year-old who refuses to go to Grandma's, and that is the yuppy father who gives way, because the child has made his 'choice', which must be 'respected'.

All these things – casual deprecation of blood ties, endowing children with premature sovereignty – would be thought appalling by Indians; and so would the way we treat our old people. Many good, honest Britons are furious these days to find, in middle life, when they have their own children to look after, tuition fees to pay, pensions and mortgages to worry about, that the state will not do more to help them look after their elderly parents.

Most Indians, on the other hand, would be amazed at the idea. They don't put old people into homes in India, even among the vast and growing middle classes. It is not just a question of repaying the benefits of nurture. Anything else would be a breach of family obligation. None of this is to say that there is something intrinsically superior in the traditional Indian reliance on the family, or that it is necessarily pernicious to create a taxpayer-funded safety net.

It is all too easy, in fact, to see how we have allowed the state to encroach as the family has retreated. The state looks after us, in ways that families cannot. It legislates on such matters as health and safety, and anyone touring the dilapidated and precipitous Rajput fortifications of Jaipur could happily wish for a visitation from the most high-minded Dutch-Belgian hygiene inspectors or Scandinavian child protection units. The state does not disapprove of us, or maddeningly insist on judging us by the standards of our nearest relatives. The state does not fuss and cluck, or start weeping if we fail to wear the tie it bought us. The state does not demand any token of reciprocal love, or even of respect. The state just gives us the money.

The state is not oppressive, or claustrophobic, or feud-riven, in the way that a large family can be. It is not the state that is the model of the greatest criminal organisations, in which a code of honour co-exists with terror, and a rule of silence among outsiders. It is the Family. These may be among the reasons why sophisticated western folk have come to prefer the ministrations of the state to those of their relatives.

You might also say that the welfare state deprives people of genuine warmth, and a genuine sense of the need to look out for others, and also deprives them of a great deal of their hard-earned cash. Perhaps, to judge by a paper I bought for 150 rupees, the Tories will one day return some of the cash that is currently being wasted. That is not my point.

My only point is that the Indians stand to lose some good things, as well as gain some good things, if they approximate themselves to our ways, and not just their immemorial skill in making an elephant move in the right direction.

We banned a berry – and it took Brussels to stop us being so silly

And while we are on the subject of demented British regulation, and this Government's lust to interfere in every aspect of our daily lives, let us not forget the breakfast habits of Mr Ron Jones, of Chinnor, in the beautiful county of Oxfordshire, and the insane, costly and ultimately abortive attempts to stop him eating a particular type of berry.

You may not have heard of a saskatoon, and nor, frankly, had I. But Mr Jones is widely travelled, and had come across this odd purple fruit in Canada. He put it in his mouth, as the Indians have done in those parts for thousands of years. He chewed. He was hooked. I hope I don't misrepresent him if I say that he became this country's leading saskatoon fanatic, and who can blame him?

You may not have been aware that the saskatoon is to berries as the Cohiba is to cigars. It is the king of the bush.

It is used all over Canada to make jams, syrups, salad dressings and even crème brulée. According to some bumf I have from the Canadian High Commission, it is standard practice, at all Canadian state banquets, to sprinkle every course with saskatoons. When one contemplates the volcanic energy of this century's great Canadians, from Mark Steyn to Conrad Black to Margaret Trudeau, one can only ascribe it to the saskatoon-based national diet.

The saskatoon (*Amelanchier ainifolia*) is also known as the juneberry, serviceberry or shadberry and grows on tall bushes in northwest Canada. It is related to the rose family, and can be used to make all sorts of things, including saskatoon cider, not least because it has sensational nutritional characteristics. For instance, it has 84 calories per 100g, compared with a piffling 51 Ca for blueberries, 37 for strawberries and 49 for raspberries. It has more protein, more carbohydrate, three times as much Vitamin C, far more potassium, more fibre and more iron than any of these rival berries.

And it has less fat. It is a miracle fruit, and when, in February this year Mr Jones saw it on the shelves at his local supermarket, he gave a hymn of thanks to globalisation, and for three blissful months he had barely a saskatoon-free day.

Alas, he had underestimated the vengeful meddlesomeness of the bureaucrats. It turns out, of course, that there is a law against this sensible exercise of free trade, whereby British people can eat at breakfast what their kith and kin enjoy in Canada. It is called the Novel Foods Regulation (EC 258/97), and it came into force in this country in 1997, and means that you cannot expect the authorities to accept that a food is safe, just because the Canadian population swears by it.

Oh, no. That's not good enough. Under the Novel Foods Regulation, anything new to the EU market must undergo at least two years of tedious tests and safety demonstrations before it can be put on the shelves. As it happened, the original importers of the saskatoons just ignored this regulation, because it was obviously absurd, and that is how Mr Jones came to find the berries in his supermarket. What seems to have happened then is that someone sneaked to the authorities. There are companies that specialise in helping firms overcome demented anti-berry regulations, and it seems that the saskatoon importers made the mistake of ignoring them. These saskatoons are just like blueberries, the importers told the Customs people; just a sort of Canadian blueberry. Oh no they're not, said the middlemen, angry at losing some business: they are related to the rosehip! Nothing like a blueberry! They are a Novel Food!

And they reported the arrival of the saskatoon to that new and ludicrous body, the Food Standards Agency. In May, the 550 bureaucrats of the Food Standards Agency launched a vicious anti-saskatoon sweep of Britain, and the berry was cleared from the shelves. Mr Jones was indignant; he wrote to me; I wrote to the Department of Health, the Department of Agriculture, and the Food Standards Agency, and I have a full set of preposterous letters telling me that no, sorry, the berry is illegal in Britain, and will be for as long as two years while tests are conducted to find out whether the population of Canada is right in thinking it to be edible, and that is all there is to it. That's right: this berry is now banned. It's as illegal as heroin. It is only thanks to the bravery of the importers, J. O. Sims of Spalding, Lincolnshire, that I have on my desk some of the contraband berries. They are by no means fresh, and have shrivelled to the size of blackcurrants, and as I munch them now I pick up only a suggestion of the flavour that must have entranced Mr Jones (likened, when newly picked, to a mixture of almonds and cherries).

Pathetic though these relics are, they could still in theory be seized by Food Standards agents in black pyjamas crashing through my windows. But the final absurdity is that the FSA fatwa is about to be unexpectedly overturned not by Parliament, but by Brussels!

The other day the German government decided that there was nothing wrong with the berries, and that the Finns had been eating them for yonks, and under basic EU single market principles, the saskatoon is therefore deemed fit for consumption in all member states, Britain included. In other words, the FSA ban has been rendered meaningless, at which moment you may ask yourselves, what is the point of this agency, invented by Labour in 2001, with its 550 officials paid for by the taxpayer? What do we pay them for, when their cretinous bans can be undone by the good sense of the Germans? What is the point of them?

The answer is there is no point. But if you want to understand how Labour has created 530,000 jobs in the public sector, and squandered untold billions in the enforcement of vexatious regulation, remember how they tried to ban the saskatoon. A berry Christmas to all my readers!

We futilely yearn for someone to blame

We can supply them with fresh water. We can get them sticking plasters and body bags, and we can ring up the helplines and pledge our cash, and so we should.

But, as we contemplate the thousands of dead on the shores of the Indian Ocean, there is one thing the whole planet wants, and that we cannot supply. We all want someone to blame. Deep in our souls, we want to find some human factor in the disaster, in the way that our species has done since – well, since the Flood.

What was the cause of that first great inundation, back there in the Old Testament, the one that Noah rode out? Genesis is clear: 'And God saw that the wickedness of man was very great in the earth, and that every imagination of the thoughts of his heart was only evil continually. And it repented the Lord that he had made man on the earth, and it grieved him at his heart . . .'

And anyway, God sent a lot of rain. We find the same myth in the Greek tradition, where Zeus is fed up with the bad behaviour of men during the age of bronze, especially the conduct of Lycaon, who feeds his guests human flesh. The king of the gods causes a flood, which Deucalion escapes by building a wooden chest, in which he floats with his wife, Pyrrha, for nine days, before the waters subside and they repopulate the planet.

In the Sumerian tradition, the Noah figure is called Utnapishtim, and the causes of the flood, again, are divine anger at human decadence; in the Akkadian myth, the man in the boat is called Atrahasis, and the cause of the flood is the anger of the god Enlil, who is annoyed at having his sleep disturbed by the booming human population.

There are similar accounts in Hindi myth, in the Norse sagas, and even among the Hopi Indians of Latin America. Scholars have speculated that it may be all a coincidence, in that human societies have tended to evolve in flood-prone areas, on the banks of rivers; but several of the myths – such as Noah, the Greek and Sumerian accounts – may hark back to a single event, a catastrophic deluge in about 5,600 BC, when the Mediterranean appears to have poured into the Black Sea.

The important point is that all peoples have reacted to memories of the flood in the same way – by ascribing some fault to human beings; and one can see why this is so psychologically satisfying. With the idea of fault go notions of human agency, and the implicit suggestion that, if we did wrong on one occasion, we can do better the next time. If we can persuade ourselves that there is some divine justice in a terrifying flood, then we have the consolation of believing that man may be in some sense the author of his own misfortunes.

Of course, we are no longer quite so primitive as to think, with the writers of the ancient scriptures, that natural calamities may be causally connected to human bad behaviour. If there are any loonies out there who think that Phuket is being punished for being the modern Nineveh, they have had the good sense to keep it to themselves.

In this largely godless age, we have a more subtle interpretation of the relation between human excess and natural disaster. Our new high priests are the environmentalists and, when the icebergs calve early or the swallows fly the wrong way, it is they who cry woe and say that it is a judgment on us all, and our wicked ways; and that is why, in the case of a colossal undersea earthquake, you can sense the silent frustration of the told-you-so scientists.

Whatever you say about the slipping of tectonic plates on the sea-bed off Sumatra, it had nothing to do with global warming. It was not caused by decadent use of Right Guard, or George W Bush, or the flouting of the Kyoto Protocol, or inadequate enforcement of the Windows and Doors Regulation of April 2002. There may now be six billion of us crawling over the crust of the Earth, but, when things move beneath that crust, we might as well not exist for all the difference we make.

And if the priests and the scientists have nothing useful to say on the matter, the same goes in spades for politicians and journalists. We yearn, with that immemorial human ache, to find someone to blame – but whom? Pathetic efforts have been made already to blame the Americans, for failing to equip the littoral of the Indian Ocean with adequate tsunami sensors; and as ever, in the wake of some random and pitiless disaster, there are calls for some kind of preventive action against the next one.

A magnificent article in yesterday's *Guardian* argued that a chunk of the Canary Islands should be pre-emptively detonated, in case a landslip caused a tsunami to race across the Atlantic and destroy New York.

Well, perhaps this would indeed do more good than harm, and perhaps we should see whether there are any other suspect islands – Ibiza? – that could be usefully blown up; but it would do nothing, of course, to prevent further Indonesian earthquakes, and the same point could be made to those Euro-MPs now calling for the building of some Battlestar Galactica to fight off asteroids.

One can see that this is in the spirit of the hysterical precautionary principle that now bedevils our legislation, but it is mad. It may offend our species' sense of self-importance, but when a thunking great hunk of rock comes hurtling out of space, to splat this planet like an egg, it is time to admit gracefully that our number is up.

A long time ago, an English king made this point, in the very matter of waves. He sat on the beach and ordered the tide to withdraw. Canute was not a megalomaniac. He was just showing that there are some things that are beyond the scope of kings, or laws, or regulation.

PERSONALITIES

What an odd business it is, the big feature interview. In a sense it is an illustration of the rebalancing of power in Britain, in favour of the media. In France or America, you can still read interviews with politicians or celebrities which consist of reverential Q and A transcripts. British readers, with their jaded palates, want something stronger. They want the revelations, the confessions. They want the sudden grabbing for the hankie. That is why the British hack approaches his interviewee with what is sometimes a frankly treacherous smile.

The interviewer fawns, he beams, he keeps one eye on the little red light on his tape recorder; and then he pounces. If you want a perfect example of the disingenuousness of the modern interviewer, consider the episode of Martin Bashir and Michael Jackson. When the programme was broadcast, it appeared to be a remarkable indictment of whacko Jacko's approach to fatherhood, with the implication that Bashir thought his subject more than slightly weird. But the pop star then turned the tables, by producing the out-takes. These showed the simpering journalist apparently with tears in his eyes congratulating Jacko on his parenting skills, and generally sucking up in a disgusting fashion.

It is because interviews involve these betrayals that PR men have become ever more ruthless in handling them: sitting in, cutting in, turning off the tape, and so on. Journalists, in response, have become ever more ratlike in their cunning. In principle, of course, I am on the side of the hacks.

After all, journalists have to turn these maunderings into something readable, and it is sometimes very difficult, faced with a great dumper truck of verbal gravel, to pick out the pebbles for the mosaic. For my own part, I have always tried to be faithful to the drift and mood of the conversation, even if there is a lot one must necessarily cut. I also tend to like my subjects, though Chris Evans and I were probably quite relieved when our game of golf was over.

Ken Clarke

One could swear there is something deliberate about the way one of the scuffed brown shoes has its lace undone; something calculated in the uninhibited convexities of his frame; the frequent laugh that gurgles from his merry face. And when he vanishes to an antechamber to slick back his hair for the photographer, it is, perhaps, a sign of the underlying self-possession that has made him among the most durable of modern politicians.

For the followers of political Wisden, the Treasury is Ken Clarke's seventh department of state. Along with Malcolm Rifkind and Lynda Chalker, he is the longest continuously serving minister since Lloyd George; and you don't survive that long in British politics by tactlessness alone. He is the bull in a china shop who is actually rather careful about the china.

'You're not going to talk about Europe,' he says with an air of mock dread. People are so obsessive about the subject, he complains. We both chortle. Of course I am going to ask him about Europe. But first, how does he propose to save the next election?

Will he guarantee to cut taxes in the next Budget, assuming there is one? He has a way of drowning his opponent by repeating the word he happens to be stuck on.

'I, I, I had this disagreement with the Conservative press, or what used to be the Conservative press, last autumn. I don't think the fortunes of the Government entirely depend on us producing enormous tax cuts for the population.

'To offer tax cuts purely as an electoral bribe, I, I think underrates the intelligence of the electorate. In fact the electorate is rather cynical about us, and it does not want to have the Government behaving as though just giving them big tax cuts before an election entitles the Government to be re-elected.

'I want to offer the public the prospect that any tax cuts we have made will last, and that there may be more to come if we're re-elected.'

'What do you mean bribes?' I say, feigning outrage at this sensible answer. It's our money, isn't it?

'It's our money, it's our money. That's right. The Government should restrict the extent to which it takes away people's own money. But first you control the Government, then you make tax cuts.'

Yes, but are you as macho about budget-cutting as you should be? John Major and William Waldegrave, the Chief Secretary, seem to think government spending could fall to 35 per cent of GDP. But Mr Clarke was lately reported to believe 40 per cent was the minimum in a civilised society.

Get away, says Clarke. 'I was the guy who *set* a 40 per

cent target in the first place. I've had the three toughest public spending rounds I think since the war, in getting down to the 42 per cent we're at now, and still falling.

'So I don't personally regard myself as the last of the big spenders', chuckle, chuckle, chortle. I try a different tack with this One-Nation Tory. What, I ask, is the difference between you and Tony Blair?

'Between myself and Tony Blair?' He leans back. Clarke thinks he's rumbled the point of the interview. I'm out to paint him as a Lefty.

'Firstly, my instincts for a market economy, my instincts for a deregulated economy; my instincts for a flexible Labour market; my instincts against the power of the vested interest lobbies, have always set me well apart from anyone in the Labour Party.

'If he's a One-Nation Tory, I'm a monkey's uncle.'

According to Clarke, Blair would never have taken on the vested interests of the nurses, the police, the doctors, the teachers. He is proudest of the NHS reforms and attributes his success to 'strong convictions and, ha ha ha, probably an excessive self-confidence'. Self-confidence is right. Whence does it come?

'My self-confidence? I suppose it comes from the process of having done it for a long time and being reshuffled a lot, and learning from one's mistakes.'

Ken Clarke was born in Nottingham in 1940. His father was a pit electrician. His grandfather was a communist. 'He was a very formidable character, my mother's father, a very, very nice man, a communist and not remotely a Marxist, who fell for the Uncle Joe Stalin bit.

'The only newspaper he would take in the house was the *Morning Star*. He said it was the only one you could believe.'

And did his upbringing ever trigger any Left-wing impulses? 'Yes, but only at school. When I went up to university I joined all the political parties because everybody did. I wasn't sure what political party I had any allegiance to when I arrived.'

The Cambridge Tory mafia which Clarke joined was characterised more by ambition than Right-wing fervour. But he was reactionary in his way. For instance, he voted against women joining the Union, of which he was President. 'I now think that was a mistake,' says Clarke. 'If the Garrick club had a vote now on the admission of women, I'd vote for them.'

I tell him that in Edwina Currie's latest bonkbuster he is portrayed as Bampton, the pot-bellied, cigar-puffing Health Secretary from the Midlands, conventionally married with two children. Bampton is a cynical sexist who lets the heroine down. Let's take these charges of Currie in order.

Pot-bellied? That's Clarke. 'Do I look like a man who goes to an effort to keep fit? I enjoy robust good health', says the man who was a wonderful, walking reproof to the nannying tendencies of other Health Secretaries. 'My outdoor activities are the occasional good long walk and bird-watching.'

Cigar-puffing? Check.

Conventionally married? Well, Clarke's wife, Gillian, an exceedingly clever medieval historian with an auntyish appearance, is not exactly an Edwina Currie heroine, but the Clarkes are said to be devoted to one another. The Midlands? Yes, that was where Clarke practised as a barrister for 16 years.

Two children? Spot on, Edwina. Now both married, the Clarke children were educated in good One-Nation Tory fashion, leaving their state primary schools at 11 for the independent sector. 'I went through the same process Mr Blair is supposed to have gone through, but in my case there was no hypocrisy or crisis of conscience,' he says.

And what about these allegations of sexism, Mr Clarke?

Did you let Edwina down when, as a junior minister in your department, she issued her *fatwa* against eggs?

'Yes, she has a grievance against me over the eggs saga – even though I was about the last member of the Government to argue that she shouldn't be driven out over it. I tried to defend her.

'She, she, she criticises me now for telling her to stop making public statements, but the reason I did that was she kept repeating the original error. She says it is sexism. That is rubbish, absolute rubbish. Well I don't think I'm remotely sexist. I don't think anybody in the world would regard me as sexist.'

But Clarke has far more powerful opponents on the opposite end of the party: the men of the New Right – no names, no pack-drill – who see him as the last and most dangerous exponent of what used to be called 'wetness'.

'If you ask me to answer my Right-wing critics, who I am told do regard me as a sort of slightly worrying character, I regard it as baffling,' says Clarke. 'Because I regard myself as someone who's followed a very straightforward approach of being a market economist, and a fairly orthodox one.

'Some of today's Thatcherites are not in my opinion the real thing. I'm not going to name names. But people who proclaim themselves Thatcherite now hold views which were not the views of the Thatcher Government. Ten years ago, when the health reforms were at their most difficult, I was regarded as a very Right-wing, rather thug-like, Conservative.

'So it's Europe,' he says almost sadly. He brings it up, not I. 'People have got this curious idea that if you're Europhile you're Left-wing and if you're Euro-sceptic you're Right-wing.

'I don't regard myself as a federalist and never have. I believe in a union of nation states,' he says. No, Mr Clarke.

But the issue is the single currency, of which you are emphatically in favour.

'I am sympathetic to the idea,' he says, though he enters the usual caveats about achieving economic convergence. 'I think if it happens it will matter a lot to us whether we're in or out.'

A fellow cabinet minister says if and when the moment comes, Clarke will lead a splinter group of 40 Tories who favour a single currency. That moment may never come. But if it does, the great thing about Ken Clarke is that we know exactly where he will stand.

Clare Short

Whoever handles Clare Short's PR does a fine job. The advance billing was becoming positively wearisome. Everyone who heard I was going to meet Labour's transport spokesperson seemed to go into a kind of fit. Oh, Clare! My dear! 'You'll love her!'

'You'll fall in love!' It was her crusty glamour, apparently. Her gipsy charm. So authentic, so real. She's not at all like her public persona, I was assured.

I was told to forget about how the tabloids try to portray her as Killjoy Clare, the grim-jawed persecutor of the tit-and-bum merchants, the militant, childless, snaggle-toothed Fenian feminist of the hard Left. And, of course, the more I was urged to sit back and enjoy the Clare Short experience, the deeper the iron entered the soul.

One does not like to be schmoozed. We hacks are desperadoes, professional cynics. We do not lightly allow our prejudices to be brushed aside. So I entered her office in No 7 Millbank determined to uncover the Stalinist harridan within; an hour later I left in a state of rout.

She took my coat. She brushed my arm. She laughed with a great throaty cackle at my excuse for being late (no trains to King's Cross from Highbury), which delighted the transport spokesman on the eve of her cunning announcement about how Labour intends to buy back the railways without, supposedly, spending a dime.

And it was when she plied me with coffee in a mug bearing the insignia of Emily's List, the ginger group for getting women into politics, that I remembered my mission.

Thanks largely to Clare Short's lobbying of John Smith, Labour muscled another 35 women on to its candidates' list. The European Court has lately banned the practice for flagrant sexism; yet if Labour comes to power, they can expect about 90 female MPs in the party alone.

When you listen to the Commons in the next few years, don't be surprised if the baying has gone up an octave. Starting from tomorrow night, the BBC will be giving us a taster of the coming feminocracy with a series called *Ladies of the House*, featuring Voortrekkers such as Barbara Castle and Gillian Shephard.

Clare Short stars in the first programme. The question, though, is whether she will be rewarded in person for her pioneering work. Will she, like them, make it to the Cabinet?

For if she has one engaging characteristic, it is a failure to watch her mouth. The word in Westminster is that the Blairocrats were none too chuffed by her recent performance on the *Today* programme. The hard young men say she was slurred; forgivable, one might think, since it was not yet 8am.

Rumour tells of a feud between her and Brian Wilson, an able and sharp-suited Scot who understudies her at transport and is said to be nipping at her heels. And popular though she is in the parliamentary party, it has not been forgotten that she did not vote for Blair in the leadership election.

So come on, Clare, what do you think of this Pied Piper turning you all into an SDP Mark II?

'We've got a good working relationship,' she says in her Birmingham voice.

Aha. Not soulmates, then?

Actually, says Clare, she recognises in Blair the same sense of moral indignation which, she says, is her own motivating force. 'Because he's glamorous and pretty and good at soundbites, he can look more synthetic than he is. I go for the firm interior rather than the glitzy exterior.'

Very well, then. What about Harriet Harman sending her child to that grant-maintained school? We saw on television how that got up her nose. New Labour cracked open, and Old Labour came bubbling through.

'In reality I was saying, I don't know all the facts, and that I was not going to sit here and pontificate about Harriet's choices.'

Okay. Now that you know all the facts, what do you think?

'Well,' she says, 'I am not going to sit here and pontificate about Harriet's choices. I have my views.'

Now if she had been a real Blairite, Clare would have worked out some weasely formula exculpating Harriet Harman for her sin – using an educational option officially anathematised by Labour policy. She would have found some way of blaming the Tories.

But she didn't. Her views were written all over her face, which, while we are on the subject, is far more handsome than it appears on television or in most photographs; her hair and skin seem vaguely lustrous, though when the photographer comes, she claims, somewhat against the evidence, to have a spot on her chin.

She's honest, Clare Short. She left the Catholic Church

at 16 because she thought it was silly to say people shouldn't use contraception. She recently found herself in piping hot water with the Blairocracy, when she was deemed to be in favour of legalising cannabis. As she now explains on the cannabis front: 'What I should have said as a member of the Shadow Cabinet is that this is a matter for Jack Straw, and I gather this is not his view at the moment . . .'

Er, it's not his view *at the moment*? How often does he change his view?

She laughs like a gurgling drain. The flexibility of Jack Straw's opinions on law and order is a subject for Left-wing Labour despair. 'Sorry! It's not his view, full stop.'

The outlines of authentic Old Labour are beginning to emerge. Given that Blair may yet face a schism in his own party on the single currency, she is embarrassingly honest, too, about European monetary union.

Clare has nothing against currencies circulating freely: 'I remember when I was a child, we went on holidays in the west of Ireland, and you could buy ice-cream with your Irish money or your Birmingham money.'

But EMU fills her with old-fashioned Left-wing dread. 'The Maastricht criteria are so deflationary that they would drive Europe into the most terrible recession with the most dreadful social and economic consequences if it goes too fast. For countries that are economically less successful now, it could entrench them into a second-rate position in the EU, and Britain could be in that position.'

Clare Short was born not quite 50 years ago in Dudley Road Hospital, Ladywood, Birmingham. Her family is Irish, and she is an instinctive supporter of the republican cause. 'My father came from Crossmaglen, three miles north of the border, in the bandit country of South Armagh.' (For bandit, read murderer, I suppose.)

'My family come from an area which straddles the

border, and the border is irrational in that area. My father, who was a brilliant guy, felt very deeply about it, very hurt, very angry that they'd drawn this line in his country, and I grew up with that. That affected our world view.

'We grew up thinking that the British empire wasn't a good thing, and that it was a good thing that India gained its independence and that slavery was abolished.'

Do you really mean to say the empire wasn't a good thing?

'No, it wasn't.'

The British empire ended slavery, though; no one else.

'The British empire helped to *organise* slavery.'

Well, I say, it was the native rulers of West Africa who invented and also helped to organise slavery.

'It was the black African kings who had feudal friends in Europe. They both organised slavery,' says Clare, and our discussion on slavery ends with a nil-nil scoreline.

'It all depends where you come from,' she goes on. 'My ancestors were depicted historically as ape-like creatures. There is a "mass" rock near the village where my ancestors came from, and I go there because I have got aunts who are getting older and more precious. The rock is where my ancestors went for mass because the Brits were persecuting them for practising their religion.'

Clare Short has had a hard life in many ways, not least witnessing the slow and miserable death of her husband, former Labour minister Alex Lyon, from Alzheimer's disease in 1993. But she seems to be one of those school-of-hard-knocks types whose temperamental reaction is to stand up for the underdog.

In that same group she would put the poor, the old, the PLO, the IRA, and aspirant female politicians. I ask her, finally, why it is so essential to have more women in the House of Commons. Is the place really so disreputable?

She admits that the Commons can have great moments

of theatre, such as Mrs Thatcher's resignation speech, or Sir Geoffrey Howe's attack on Thatcher . . .

Or Michael Howard's demolition of Jack Straw?

'Ye-e-,' says Clare, and then catches herself. 'Well, I wasn't there for that,' she says diplomatically.

But she says the problem with the Commons is that it's full of Billy Bunterish males, all going yah-boo. 'It's second-rate grot,' she says.

Women would be more reasonable, she says. They speak their minds. 'I don't think women are of superior moral quality to men. But we tend to be outsiders, and that's where being less sleazy comes from.'

But will women always be less sleazy than men? 'Oh, I think if 100 years from now, women are as much part of the institutions of power as men, they will have equally undesirable characteristics.'

So if you get your way, I say, we are all doomed to endure the transformation of the Commons from a bearpit into a touchy-feely Finnish-style seminar with everyone sitting in the round and being careful not to disagree.

'People like you create such distortions because you find the idea of women being as bright as men terrifying,' she says. 'Well don't worry!' and she laughs so much that the idea seems almost benign.

Tony Benn

Aargh. I almost popped out of my skin. 'It'sh down here,' says a voice and there is a faint whiff of tobacco. And I boggle because there appears to be a head sprouting from the brickwork at my feet, the silver head, the cartoonists' beloved eyes and pipe that all my life have stood for the same set of ideas.

How typical of Anthony Wedgwood Benn not to live in this house in Holland Park Avenue but in the basement flat, a bit like being Viscount Stansgate but giving up the title.

He leads the way into his study, full of bits of once-high technology, a pipe-shaped model of Big Ben, tributes from Left-wing organisations and a deep arm-chair. 'Would you like some tea or coffee?' he asked, and as I look at his trim 71-year-old form I think of the billion cuppas, the muggas, the pintas that have allegedly preserved his vigour, the tannin tanning the Benn innards like some Aztec formula.

I go for the tea. Soon he is back with a tray, launching into a virtual soliloquy.

'Well I've lived a very long time 'cos I was brought up in a political home, I mean, Ramsay MacDonald sat me on his knee and I've looked at Labour leaders in a funny way ever since,' he says, off the starting block before I have barely asked him a question. And on it goes in a lisping cataract as he expounds his theory of what really happened in the twentieth-century. The insight hit him – Pow! – about 20 years ago when, for such is Benn's instinct for charm, he says he bought a *Daily Telegraph* historical wall chart. 'And at the top it had the words: *the first part of the 20th century was the advance in political influence of the industrial working class*. If I take my life and divide it in half, the first half was the enlargement of the power of ordinary people.'

But in the last 40 or 50 years market forces have counter-attacked against the advances of democracy. And here he figures we must be soulmates, for nothing, says Benn, has been as anti-democratic as Brushelsh; the bureaucrats who tried to stop him nationalising North Sea oil, who tried to put the kibosh on his plans for industrial subsidy.

'The first time I went to Brushelsh I felt like one of those Angles who paraded before the Emperor in Rome. I think politicians in the West are now maharajahs of the new raj of money. The maharajahs were allowed to remain as long as they did the will of Queen Victoria, and we are allowed to remain as long as we abide by the requirements of international capital.'

When Thatcher went against Brussels she was doomed. '"No, no, no" did for her, just as the markets did for Labour in 1976 ... I feel I'm witnessing the progressive extinction of representative democracy.' There is something so hypnotic about his discourse that only now and then one realises with a start that he has completely cut the moorings of fact.

For instance, Benn at one point is explaining that the British have always been ruled by foreigners. 'Julius Caesar arrived in 55 BC and brought a single currency and they stayed until AD 610 when the 7th Legion had to go back to Masada.' Eh? I say. I thought the Jewish wars were in AD 17? It's a bit like Benn's theory of 20th-century history. It's hogwash, but it sounds so seductive because it is based on a half-truth.

Of course he's right to say democratic politics have often impeded the free market. As the franchise has widened, politicians have tried to win the votes of more and more people by spending more and more money, whether taxing or borrowing. That is why the state has taken and spent an increasing part of the nation's wealth as the century has gone on.

But when Thatcher fell over Europe, that was hardly because she opposed the free market. The Europe of Delors, Mitterrand and Kohl was in many ways *anti*-free market. Benn has ignored this simple point in his desire to make the facts fit the theory. The wonderful thing about Tony Benn is that he still believes that British manufacturing industry could have been 'the best in the world' if he'd been allowed to lubricate it with the entire receipts from North Sea oil. He reminisces fondly about Meriden, the ludicrous workers' co-operative he invented in a doomed attempt to revive the British motorcycle industry.

I've always wanted to meet Mr Benn, and now I understand the mixture of sweep, vision and nuttiness that inspired his followers and kept Labour in the wilderness. Of course, he's scathing about New Labour. He is, though, full of hope. If Blair is elected, he believes it will not be long before the great public desire for a change wells up, as it welled up over Dunblane. 'I think the pressure will build up for a fairer society.'

Well, I wonder. His real problem is not that the free market has stifled democracy. It is that democracy has rejected Bennery. Not that he minds. 'Really I have no chip on my shoulder. That must be very apparent to you. If I did, I would be able to open a fish and chip shop.'

Frank Bruno

It was always possible things would get rough when I went to interview the former heavyweight champion of the world. OK, so he's Uncle Frank, the nation's favourite rear-end of a pantomime horse. He's the gentle giant, know what I mean 'arry, the dedicated family man.

But he's still 6ft 3in of chestnut-hard menace, with a punch likened by the Royal College of Nursing to being hit by a half-ton car. And he is not in the sunniest of moods when he finally leaves the tint-windowed muscular Merc where he had been having a long, agitated conversation on his mobile. He grasps his close-cropped bonce.

'I don't need these anxieties in my head,' he tells the person who had agreed that Frank could be consulted on the issue of the hour: what was it like when he went the distance – the distance of two and a half rounds – on

March 17, 1996, with Tyson, the former World Chomp? Is it true, as Bruno is reported to have said, that those steel gnashers also closed on a piece of Frank?

He's standing in a school theatre, where he's doing some television work, and still talking to his hapless minders when he suddenly says, *basso profundissimo*: 'Why are you looking at me like that, Mr Johnson, brigadier? Are you trying to suss me out?' Gracious no, I say, noting that the peripheral vision is phenomenal from those big, ironical brown eyes. And it's ding ding, round one of one of the shortest interviews in history.

Mr Bruno, Frank, I say, it always strikes me as amazing that you can do such violence when you're obviously so pacific in temperament . . . He starts a kind of Ali patter, shuffling in his cool blue suit and snakeskin bootees. 'I'm no nicer than you, no nastier than you, I've got the same arms, same legs' – he reaches down to prod my legs and squeeze my biceps – 'the only difference is I'm black and you're white.'

And then his fists are up, giving me a chance to see his jewellery real close, the doubloon on his ring, the watch, everything scabbed and crusted with diamonds.

'Are you going to tell me that when I hit you, you're just going to say *(falsetto)*: "Oh stop that, old bean"? Are you going to be that nice to me? When you do your job you do your job. It's survival. I'm doing a job to make a living for my family and myself; lock me up if that's a crime.'

It's time to close in. Tell me about when Tyson bit you, I say. Apparently this is a low blow. 'I don't like to get involved in boxing questions. I'm not giving no exclusive interviews. Boris, what I'm trying to say to you man is that I wasn't there at the Tyson thing.

'I don't know whether you're kinky and you like that sort of biting thing. I'm not kinky. Tyson he come up and give me the elbow, things like that, but he won fair and square and at the end of the day he's got to be punished, he's got to be stopped. I haven't got time for these loaded questions. I'm not sitting on my backside drinking beer and saying I rocked Tyson once, and if that's a crime lock me up again.'

And now the seconds are crowding into the ring. 'You've had 20 minutes,' says a frightening looking man with a very short haircut. Have I? According to my watch, it's more like five.

'Relax, man,' says Bruno. 'Don't get out of your pram.' And now the former world champion has extended his 82-inch reach and he's got me in a playful headlock. At least I assume it's playful. 'Relax, Mr Boris brigadier,' he says, massaging my neck muscles with his thumbs like a man preparing to ease a Champagne cork out of the bottle. 'You're getting all tense here. I don't want to give no exclusive,' he says. It's all right, I gasp. I don't want an exclusive, really and truly.

And then ding ding, a man in shorts and various girls with clipboards demand an end to this degrading spectacle, saying I've taken up far too much of Mr Bruno's time. He's got to get on with the serious business of being a roving reporter for ITV, before appearing in the Spice Girls movie. I'm seriously out of my depth here.

But Uncle Frank relents, waving them aside. 'I'm trying to be as nice as possible,' he says. 'I don't want to tell you to go to the toilet and have a vindaloo,' and the interview staggers on for a few more seconds. He thinks Muhammad Ali was the all-time greatest, Bob Marley the greatest musician, and no, he's not planning a come-back.

'If you gave me all your money, all your mother's money, and I can tell you've got a lot of money, I wouldn't go back. I've made enough corn . . . There you are Mr Johnson brigadier. I've given you more than just a few crumbs, I've given you a loaf.'

And then for Uncle Frank, the warhorse-turned-circus

horse, the man who rocked Tyson, it's back to the shaded interior of the Merc, for a long gesticulation on the car phone.

Chris Evans

There is panic when the call comes through. For two years, the features department has been lobbying the ginger binger for an interview, and then – jackpot: not only will Chris Evans consent to see us – he will give *The Daily Telegraph* a game of golf!

The multi-millionaire proprietor-star of Virgin Radio is ready to plug a new television series called *Tee Time*, and he requires a partner. Just when he is needed most, Bill Deedes, the paper's answer to Arnold Palmer, is in Sudan.

Someone, anyone, is needed to play golf with Evans. Have you ever swung a club in anger? the features impresarios ask and, like a fool, I say yes.

It is when I arrive with George, a *Daily Telegraph* features executive turned caddy, that it dawns what we are letting ourselves in for. In the car park of the Buckinghamshire Golf Club, an official looks ruminatively over our Fiesta.

Uh-oh. There are Rollers and Beemers here, but no Fiestas, and I have a sense of impending doom. This man Evans once humiliated an employee on air by reading out the details of his expenses fiddle. He said Anthea Turner should be kicked in the teeth. What will he say when he twigs the quality of his opposition?

'Are you going to change?' asks the chain-smoking PR, Patrick Keegan of Freud Communications, looking incredulously at my trousers. It's all right, he says at length.

'Chris won't mind. He's not at all precious. He's easy-going and generous.' Pathetically, we ask what Mr Evans would like to discuss with us.

'Golf is his big love,' says Patrick, Our Man In The Navy Corduroy Suit, as if to say: 'Keep it to golf, my son, and you'll be all right.' The woman in the Buckinghamshire Golf Club shop speaks of Mr Evans with reverence, and all at once it hits me where I have seen all this before.

It's pure James Bond. The shrubs, the scurrying minions, the golf club built by the Kajima corporation of Japan which has a vaguely oriental atmosphere – something, no doubt, to do with the samurai swords on the walls – and lowering over it all, the impending arrival of the man of power, the tycoon-golfer.

In the mind's ear, I hear Shirley Bassey: 'Goldfingaah! The man with the Midas touch! He's just too much!' He's turned his blatherings to gold. He's paid £85 million for Virgin Radio, and they say it's worth twice that now. He's ranked 668th in the *Sunday Times* top 1,000, with £30 million to his name, he has just won yet another Gold at the Sony Radio awards and – Omigosh . . .

Just as Evans arrives, wearing his baseball hat, a mere one and a half hours after the appointed tee-off time, I notice that the PR bumf says he is a 'junior member of the professional golfers' association and an ex-golf shop assistant'. This is bad.

The last time I played golf was at school when one Major Morkill expelled me from the course for using only one club. 'There you go, making excuses already,' says Evans. 'It's all in the putting. What's your handicap?' I am tempted to reply: 'Wooden leg and glass eye.'

Evans insists on showing us the Kajima corporation's shower rooms, equipped with three-legged milking stools: apparently, Japanese businessmen like to hunker down for a really good go at the toes.

We walk towards the first tee and I try to contain my anxiety. Japanese businessmen fly over here just to play golf, says Evans. 'It's cheaper than playing in Japan. The presidents of Mitsubishi and Toyota play here, and they take no prisoners.' He played here recently with Gazza, the footballer. 'Gazza had never played before, but he was a natural. He beat everybody.'

As we reach the first tee, Chris and David Granger, the producer of the golfing series, announce that they are playing a game called camels, starfish, snakes. You are a camel if you land in a bunker, a starfish if you land in the water, a snake in the rough.

The stakes begin at 12½p and mount in geometrical leaps to thousands of pounds. George, the *Telegraph* executive-cum-caddy, declines to bet on my prowess.

David goes first, thwacking it very nicely, and then it is the turn of Evans. He's wearing Oasis-style Adidas trainers and green army-surplus fatigues. He is much taller than I had imagined – 6ft 2in, with greying temples – and he bends artistically at the knees, leaning into the shot.

There is a professional sounding clack. 'Good shot, Chris,' says David the producer. Unless I specifically say otherwise, David has a very high opinion of Chris's golfing ability, which he is not shy of expressing. Now it falls to *The Daily Telegraph*.

'You want a five iron if you haven't played since school,' Evans says. George hands me a putter, which Chris kindly intercepts. He finds me the right tool. *Whack*.

I am in the rough, and the grass has swallowed the Titleist. David finds another from his bag, and it seems a good idea to move the interview along before being banished again by the authorities. In America, recently, I was listening to Howard Stern, the supreme shock jock. Does Evans model himself on Howie?

This is a *faux pas*. 'A lot of people compare me to Stern, which is so wrong. We are both the most talked about DJs in our country.' It seems that the difference between them, in the view of Evans, is that Stern relies on shock tactics, Evans on talent.

Chastened, I fall back into the abject role of Goldfinger's golfing pal. I paint a picture of his triumphs: the Jags, the Aston Martins, the fling with Kim Wilde, the show called *Don't Forget Your Toothbrush* he invented and franchised around the world, the triumph at the BBC, where he boosted Radio One's ratings by a million.

What will you do now that you have achieved everything? 'Well, I haven't achieved anything,' he says, arriving on the green after a spell in a bunker. 'Good shot, Chris,' says David.

Evans and I are now putting, and it becomes clear that putting is a serious problem. The *Telegraph* ball zooms from one side to the other, as though over a billiard table. An aerial map of the strokes would look like a spider's web. At last, we both get sufficiently near to be given the hole, and Evans continues his self-analysis.

'I am trying to look over the mountain and let everyone get on with climbing it. I am trying to look over the other side,' he says. Aha! I scribble the quote, and as we launch into the second hole, my spirits begin to rise.

Evans is not, in the literal sense, a big hitter. 'I'm very weak,' he says, and indeed, our shots from the tee are not dissimilar.

'Nice one, Chris,' says David as the megastar's second heads for the green, and then – shame and despair. I square up, swing violently, and instead of the ball, a large chunk of Buckinghamshire floats through the air, followed by several smaller clods. The ball trickles a few feet.

Evans retrieves the divots. My next two shots are like hitting the top of an egg. The ball spangs uselessly a few yards at a time; and then Evans does a wonderful thing. He gives me a piece of advice.

'Always swing through it,' he says. 'You're trying to hit it.' And do you know, he is right. 'I talk a great game,' says Evans as we move on. By now, though, three golfers behind us are signalling a desire to play through, and we sit down in the rough.

It is a balmy day; high clouds, soft sun, and Evans seems happy to talk. Others have excavated his past – the father who died of cancer when he was 14, the working-class upbringing in Warrington, the £150 a week job as a Tarzanogram, the way he wangled himself a job on Manchester's Piccadilly radio. But never mind the past; what about the future? Where is he on that mountain he mentioned on the green?

It seems that, in fact, he's not at the top. He's just having a breather, while everyone else scrabbles vainly on ahead. 'If you have the luxury of stopping – having other people do things for you – you can look around and look into the future,' says the 32-year-old. 'That's what Rupert Murdoch does. He thinks about the future.'

There it is again! I can hear Shirley Bassey singing the theme tune of the great tycoon. All we need is David to play Oddjob and decapitate someone with a bowler hat.

So what aspect of modern life does Evans propose to dominate next? Books? Film?

'It's not about that. Books have been done before and feature films have been done before. It's quite easy to turn the media upside down, but nobody has ever done it before. I was really angry after the Montreux television festival. This is supposed to be a ground-breaking weekend, and the BBC people came back after getting completely trolleyed in Lake Geneva, and the biggest headline was that they have re-signed Dawn French and Jennifer Saunders.'

The full horror of this is not obvious. Even more puzzling is his objection to drunkenness. What about his friendship with Jimmy Five Bellies, the benders with Gazza? 'That's my style. I enjoy drinking too much, but I think it's quite bad for me.

'I've been so drunk I haven't been able to pronounce my name or give my address to the taxi driver. I had to move from Kensington Park Road because it is difficult to pronounce.

'Arundel Gardens is easier. Pont Street is a piece of piss. Try Prison Officers Association when you are drunk. No chance, absolutely no chance.'

What about drugs? 'I smoke the odd spliff. I don't have a problem with that. I've been cornered by people talking about nothing for an hour with their noses six inches from your face. Now, I know to walk away, because they are on coke.

'I have been offered coke millions of times; but I've never taken it because I am not interested. A lot of people who work with me take it, but I don't think it does them any good.'

Just then, Patrick comes tripping across the sward in dark glasses. He pretends to be worried about an appointment I have in London, but the real reason is obvious.

Another golf cart has drawn up some way off. Our time is drawing to a close. We can see the *Sun* snappers, with lenses the size of milk churns.

'One more hole,' says Evans, sensing perhaps that I need to salvage some golfing pride; and on the way, he describes his cultural life. He is famously a man from the post-literate age. He used to boast that he had read only three books, including *My Family And Other Animals* by Gerald Durrell, and *Lady Boss* by Jackie Collins, but the tally is rising. He's stuck into *Sophie's World*, and Jeffrey Archer gave him his latest in the hope of securing Evans's support in the race to be London's mayor.

'I said, "I can't give you my support while Ken Living-stone's involved," and he said, "I think Ken's going to drop out pretty soon".

'*I'd* be a great mayor,' he adds, and then qualifies this quickly. 'But I don't think I'd know enough.'

It is time for the last tee-off. Whoever is the god of golf – Hercules, I suppose: he had a club – took my elbow, and good heavens, the ball soared from the tee to the green in one.

'Look at your pitch, mate,' says Evans, pointing to the impact hole with real delight. 'We're so intimidated, aren't we? That will be a birdie – one under par.'

If only it were. The match ends, and we reflect what a genial chap Chris Evans is, though, funnily enough, he's not that good at golf; unless – ghastly thought – he was only being polite.

Kelvin MacKenzie

Health warning: this article should not be read by those of a sensitive disposition, or by anyone having breakfast.

It is only a couple of hours since the coup. The radio station has barely capitulated and already Kelvin Mac-Kenzie is firing on all cylinders. In fact, he's fired three senior executives already, and seems frightfully bucked by the experience.

'It's only 20 past four,' he boasts, meaning there's plenty more firing time left in the day. You may never have heard of Talk Radio, a so-far unsuccessful attempt to mimic the speech-only programmes of America and Australia. But if anyone can justify the £24.7 million he has just spent on a business losing £8 million a year, it is Kelv; because any journalist would admit that he is a master of his trade. He is the privately-educated wordsmith who reduced newsrooms to jelly with his sarff London bawl.

His name stands, in some eyes, for all that is coarse, brutish and base, and yet his reign at the *Sun* yielded such gems of the sub-editor's craft as 'Gotcha' (the sinking of the Belgrano), 'Hop Off You Frogs' (the lamb war), 'Up Yours Delors' (plans for a single currency) and 'Freddie Starr Ate My Hamster' (speaks for itself, I think). 'It's highly unlikely that the editor writes the headlines,' says Kelvin modestly. 'He takes the credit for the ones that go down well and, with the ones that go down badly, someone has to be dismissed at once. The headline "Paddy Pantsdown" was written by the picture editor, but I don't like to reveal these things because it affects my after dinner speaking price, hur, hur.'

Kelvin took the *Sun* to the height of its political influence, as John Major discovered on Black Wednesday, Sept 16, 1992. 'He said, you know (imitates John Major), "Heh, exciting day, how are you going to play it?" This was 7.30, quarter to eight, and interest rates had been going up and down all day like a whore's drawers – no, you can't say that in *The Daily Telegraph* – like Ron Davies's trousers. So I said, "Look, I've got a bucketful of **** on my desk and I am going to pour it all over you" and he said "Hmmm, you are a wag". Which showed me that he was totally out of touch with ordinary people and the danger of Prime Ministers having relations with tabloid editors, because in the end the one loyalty an editor should have is to his readers.'

Doesn't he regret any of his rubbishings and monsterings? 'No, absolutely not. All those guys who employ PRs to give one image of themselves have virtually no defence. They all live in these great big houses and all the rest.'

353

And what about the not-so-famous, such as that man who glued himself to the lavatory seat. Did he deserve such humiliation? Kelvin hoots. 'He went into the bathroom and thought he was getting some haemorrhoid cream, and for some reason it was superglue and he glued the cheeks of his **** together, and it took half an hour with a hacksaw and half of Derbyshire Infirmary to help. That was raised by Joe Ashton MP, and the point was that the guy was quite happy to talk about it.'

What about the children he sent crying home from school? His mood subtly alters. 'Are you all right? Did you have a long lunch, Boris? Crying over what? Perhaps their parents should have thought about that before they did it. Lots of people, including me, get tubloads poured over them.'

Actually, *Sun* victims have one modest consolation. Kelvin himself appears to have undergone a mid-life crisis, and disappeared to the West Indies with a girl. At which point he was 'fronted up' by another tabloid. 'Well, what could I say, what could I do? The *Mail on Sunday* were doing their job. There was a young lady who was euphemistically described as not my wife, and that's fair enough. You can hardly complain.'

There were more serious goofs, like the *Sun*'s handling of the Hillsborough stadium disaster, and the libel of Elton John. But MacKenzie survived. After 12 years he took his pungent gift of innovation to Sky and then to Live TV, famous for topless darts and the News Bunny.

Now he has pumped his entire savings into Talk Radio. 'When I told my wife she didn't say anything except, "I'm not moving house and I'm not living in a semi in Whitstable."'

A man from Apax, a venture capital outfit that is funding Talk Radio, puts his head round the door. 'I'll be back in a minute,' says Kelvin. 'I've got to sack him.'

As I leave, our photographer is striving for the most flattering angle. 'It does look a bit chinny,' he says, indicating the MacKenzie dewlap. 'I'm not surprised,' says Kelvin. 'There's a lot of Chardonnay gone into that.'

Dancing with Ulrika

The ancients believed that sometimes a goddess or nymph would descend from Olympus or Parnassus or some such top address, and, finding a horny handed goatherd, reveal to him the secret of a key advance in human civilisation: the notes of the musical scale, bee-keeping, wine-making, and so on.

They further held that this goatherd, regaining the power of speech after the shock and beauty of the epiphany, would spread the word among his fellows. Think of that antique peasant, my friends, and you will understand the feelings of this hack.

First they hooted, the cackling crows in the office when the idea was discussed. Then you can imagine the blank, hostile jealousy when the sensational news came through from Ulrika's people. Not 90 minutes, old son, they said, white-lipped. Not you and her, cheek to cheek. Naaah, they said.

And yes, as the Weekend team stood in the graffitied murk of the Ministry of Sound, run by the ever so slightly terrifying Jamie Palumbo, we were none too sure that the visitation would really take place. In the anterooms of the 'Ministry', a *boite de nuit* in Elephant and Castle, boardroom meetings full of black polonecks were charting a course of world domination.

The vulpine figure of Palumbo himself could be seen in a raised glass-walled office, greenlighting new discos in

Manila and Vientiane. The clock advanced. Our hearts sank.

Then, when we had all but given up hope, the metal door clanged. Somehow the shades of the discotheque seemed to melt in bashful awe as she approached. The janitors ceased their sponging of the begummed and butted floor. 'Hello, lovely Boris,' said Ulrika, with the easy familiarity of Athena addressing Odysseus, and her teeth lit the room like a lamp.

Bowing low, I led her to a special disco place in the heart of Palumbo's darkness, called the VIP bar. A tape machine was turned on and began to spool silently. She looked at me. I looked at her. There was nothing for it.

You know the problem. Or if you've forgotten the embarrassment, it's coming up again in the next couple of months. Yup. It's time to get that party hat on, get those shirt tails out, get legless and get on down.

It's not that all men are bad at dancing. It's just that most of us are. Our strategy is to shuffle ambiguously, until the Rolling Stones come on, at which point we do a kind of vertical squat-thrust, like Gianni de Michelis, the 18-stone former Italian foreign minister and global authority on Milanese discotheques; and having raised ourselves about six and a half inches, we come down with enough violence to rattle the parquet, were our descent not checked by the ingrown toenail of the nice woman in the expenses department.

Or else we stick out a tentative foot. We jut our chins. We wiggle stertorously down into a squatting position, whereupon our pants split. That, frankly, exhausts our repertoire, and that has been good enough for me; good enough, that is, until a month or so ago, and I realised that times have moved on.

It was in Nice, and I was doing my Denis Thatcher routine at a conference of European lawyers, hoofing it,

356

as one does, in the Negresco ballroom. All of a sudden I realised that everyone was doing the same thing. Out of the jumble a phalanx had been formed. Cummerbunded QCs, chaps who spend their days explicating article 85 of the Treaty of Rome in Luxembourg, were touching their elbows and wobbling their bellies with perfect synchronicity, and then, as one, shouting in Spanish.

Someone later told me it was called the *Macarena*. Apparently Al Gore, the catatonic Democrat, is an accomplished exponent. Even Newt Gingrich can do it. Try as I might to keep up out of the corner of the eye, I was nowhere. I blushed. I stammered.

It was like being suddenly invited to chip in to a seminar on particle physics. That is why, for the sake of all of us easy skankers, kibe-gallers and toe-squashers, we begged Ulrika for a lesson. She could tell us, we reasoned, what challenges chaps like us face this festive season.

To my astonishment, in an act of golden-hearted charity that one might liken to Brigitte Bardot's compassion for some stricken donkey or condemned mutt, she consented. The former Rear of the Year, she with the Red Devil tattooed on her left buttock, the woman opinion polls say most men would like to sleep with, agreed to come down from her Olympus – in Datchet, I think – and give us, the Hopeless Ones, the gift of the dance.

So we waited ominous seconds for the music to begin. She observed that it was parky in here. Those Ministry of Sound tycoons don't waste money on fuel, I agreed, my breath hanging awkwardly in the air.

'I've got cold hands,' she said, blowing on them, 'but a warm heart.' Now there were drums. It sounded promising. Aha, yes: Sympathy For The Devil. The Stones. No problemo. Up. Kick. Down. Kick. 'No, no,' said Ulrika. She wanted something else, and soon it was procured.

Whooh. I wonder why. Whooo. He's the greatest

dancer. Ulrika did something oriental with her neck, causing her head to move along her shoulders in a kind of smooth Thunderbird click that only my mother-in-law can surpass.

I wonder why. Whooh. That I've ever seen. Another problem about dancing: what on earth are you supposed to say? You think of some banality, and bellow it, and she says 'What?' and then you try again, and she says 'What?' and by the third or fourth go, you've rather lost heart in the thing you were going to say.

So I asked Ulrika, did she, er, go to many clubs and raves and that sort of thing? 'Do you come here often?', she shot back, with a mellow laugh. I ventured to compliment her on her long black leather coat, a sort of SS commandant's dream.

'Ve have vays of making you dance,' she said, looking appraisingly at my style. 'Boris,' said the former weathergirl and all-purpose comedian-cum-megastar in warm, understanding tones, 'the whole thing is about absolute freedom of the body.

'You can do things you can do on the dance floor that you wouldn't do in the office. You can afford to push back the boundaries of your sexuality.' Now she was like an oscillating osier in a warm, wet, wind.

'Think snake,' she urged. Perhaps because it was so nippy in Palumbo's dungeon, my efforts were if anything a shade more lumpy and disjointed than normal. 'Slow down,' she advised. The problem was partly in the shoulders, she diagnosed, and partly in the legs.

'Think sssexy,' said Ulrika, running her hands over what her fellow metmen used to call her frontal systems. By Zeus. Now she was undulating like a Sikh Queen approaching the divan of her moaning king, before bumping him off with a draught of khat or ghat or whatever.

Or perhaps she was, indeed, a snake, a leather-coated

mamba hypnotising a gerbil. Inspired by a distant memory of rugby warm-up exercises, I started to rotate what I believed to be my pelvis.

Ulrika was polite. 'In dancing, you should use your greatest asset, which in your case is your face,' she said. This seemed uncommonly civil. 'When we get to the really sexy tune, you'll want to be telling everything with your face.'

Aha. The sexy tune, eh? I was all set for that one. By now, Ulrika had taken her coat off, and it was obvious why Palumbo didn't bother with the heating in here. When the place is stuffed with semi-nude teutonic tourists, as it apparently is every weekend, it must become an inferno.

But for some reason the next tune was a species of techno-jangling House or Garage or Carpark, and Ulrika wasn't having it. 'That is for people who've taken some tablets,' she said. Followers of Ulrika will know that she can drink a pint of lager in one, but pills are not for her.

While someone rootled for a new tape she walked over and read the Sports section of the *Daily Telegraph*, or, to be more exact, an analysis of the latest infamy perpetrated by her man, Aston Villa's Stan Collymore. This Collymore, you will recollect, is the brute who tendered his resignation from the human race when he struck Ulrika in a Paris bar, just because she was showing everyone else her lager-drinking trick. The amazing truth, according to the tabloids, is that Ulrika still feels affection for Colly. This cowardy Custard. This big girl's blouse. It would have been tactless to bring the subject up. But her continuing devotion to the Colly must be rated one of the mysteries of evolution.

'Huh,' she said, after absorbing the truth about Collymore's foul, and its part in Villa's defeat. She set her jaw in an unreadable line. Whatever her inner thoughts, the tutorial seemed to gain momentum after that, as Sister Sledge came on with the new theme tune of Tory social policy.

'We Are Fam-i-LY!' She took me by the middle and we leant backward together, a bit like the cover of that old Madness album. 'You're collapsing,' she said, which was quite wrong. Perhaps the odd bead was by now dewing the brow, but the legs were as tungsten girders. Pretty soon, I must confess, it would have been good to have that old slow number; and what man in my position would not have conceived the same hope, if only for the sake of a breather? *Honi soit qui mal y pense*, that's the motto.

But, no, there was no let-up from the lactic-acid build-up in the legs. 'Night fever, Night fev-AAAH,' sang the Bee Gees. 'Pout, pout!' said Ulrika, showing me how. 'That's part of the flirting. It's communicating without sending memos.' Indeed, I assented, composing the features into a cast-iron pout.

'You look like an orang-utang,' she said, indulgently of course. Things must have started to look a bit more systematic because Eleanor, the photographer, shouted, 'No, Boris, not so close!' and I sprang away like a startled frog.

'I would say closer,' said Ulrika, with what can only be called supreme sportsmanship. Struggling to get my mind back to the question of office parties, I asked her advice for damsels pursued, as they will be in the coming weeks, by corpulent executives of middle years. 'Outdance the bastard!' said Ulrika, showing her pace, and now she was doing something complicated with her arms.

Stop! In the name of love! said the song, and she imitated a policeman holding up traffic. *Before you break my heart!* and she quickly made a snapping motion with both fists, and then drew a picture of a heart in the air. Disco kings have since told me that this is a well-known dodge, but to my joy it came pretty easily, and soon we were two minds with but a single thought, two hearts which beat as one . . .

'That's the kind of song where you can make your feelings very well known to someone,' she said, and her blue eyes locked on mine. And then for one brief, flame-like moment that somehow seemed an eternity there on the floor of the Ministry of Sound, we came together and . . . Relax, relax, everyone. I made that bit up. Take it easy, Stan. Easy there, boy. Anyway, we *Telegraph* hacks, it is well known, are expert in the arts of self-defence. The wretched truth was our time was drawing to a close.

'We're not doing a slow number?' she asked, with what sounded pretty convincingly like disappointment. We were not.

'It needs more than one session,' she said. If that isn't politeness on a heroic scale, I don't know what is. So, my fellow rugcutters and curvetters, what did Ulrika teach me, apart from 'Think snake'?

At the end of our session she had given instruction in 'the cauldron', in which you make a stirring motion, while moving your body at half the speed. Very tricky. There was the 'Nefertiti and Akhenaton', where you imitate an Egyptian frieze with sideways-on jabbing motions of the arms. And there was the ever-popular 'shelf-stacker', in which you pretend to heave six-packs from the floor to waist height.

Schooled in those, none of us will ever seem inadequate on the dance-floor again. Such was the revelation from on high. She was gone, Terpsichore or Melpomene or some other muse, convincingly disguised as a Swedish wunderfrau, back to Olympus or Parnassus or Datchet, or at least back to her prowling limo outside.

Soon she was talking happily on her mobile, and waving to us as we trudged on blistered feet back to our ploughs at Canary Wharf. Actually, she said she was off to see her osteopath. It was completely coincidental, she said.

Robert Harris

As we cross the foot-bridge and see the house he laughs lightly. 'Rumours of its opulence are greatly exaggerated,' he says. Surely not.

What a vision. Here, rolling immaculately down to the Kennet, is the sward where Blair rests his weary limbs, where Mandy sports on a summer afternoon. There the XJS squats butchly on the gravel: all trophies of Robert Harris's coruscating pen. Within is Gill, his wife, assorted staff, and one of his three children.

He's the Labour answer to Jeffrey Archer – and what a withering retort he is.

I speak as one who has been kept awake by *Archangel*, his latest bestseller. We mere journalists, we who are as he once was, grind our teeth as we contemplate not just his success, but the elegance, the neatness of his creativity. Why didn't I dream up this yarn of a brilliant-but-bibulous British history don (Norman Stone) discovering something spooky beginning with S in the Russian north?

In the study, Harris explains that Stalin came to him in a dream. 'There was this sense of violence crackling round him, though he was quite friendly.' History does not relate what Stalin said to Harris. But we can guess. 'Good work, Comrade, with your what-if-Hitler-won book, *Fatherland*. $1.8 million for the US rights alone! Not bad. Six million copies sold of *Fatherland* and *Enigma* combined, and now Mel Gibson has bought the rights to *Archangel*. But, Tovarish, now is the time to achieve power! Socialism needs you . . . ha ha.'

And with a horrible cackle the Georgian melted into the Kintbury night. Shaken, no doubt, by this epiphany, the 41-year-old Harris is changing tack again.

He is the son of a Nottingham printer, and 'born into the Labour Party'. He went to the local school in Melton Mowbray before going to Cambridge, where he managed to edit the university magazine and be president of the Union. He has scaled the summits of hackery. He has done the novels. Now he's trying to be a New Labour media tycoon, prising the *New Statesman* from Geoffrey Robinson's grasp.

The other week he wrote a column in the *Sunday Times*, which might have been called My Friend Mandelson the Martyr. Pah, he said, pressing the smelling-salt-soaked hankie to his nose. He was appalled at the way dear Peter had been treated. For the first time, he felt ashamed of his profession. They were a bunch of 'skinheads'.

'Ere, said the rest of us, 'ow come you're calling us skinheads, Mr Fancypants? Think you're too good for us now, just cos Tony Blair's yer best mate?

'I don't knock the media for one second for getting the story,' says Harris. 'The column was written on Boxing Day morning,' he says plaintively. 'But the idea that I shouldn't even put in a word for the poor old sod [Mandy] honestly never even occurred to me. I took the view that my name had been linked with his in the good times and it would have been morally weak to dissociate myself.'

Indeed. Harris it was who first tempted Mandy to error. He took him into a high place, Notting Hill, and showed him the fleshpots of west London; at one point, Harris was going to buy the house for him.

For better or worse, something has happened to Harris the Hack. He has become a New Labour figure. 'Politics,' he says, 'has become like late 19th century France, all about who is sleeping with whom. Society hostesses strut across the stage. It is like *Vanity Fair* – there's this extra-ordinary group of people.'

He detects a whiff of puritanism in some of the Mandy-bashing. 'Oooh!' he says in mock horror, 'his £1,400 chair. They [the critics] are the new Bolsheviks.'

But surely there's a kind of logic in feeling cheesed off with people who put up your taxes, when they are cushioned from life's realities by Robinson's millions? 'Huh,' he says, 'maybe Labour has made some marginal difference in tax. But not as much as John Smith or Healey would have made.'

So what ethic does he have in mind for the *New States-man*, bible of Britain's sandal-wearing wheat-germ scof-fers? The Staggers, which drones on about 'the Third Way', loses £500,000 a year, while *The Spectator* has double the circulation and makes a profit. He wants the *Statesman* to be a pleasure to read, he says, 'but those very character-istics which render people Left-wing render them reluctant to be seen having a good time'.

'Moneybags', as Harris is affectionately known, is writ-ing the biography of John Le Carré, with whom he bears some comparison, and has a contract to write three more thrillers. This dabbling in hackery and politics is only 20 per cent of his life, he swears. 'I don't want to keep opening a paper and reading something about me and my life-style and my friends.' But 20 per cent of him does.

Jenny Agutter

Phwoar, we said, and who can blame us? It was hot. The end of term video was *American Werewolf in London*. Jenny Agutter appeared on screen, and, let me tell you, she went down big with her 12-year-old audience.

We stamped. We cheered. We toasted her with orange squash and Nice biscuits. And that is why, decades later, when I am slumped before some zoo-like late night discussion show, and there she is, tip-tilted as ever, I feel a sudden spasm, a memory of those pent-up feelings. Even Glenda Jackson's Stalinist features melt in the penumbra of her charm.

Jenny Agutter is talking passionately, persuasively, and – good grief – according to the caption on the screen, she represents 'Transport 2000' the anti-car think-tank. Wouldn't it be grand, I muse, if someone like that could be persuaded to appear on the back page?

Wouldn't that be the stuff to give the troops? So imagine my feelings when, the following day, she actually rings back, within 10 minutes. 'It's Jenny Agutter,' she says melodiously, her surname scanning like Agatha rather than a piece of road drainage; and barely two hours later my cab has groaned through south-east London, and here we are in the cosy parlour of her newly done-up Camberwell schloss, she in her lacy white shirt, black waistcoat and flowery skirt. Yes, who can forget how she took off her red knickers in *The Railway Children*, and waved them at the train? This event is seared in the memory of the boffins of Transport 2000 because, she admits, it inspired them to ask her to be a patron, and to speak in their cause on TV.

'In truth, I have always loved trains,' she says, and speaks fondly of travelling from Waterloo to Camberley, where she was at school. Indeed, it would be a mistake to think that Jenny Agutter is just lending her name, on the strength of being a Railway Child.

So volcanic are her feelings that if a car should go past her at speed in Camberwell, 'I stand and shake my first, or stand in the road to slow them down.' Paragraphs bubble from her lips as we sit in the gloaming, ideas for 'diamond lanes', and car pools. She denounces the 'hideous' school run, and wonders why supermarkets cannot lay on buses like Ikea in New York.

She is about to set off for Cornwall and points out that a first-class return costs more than a transatlantic flight. She asked Glenda Jackson why the Government subsidy could not go towards cutting fares, rather than boosting Railtrack's profits. 'She gave a very complicated reply,' she says.

'Why will people stand waiting for a taxi for 15 minutes when they could have walked in that time?' Why, she wants to know, can't the staff on public transport have some sense of where they are, instead of thinking of stops as blobs on the line in a white desert? And as her fervour mounts, it suddenly hits me: there are two great themes to the art of Jenny Agutter. They are environmentally-friendly transport, and nudity. You will remember her sensational role in *The Eagle Has Landed*, where she rides a horse to the beach, and then takes her clothes off. Then there was *Equus*, in which horses play a key part, and in which she also took her clothes off.

Then there was *Walkabout* which, I gather, involves a lot of walking about with no clothes on. We have already discussed *The Railway Children*, and her bloomer-removing approval for public transport. In fact, we've covered the first key theme of her oeuvre, transport, pretty well. We've got to the core of the problem: viz, that if you do succeed in persuading a large chunk of the public to

366

stop using their cars, there will come a point when people will suddenly notice that the roads are nice and clear and, hey presto, traffic's back.

By this stage, well, I am mentally trying to formulate a question on the other aspect, you know, the nudity business and am finding it quite tricky (and so would you) when clunk, thunk, dunk . . . Uh-oh.

A very large blond man comes in to the room.

'Hello,' he says challengingly and thuds down a big black briefcase. I say, idiotically: 'I'm just taking the chance to grab a quick interview with your wife.'

'Well,' says Johan Tham, the proprietor of the Cliveden hotel, 'I'll just take the chance to grab a quick drink.' He crashes into the kitchen, pours a glass of white wine for Jenny and himself, and heads upstairs.

'I don't use public transport,' he announces, at the door. 'Never'. In fact, he has an Audi A8 with an engine of no less than 3.7 litres. Somehow, perhaps because Johan can be heard on the phone upstairs, I never get round to the no-clothes-on business. But who cares?

Buoyed up with the pleasure of meeting her, I leave determined to do my bit. This means walking some way to the bus stop. After quite a long wait in a dodgy-seeming area a bus arrives, shudders to a standstill, and a sign says 'Not In Service.' After a while another bus arrives, and . . . to cut a long story short, I get a cab.

RIP Alan Clark

The thing about charming people, the catch, the downside, is that the greater their charm, the more painful it is when, almost certainly inadvertently, they say something that is in some way wounding. There I was in the Committee

Corridor of the Commons. It was the day of the 1997 Tory leadership election.

Here came Alan Clark, swaying down the corridor with his lizard-hipped gait, eyeing the pustulent throng of lobby correspondents through narrowed, amused eyes. 'Alan!' I cried, since we were, so I imagined, on good terms, or rather, we enjoyed the treacherous chumminess of journalists and politicians.

I had once interviewed him fairly sycophantically, with lots of stuff, which I stick by, about how he was arguably our greatest diarist since Pepys, and how he could detect a bogus Bellini at 50 paces and a bottle blonde at 100 yards. The article had drawn attention to his power and originality as a historian; and he had once, in public, been embarrassingly kind about me. And so, fortified by this vague sense of matiness, I hailed him there in the corridor, surrounded by my friends and colleagues in the Lobby.

'Alan,' I said, and asked him a wholly reasonable question, a question we had been asking every one of the smirking Tories who came and went from Room Five, after voting for William Hague or Ken Clarke.

'Who are you going to vote for, eh?' I asked. And then he slowly turned that dolichocephalic skull with its woolly iron quiff, and around me I could feel the crowd of journos tense over their notebooks, since Clark was an unknown quantity in this question, and he gazed at me briefly in a saurian sort of way, and he spoke, this belletrist, this curling-tonged epigrammatist, this adornment of the English language; and do you know what he said? He said: 'Sod off,' though he managed to fit about five syllables into the word 'sod'; and I must confess that I felt ever so slightly crushed.

Yes, I thought, of course he is right: I should set about sodding off immediately. Off is exactly the direction in which I should sod. That, I thought, as all the other hacks gurgled with pleasure and my ears turned pink, is a jolly good piece of advice from Mr Clark to an impertinent journalist. All of which serves no purpose other than to prove how frail our egos are and, in that key respect, of course, Clark was the same as the rest of us, only more so.

When you think of the cultural impact of Alan Clark in 1990s' Britain – as great as that of his father in another decade – you could not solely attribute his popularity to his diaries. These were, as everyone has said, a kind of masterpiece; not because of the lascivious stuff, the studied indiscretions about the bouncing globes of girls on trains, and the Red Box winking at him in the luggage rack above.

Clark's achievement was to produce a melancholy and absorbing thriller, in which he understood the central role in politics of failure. He takes us through his worship of Margaret Thatcher, his craving for approval, his pathetic, spaniel-like attempts to get into the Cabinet; and then, symmetrically, we see the comeuppance of that rare woman who has refused to go all the way with him, and to whom he remains devoted – particularly devoted – in the hour of her political extinction.

Those diaries reached a vast readership; they made politics interesting to people who would not normally bother with the *Today* programme; but they don't, in themselves, explain the impact of Clark. To understand his success, you have to grasp what was happening to the entire male sex, or at least its British representatives, in the pathetic post-feminist uncertainties of the 1990s.

Here was a man, just like the readers of *GQ*, *Esquire*, *Loaded* – all the reassurance-craving magazines that have sprouted in the past 10 years – who was endlessly fascinated by the various advantages and disappointments of his own gonads. He was interested in cars; he had Bentleys, bulging with tinplate testosterone; he had Rollers and Aston Martins and special chickwagons for arriving at *The Spectator* party; and in that respect, of course, he perfectly echoed the hedonistic juvenile vroom-vroom obsessions of anyone who reads a lads' mag.

He even went so far as to share with the former editor of *Loaded* magazine an unhealthy interest in Nazism, or at least in the style of the Nazis; though Clark, naturally, was more outré. He seemed to share the autarkic tenets of Nazi economics, and would, had he ever been allowed to by Mrs T, have pursued a Goldsmithian agenda of agrarian self-sufficiency and protectionism.

Like the readers of the modern lads' mags, wondering vaguely what to do with themselves now that women seem so keen on running the world, Clark also exhibited a certain insecurity. Behind all that ostentatious boasting about sex, there must have lurked, one assumes, an element of self-doubt. Above all, like the ideal *Loaded* reader, he had a selfish side to him.

He dumped his colleagues in it over Matrix Churchill, and some of them have not forgiven him. He was loyal to John Major, after he had made the mistake of giving up his Plymouth seat in 1992, but that may have been because he wanted to get back into the Commons. He was certainly not loyal to William Hague when he re-entered in 1997.

My last visual memory of him is watching him break ranks over Kosovo, shaking with anger as he attacked the bombing of a 'Christian' country. That was Clark all over: provocative, brilliant – but carrying you just further than you wanted to go. There were many reasons for finding fault with the Kosovo war, but not that we were backing Muslims against Christians.

And thinking of selfishness, and party unity, we come to his successor in the Royal Borough of Kensington and Chelsea. It would be good for the Conservative Party, and good for Michael Portillo, if he were the man. Let us hope he 'allows his name to go forward'. It will work, though, only if he sticks to Hague like glue, if he expends all the devotion on the party leader that Clark expended on Thatcher. The last thing the Tory party needs is another scene like the one we have mentioned in the Committee Corridor, or another defenestration to be secretly recorded by whichever political diarist has the nerve to follow in the footsteps of Alan Clark.

Martin McGuinness

What a place, I think to myself, as I arrive at Stormont. You drive up past the enormous lawns, and the great bronze statue of Carson, the Unionist leader, waving defiance, and everywhere you look there are signs of the British imperium: the vast ghostly pediment fringed with marble palmettes, the ceilings painted eggshell blue, and terracotta and silver; the lion, the unicorn, and *honi soit qui mal y pense*; the red despatch boxes; the Speaker's Chair, the dedications to those who died for king and country. But if you keep going down the marble corridor, and up about three flights of stairs, you will come to something rather odd. 'Crinniu ar siul bain usaid as an doras eile', barks the notice on the door, in what one takes to be a Gaelic demand for privacy.

Behind it sits the blond-curled and sweatered form of a man who has spent his entire adult life engaged, as he confirms, in a programme of terror, whose objective has been to destroy British power in Northern Ireland. He has almost succeeded in chopping the Royal Ulster Constabulary; he has brought about the release of hundreds of terrorist prisoners; he is on this very morning conducting a war of words over whether the Unionists have the right to insist on the Union flag flying from this building where, if and when the executive returns, he will once again serve as education minister; and he has done it without renouncing violence, or even causing a single weapon to be handed over.

Some see Martin McGuinness as a cherubic grandfather and fly-fishing fanatic, a man of religious conviction who rose to the leadership of Sinn Fein/IRA through his manifest integrity, and who has just persuaded them to make the huge concession of offering their weapons for inspection. To others he is the *capo di tutti capi*, the godfather of the IRA, a pale-eyed killer. In the words of the IRA historian Kevin Toolis, 'no other living person is a greater threat to the British state'.

He welcomes me with great friendliness, and his charm perhaps partly explains the chronic weakness of the British government in dealing with him. On the wall is a poem about the death of Mairead Farrell, and a child's pencilled scrawl in praise of Sinn Fein.

What's it like being dwarfed by these emblems of British rule? How does it feel to come to work every day under the salute of Carson, to be a member of the British government? 'No, I'm not actually – uctually – I don't swear an oath of allegiance to anyone other than the people who elected me.' This is still part of the UK, isn't it? 'Well, the British – the Bratash – tell us it is, but we want to change that.' Come on, Martin: are the salaries of your officials paid for by London or by Dublin? 'Obviously the salaries are paid for by the executive and by the considerable subsidy that comes from the British government.' And might you not have a car and a driver, paid for by us, the British taxpayers? 'No "might" about it. I will get one. I didn't want a BMW. I didn't want a Mercedes. I just wanted a car that would be adequate and would not be over the top or anything like that.'

What was the best bit about your eight weeks in government, before Mr Mandelson closed down the assembly? 'I announced the largest school-building programme ever in the North of Ireland, £72 million for building new schools.' And I bet it was a pleasure to spend British money, eh? I ask the man who drew the dole while trying to smash British rule. 'Yeah, ha ha ha,' he laughs.

It is amazing. The butcher's boy from the Bogside is campaigning against the 11-plus, which he failed himself. He's tough on EU integration. 'We're anti a common European army, that's what we're anti,' he says, and chuckles at the thought of a Sinn Fein–Tory agreement. He's in and out of Downing Street; he's penetrated the highest levels of the British establishment; he's bombed his way to power. Don't you feel a sense of triumph, I ask him. 'Triumph? Why? You have to understand that we are Irish Republicans. What we want to bring about fundamentally is an end to British rule in the North and the establishment of a 32-county republic.'

Martin McGuinness's mother was from Donegal. His father worked in a foundry. The second eldest boy in a family of six children, he had his first experience of sectarian prejudice when he tried to get a job with a local garage; when it emerged that he had been to a local Catholic school, the interview ended. He was at the battle of the Bogside in 1969. In 1971, as 'officer' commanding the Derry Brigade of the IRA, he set about blowing the heart out of his own city. Of Londonderry's 150 shops, only 20 were left standing by the time he and his comrades had finished.

Then, on 20 January 1972, there was Bloody Sunday. According to an intelligence source codenamed Infliction, McGuinness fired the first shot, from a tommy gun in the Rossville flats, which prompted the Paras to return fire. 'That has since been repudiated by British soldier after

British soldier who has given evidence to the tribunal.' But you were there? 'I was on the march, yeah, like thousands of others.' But you did no shooting on that day? 'That's all nonsense.'

Actually, Sean O'Callaghan says that Infliction is wrong, and that McGuinness is telling the truth. Huh, scoffs McGuinness at the idea of support from O'Callaghan, a senior IRA man in the republic who became an informer, and saved many lives. If Sean says it's the truth, it must be a lie, he says. 'What a remarkable person to be quoting to me. He's got himself in an awful predicament. I am sure it must be painful for anyone born in the island of Ireland, even in a place like Kerry, to be effectively domiciled in a place like England.' This sounds like gangster talk. Why should Sean be afraid? 'I mean if he walked down the main street in Tralee, I wouldn't give tuppence for his ability to get from one end to the other.' Sean O'Callaghan says he had dozens of meetings with you to plan terrorist operations. 'I used to have meetings with him? I think I met him once or twice in Sinn Fein HQ in Dublin, but, I mean, Sean's the past.'

After Bloody Sunday, the British state in Northern Ireland was under siege. In 1972, 500 people were killed, including 150 members of the security forces. In a panic, Willie Whitelaw flew the Provos to Paul Channon's house in Cheyne Walk. I wonder whether that was when McGuinness first sensed the irresolution of the British state? 'At that stage I was 21 years of age and never in a million years did I expect that I would be part of a delegation to meet with, effectively, British ministers in London. It was a totally unreal experience for me.' McGuinness only spoke once, clashing with Whitelaw about Bloody Sunday. The talks produced nothing. The bombing and the killing went on.

I try to explain why, as a child, I came to loathe the

IRA and why it seems so monstrous that terror should be rewarded. 'But if you were to apply that logic fairly and honestly, you would have to admit that the British security forces have used terroristic methods in the last 30 years.' Oh come off it, I say, and he reverts, as usual, to Bloody Sunday. 'I come from a city where 14 people were killed by the British army, and many others were wounded. Now outside of those deaths in that city alone, dozens of people were killed by the British army.' But how can you say that those heat-of-the-moment shootings were morally commensurate with what your organisation did to thousands of innocent civilians, in Ulster, and in Warrington, Manchester, Birmingham? 'I believe that the people of Derry believe the opposite of what you believe, and that is a huge problem for you.' He suggests that I have a sentimental pride in the British army, and repeats his experience in 1969, when the army started to shoot his friends. 'You have to imagine the impact that has on an 18-year-old kid from the Bogside.'

When I last met McGuinness five years ago it was in his flyblown HQ, at Cable Street in Londonderry. I asked him if he had ever been a member of the IRA, and he denied it, so I put the question again.

'I have never denied that I was a party to the resistance against the British government in the North during the last 30 years. I've always been very open about that.' So you'd stick by what you said in January 1973, in the Special Criminal Court in Dublin, after you had been found close to a car filled with 250lb of explosives and 5,000 rounds of ammunition? I read it out: 'I am a member of the Derry brigade of Oglaigh na hEireann and am very, very proud of it. We fought against the killers of my people. Many of my comrades were arrested, tortured or killed. Some of them were shot, while unarmed, by the British army. We firmly and honestly believed we were doing our duty as

Irishmen.' There is a long pause. McGuinness grunts and says, 'I am not ashamed of anything I have done in the past.' Did you ever use violence? 'Everyone uses violence. British soldiers use violence.' Were you responsible for anyone's death? 'I think we're all responsible for people's death.' By firing a bullet from a gun? 'Paisley has fired verbal bullets which have caused people to fire guns.' Do you have the blood of anyone on your hands? 'We all do, we all do. We're all responsible. If you're asking me, for example, in the course of the resistance to the British military in the siege of Derry, did I throw a stone that hit a soldier in the head and took blood from him, or did I throw a petrol bomb at a member of the RUC, or did I ever fire a shot that killed a soldier, you know, what's the point? What's the point of it?'

The point, I suppose, is to find out whether you're still a killer, or whether it's all behind you? 'I don't think David Trimble would be meeting with me if he didn't think we were for real,' he says, and nor would Blair or Clinton. But you did return to violence after the 'ceasefire'. I remember the Docklands bomb. 'Well, that was an IRA bomb; it wasn't a Sinn Fein bomb.' Sean O'Callaghan says you must have known about it. 'What credibility does someone have who has been out of Ireland for 15 years?'

So is the war over? 'That question has been raised by the rejectionist Unionists.' Look: your organisation has a bad record of blowing people up. Is the war over? He starts another answer, about how you have to judge people as you find them, so I cut him off. Is the war over, yes or no? 'The answer is that I don't believe the IRA are ever going to say the war is over because the Unionists make that demand.'

Martin McGuinness will not allow himself to be portrayed as the loser; why should he? And yet I come away better understanding why successive British governments have decided that, in spite of his past, he is the man they must deal with, and who, with Adams, holds the key to peace. In the long struggle of wills, he won, and the British government connived in its own defeat. The best hope now – and of course it is morally bankrupt, but not wholly despicable – is that the 'peace process' should grind on, the executive return, and Martin and his kind lose their instinct for terror, and discover the delights of spending taxpayers' money on schools, and riding in Rovers paid for by the state he would destroy.

Forza Berlusconi!

It is twilight in Sardinia. The sun has vanished behind the beetling crags. The crickets have momentarily stopped. The machine-gun-toting guards face out into the maquis of myrtle and olive, and the richest man in Europe is gripping me by the upper arm. His voice is excited. 'Look' he says, pointing his flashlight. 'Look at the strength of that tree.' It is indeed a suggestive sight.

An olive of seemingly Jurassic antiquity has grown from a crack in the rock, and like some patient wooden python it has split the huge grey boulder in two. 'Extraordinary,' I murmur. My host and I stand lost in awe at olive power. If Silvio Berlusconi, 67, Italian Prime Minister, is secretly hoping that a metaphor will form in my head, he is not disappointed.

What does it show, this outrageous olive, but the force which through the green fuse drives Berlusconi himself? And what does it stand for, this colossal cracked stone? You could try the Italian political establishment; or the European liberal elite; or just civilised Western opinion: all things which Silvio has scandalised and divided. Only last week the Swedish foreign minister, Anna Lindh, anathematised not just Berlusconi, but Italy itself.

Under the government of Forza Italia, she claimed, Italy could no longer be said to be part of Western European tradition or share its values. You may think that a flaming cheek, given that Europe's founding text is the Treaty of Rome. Where was Sweden, hey, at the 1955 Conference of Messina? You may find, like me, that at the sight of Berlusconi being monstered by Anna Lindh, your sword instinctively flies from its scabbard in his defence. But it was the attack by the *Economist* newspaper that, I suspect, got in among Berlusconi and his team, not least because it is read in – or lies inert on the coffee tables of – American boardrooms.

Twice now, this distinguished paper (motto: the wit to be dull) has given Silvio a frenzied kicking. It has said that he is not fit to govern Italy, and in a recent edition it laid 28 charges against him and said that not only was he unfit to govern Italy, he was also unfit to be president of the EU – an office he holds until December. It is the *Economist* attack which may have contributed to the presence of *The Spectator* here amid the wattle and rosemary of his 170-acre Costa Smeralda estate. Nick Farrell, our Italy correspondent and biographer of Mussolini, has flown in from Predappio. I have been summoned from the other side of the island where, coincidentally, the Johnson family has also been staying in infinitely less splendid accommodation.

When Farrell and I meet for a tactics talk in a Porto Rotondo bar, we decide that the charges must of course be raised with *signor il presidente*, as the Prime Minister is confusingly called. But we know that we are unlikely to reach a verdict on the key questions, relating as they do to the abortive 1985 sale of a state-owned biscuit company to Buitoni, the spaghetti kings. Let us leave those matters to the lawyers and the desiccated calculators of the *Economist*. We have a broader and higher purpose: that is, to establish whether or not we feel that Sig. Berlusconi is on the whole a force for good in Italy, Europe and the world.

For three hours we have been in his presence. We have sat at a table in his drawing-room, Berlusconi at the head, nipples showing through his white Marlon Brando pyjama-suit, and from time to time that table has been pounded vigorously enough to shake the glass bibelots and naked female figurines that dot the room. We have drunk pints of sweet iced tea, brought silently and unprompted, as he has outlined his robust, neo-conservative view of the world. At one stage, after about an hour, the Prime Minister has vanished into the kitchen himself, and caused the appearance of three plates of vanilla and pistachio ice-cream, as if to refuel his torrential loquacity. We have heard him extol Thatcher, praise Blair ('I have never known us to disagree on anything'), laud Bush and damn the Italian magistracy as 'anthropologically diverse from the rest of humanity'.

It has been, says Valentino, his charming interpreter, the most detailed and generous interview that the leader has ever given, and by 7 p.m. Farrell and I are feeling, frankly, a bit limp. But there is no stopping the balding, beaming, bouncing multi-billionaire. He had a brush with cancer a couple of years ago; his skin is a little sallow for a man who has spent August in Sardinia; he looks less like a million dollars than a million lire. But he is the fizziest old dog you have ever seen. '*Facciamo un giro*,' he says, by which he means, let's go for a ride.

When Berlusconi takes the wheel of a golf buggy, he does not trundle: he prefers to whang it and weave it down the swept paths of his estate, like Niki Lauda on the Monza hairpin. And as his passengers sway like sea anenomes, he gestures at a landscape which is, of course, naturally lovely, with the sun setting and the Tyrrhenian sea turning from indigo to faded denim. But everywhere he sees signs of his own handiwork and everything seems somehow the product of his own imagination. 'There,' he says, pointing to a bank of blue plumbago. 'This is the flower of Forza Italia. The flower doesn't know it, but I know it.'

Forza Italia! Come on, Italy! The very name, with its football-terrace echo, is enough to wrinkle the nostrils of Anna Lindh and the Euro-nomenklatura. Forza Italia was the movement he founded in 1994 with his $12 billion fortune, and with which he first seized the premiership, only to lose it when his right-wing allies ratted on him, and the lawyers closed in. He was indicted on various charges of bribery and corruption.[1] He struggled on in opposition. But the forza was strong in Berlusconi and in 2001 he came storming back.

From port to port went the Forza Italia cruise ship – not unlike the one on which the 17-year-old Berlusconi had sung – and adoring crowds were produced for the cameras. At a cost of $20 million he peppered 12 million Italian households with his magnificent, 128-page all-colour Berluscography, *An Italian Life*. In it they found a story of fantastic, volcanic, American self-propulsion; the early skill in Latin and Greek, a facility he hired for cash to less able pupils; the devoted friends who have remained with him as he expanded his empire, beginning with the town he built in 1960 in a swamp outside Milan which has 4,000 inhabitants and which seems from its photographs to be agreeable in a Milton Keynes-ish way.

They learnt of his first wife and how their feelings for each other turned 'from love to friendship' before he acquired his second wife, knock-out blonde soap-star Veronica Lario. There was news about his suits (Ferdinando Caraceni), his cook, his cancer and, above all, the testimony of his mother Rosella. Silvio's mother said Silvio was a hell of a guy, and whatever Silvio's mother said, other mothers took very seriously. Studded on every page were his cheery chipmunk grin and his Disneyish nose. To every small Italian businessman he stood for optimism and confidence and an ability to get things done. And here, in the first stop of our wacky races golf-cart tour, is a lesson in his can-do approach.

One day Silvio came along and found they had flattened the trees, in a 50-metre radius, to make a helicopter pad. He didn't want a helicopter pad. He was devastated. He went to sleep on Easter night, wrestling with the problem. 'At a certain point I decided that out of each evil you must find a good thing. I thought I could create a labyrinth, and then I decided to make something which had never existed before – a museum of cacti!' We dismount and admire this bizarre amphitheatre in which an audience of 4,000 prickly customers, comprising 400 species from seven countries, looks down from circular terraces on to a beautiful blue pool facing out to the bay. It is cracked but somehow brilliant.

'This is the brain of my finance minister,' says Silvio, pointing to a thing looking like a wrathful artichoke, 'ideas everywhere.' He caresses the powdery flanks of another plant to show its ingenious defence against climbing ants. 'And this,' he says, pointing to a villainous set of spines, 'is the mother-in-law's cushion. This rock came from Lanzarote!' Why did it come from Lanzarote? Was it really essential, this red pumice? Perhaps not: but it showed that Silvio could move mountains.

He has certainly moved Farrell, who is evincing signs of rapture. '*Bravo, Signor Presidente*', says the biographer of Mussolini. '*Veramente bravo!*'

Berlusconi waves aside our enthusiasm but cannot resist the moral. 'See,' he says, 'this is what the private sector can do! I did this! I did it in three months!' I did this: the boast of every alpha male. Thus the three-year-old to his doting mother; thus Agrippa on the frieze of the Pantheon.

The Italian population liked him for his energy and they handsomely returned him. In 2001 he achieved an unprecedented majority, commanding both houses of parliament. He had a huge opportunity to enact what he proclaimed was his vision: a Thatcherian tax-cutting reform of Italy. His enemies went into spasms of indignation and, in truth, one can see the cause of their unease. It is unsettling that one man should have such a concentration of commercial and political authority. It does make one queasy to think that this charming man is not only the biggest media magnate in Italy, owning Mondadori, the biggest publisher, AC Milan, the biggest football club, several newspapers and a huge chunk of Italian television – but is also Prime Minister.

We put these concerns to him and Berlusconi bats it all back in phrases honed with use. No, he didn't go into politics to protect his own commercial interests, as Enzo Biagi, a columnist, has alleged that he privately confessed. 'I couldn't work all my life in Italy with a communist, left-wing government,' he says. No, there is no conflict of interest. People can write what they like in his papers. 'I am the most liberal publisher in history.' And no, the *Economist* charges are old, footling, groundless, and the table incurs a good thudding as he iterates his defence.

It is quite the done thing, he protests, to pass a law exempting himself from prosecution for the term of his office. Chirac has done the same. But it was never our goal, in this interview, to establish the dodginess of his business practices. We were trying only to judge whether he was on balance a good thing. Our answer, when the trolley-ride finally ends and we are sitting like a pair of oiled guillemots over a beer in Porto Rotondo, is an unambiguous yes.

It is hard not to be charmed by a man who takes such an interest in cacti and who will crack jokes at important EU gatherings, not only about Nazi camp commandants but also about whether or not his wife is running off with someone else. There is something heroic about his style, something hilariously imperial – from the huge swimming pool he has created by flooding a basin in the Sardinian hills, to the four thalassotherapy pools he has sunk for Veronica, powered by computers more advanced than those used on the Moon shots.

It may or not be important that he claims never to have sacked any of his 46,000 employees. We scan closely the faces of his cook and a butler as they pass us in another golf cart and hail him matily. 'Where are you off to?' asks Berlusconi. 'We're off for a ride!' they say. Yes, they seem happy. His appeal, for me, is that he is like so many of the things he has brought to this Sardinian coast. He is a transplant.

Suddenly, after decades in which Italian politics was in thrall to a procession of gloomy, portentous, jargon-laden partitocrats, there appeared this influorescence of American gung-hoery. Yes, he may have been involved in questionable business practices; he may even yet be found out and pay the price. For the time being, though, it seems reasonable to let him get on with his programme. He may fail. But then, of course – and this is the point that someone should write in block capitals, fold up and stuff in the mouth of Anna Lindh, Swedish foreign minister – he can be rejected by the Italian people.

She may not like it but he was democratically elected and can be removed by the very people Anna Lindh insults. If we are obliged to compare Silvio Berlusconi with Anna Lindh, and other bossy, high-taxing European politicians,

I agree with Farrell: as the narrator says of Jay Gatsby, a man Berlusconi to some extent resembles, he is 'better than the whole damn lot of them'.

---

[1] This article was written in September 2003. In December 2004, Berlusconi was acquitted of one charge and the others were dropped.

AFTERWORD

I want to leave you with a final consoling thought. It is true that all journalists are endowed with these terrifying weapons. Sometimes they use them well, sometimes not. But they are never individually quite as powerful as they think. All journalists, after all, are locked in a bitter and ceaseless struggle with each other, a competition to get it first, to say it best, to mint the phrase that catches the taste of the moment.

They are, in other words, just part of that growing and all-encompassing free market system which I observed in 1988 and 1989. The free market destroyed communism because Adam Smith's invisible hand was better than collectivism at supplying lipstick to Bulgarian women. In the same way, the institutions of the free media – newspapers, magazines, the internet, radio and TV stations – are just broking houses in the gigantic bourse of public opinion. They are traders in news and views; and like all traders, they can be caught out by someone who is prepared to be original and daring.

They may all decide at once to dump a stock, and the results can be awful, especially if that stock happens to be you. But because it is a free market, there will always be someone ready to buck the conventional opinion, ready to buy when the market is low. Let us say that a charismatic Princess dies tragically young, and the whole country is convulsed with mourning. There will always be at least a few columnists happy to make a few caustic cracks, of a just-what-the-hell-is-going-on variety. If the nation decides that the Dome is a dump, there will be some journalist who will immediately test the market in Domes, and write a piece saying how wonderful it is.

If the conventional wisdom is that the war in Iraq will be over in days, someone will instantly prophesy that it could take months. Every day, every minute, the media is investigating the market in every possible proposition. They test the appetite of other journalists, who have to decide whether or not to take up these views. Ultimately, all these wares are for sale to the public. It is true that the media can to a large extent condition the public's appetite. But if for too long they supply them with an outdated product like dud Bulgarian lipstick a hidden gap in the market will be created.

If someone spots that gap, and starts to offer another stock, there will be one of those tipping points. Suddenly, everyone will stop selling and start buying. To take an example close to my heart, it has long been the conventional media wisdom that a certain political party is pretty washed up, hopeless, and has not much chance of winning the next election. I could urge you to wonder about that opinion. I could urge you to buy, buy, buy a blue chip stock that has been recklessly undervalued. But that might try your patience; and anyway, it is another story.

Acknowledgements

My journalistic debts are too numerous to mention, but I would like a special medal to be struck for Benedick Watt, who spent time ploughing through my oeuvre, and who is largely responsible for this selection.

I would like to thank the *Daily Telegraph* for their kind permission to reproduce the following articles:

So much for the pen and dagger men – 5/7/95
The 'new' gospel – 4/10/95
Tony has the smile but Gordon has the brains – 14/1/98
He went on and on, but he's no Mrs Thatcher – 30/9/98
He lived by Spin, he died by Spin – 24/12/98
This is no fight for the Tory soul – 19/7/01
Now can Blair make Mandy Chancellor? – 28/5/02
We gave Blair a gong – and then the bubble burst – 12/12/02
Kylie's bottom shows the way ahead for the Lords – 30/1/03
Revelation on the road from Hastings to Maastricht – 9/4/95

Britain: so cool it's baaad – 22/10/97
Cry grows for England and St George – 19/4/99
Yes, I did feel lucky – 6/2/99
An interview with the cat in the hat – 3/11/97
The case for Hornblower – 11/10/98
Iron Tongue – 4/8/98
Going on *Have I Got News For You* – 8/11/01
Weapons dealer found murdered – 24/3/90
Hurd warns EC of US anger at Gulf response –
    5/12/90
After Mitterrand nothing much will change – 19/12/94
The birth of the euro – 16/12/95
George Dubya Bush – 15/2/99
Flying a Scudbuster – 17/2/99
Good on you, Bush baby: you go ahead and tell 'em –
    5/4/01
Blair and Clinton – will Bill let Tony down? – 14/5/99
Arkan – 31/5/99
Incompetent swatting from above the clouds – 2/6/99
The Serbs will blame us and they will have a point –
    9/6/99
How the Serbs were turned into a nation of victims –
    16/6/99
Zimbabwe – we won't do anything for them – 17/4/00
What Islamic terrorists are really afraid of is women –
    27/9/01
We should try bin Laden first – 13/12/01
We blew the chance to finish Saddam – 21/12/98
Riches have become the bad dreams of avarice –
    27/2/95
Rights and Duties – 27/3/95
Thoughts on the ruin of Aitken – 25/6/97
Killing deer to save them – 9/7/97
Why Tony worships in the Temple of gammon – 14/10/98
Call to raise the speed limit – 12/7/01

Thoughts on an Indian elephant – 2/1/03
Ken Clarke – 4/3/96
Clare Short – 17/4/95
Tony Benn – 3/3/97
Frank Bruno – 14/7/97
Chris Evans – 12/5/98
Kelvin MacKenzie – 6/11/98
Dancing with Ulrika – 28/11/98
Robert Harris – 11/1/99
Jenny Agutter – 26/7/99
RIP Alan Clark – 9/9/99
Trust me, being sacked isn't all that bad – 2/12/04
Remember what happened to Scargill – 23/9/04
What has it got to do with the Scots? – 10/7/03
End of Blair? – 29/4/04
We need nuclear power and a new generation of boffins
    – 2/3/06
Blair is not going to get yobs off the streets – you'll have
    to – 12/1/06
Where would muddle-headed mugwumps be without
    Charlie? – 15/12/05
Cameron – 6/10/05
This is a turning point: we have to fly the flag for
    Britishness again – 14/7/05
The best way to cure ourselves of Islamophobia is to
    have a laugh – 21/7/05
Lefty thinking – 9/2/06
Even the bombs couldn't spoil this day – 17/3/05
It's simple: no democracy, no nukes – 24/6/04
Bush owes Blair – and must deliver – 4/11/04
Getting our knickers in a twist over China – 3/9/05
We banned a berry – and it took Brussels to stop us
    being so silly – 23/12/04
We futilely yearn for someone to blame – 30/12/04

would like to thank the *Spectator* for their kind permission to reproduce the following articles:

Mr Blair has learnt a valuable lesson – 18/3/95
Who was fibbing – the old Blair or new? – 29/4/95
Who *are* all these people? – 30/9/95
American revolution – 13/11/99
Congratulations! it's a Belgian – 31/7/93
Huh, I thought. Double Income, No Kids. That's what we have here. Bastards. – 18/3/00
One Nation – 8/12/00
In defence of Wodehouse – 25/9/99
Virgil's message for the Middle East – 7/4/01
London house prices – 26/3/94
Bill Clinton is right – 10/6/00
The fear, the squalor . . . and the hope – 3/5/03
Alcohol is good for you – 9/11/91
Moments of moral choice – 10/6/95
Who'd want to be a Tory MP these days? – 29/7/95
Martin McGuinness – 20/5/00
What I should say sorry for – 23/10/04
The Queen fights back – 27/3/04
The end of part of England – 19/2/05
Two wheels good, four wheels bad – 16/8/03
Way to go, Dubya – 4/9/04
The beginning of hope in the Middle East – 13/11/04
Forza Berlusconi! – 6/9/03

I would like to thank the *Guardian* for their kind permission to reproduce the following article:

'Am I guilty of racial prejudice? We all are' – 21/2/00

I would like to thank *GQ Magazine* for their kind permission to reproduce the following articles:

The iron-on lady – January 2003
You can with this Nissan – April 2005